T0220408

Oracle Solaris and Veritas Cluster

An Easy-build Guide

Vijay Shankar Upreti

Apress®

Oracle Solaris and Veritas Cluster: An Easy-build Guide

ISBN-13 (pbk): 978-1-4842-1832-7

ISBN-13 (electronic): 978-1-4842-1833-4

Trademarked names, logos, and images may appear in this book. Rather than use a trademark symbol with every occurrence of a trademarked name, logo, or image we use the names, logos, and images only in an editorial fashion and to the benefit of the trademark owner, with no intention of infringement of the trademark.

The use in this publication of trade names, trademarks, service marks, and similar terms, even if they are not identified as such, is not to be taken as an expression of opinion as to whether or not they are subject to proprietary rights.

While the advice and information in this book are believed to be true and accurate at the date of publication, neither the authors nor the editors nor the publisher can accept any legal responsibility for any errors or omissions that may be made. The publisher makes no warranty, express or implied, with respect to the material contained herein.

Managing Director: Welmoed Spahr
Lead Editor: Pramila Balan
Editorial Board: Steve Anglin, Pramila Balan, Louise Corrigan, Jonathan Gennick, Robert Hutchinson, Celestin Suresh John, Michelle Lowman, James Markham, Susan McDermott, Matthew Moodie, Jeffrey Pepper, Douglas Pundick, Ben Renow-Clarke, Gwenan Spearing
Coordinating Editor: Prachi Mehta
Copy Editor: Karen Jameson
Compositor: SPi Global
Indexer: SPi Global
Artist: SPi Global

Distributed to the book trade worldwide by Springer Nature, 233 Spring Street, 6th Floor, New York, NY 10013. Phone 1-800-SPRINGER, fax (201) 348-4505, e-mail orders-ny@springer-sbm.com, or visit www.springeronline.com. Apress Media, LLC is a California LLC and the sole member (owner) is Springer Science + Business Media Finance Inc (SSBM Finance Inc). SSBM Finance Inc is a Delaware corporation.

For information on translations, please e-mail rights@apress.com, or visit www.apress.com.

Apress and friends of ED books may be purchased in bulk for academic, corporate, or promotional use. eBook versions and licenses are also available for most titles. For more information, reference our Special Bulk Sales–eBook Licensing web page at www.apress.com/bulk-sales.

Any source code or other supplementary materials referenced by the author in this text is available to readers at www.apress.com/9781484218327. For detailed information about how to locate your book's source code, go to www.apress.com/source-code/. Readers can also access source code at SpringerLink in the Supplementary Material section for each chapter.

Dedicated to my parents

Dr. Jaydutt Upreti

Smt Kamla Upreti

YOUR BLESSINGS ARE DIVINE POWER

Contents at a Glance

Contents

About the Author

Vijay S. Upreti, is science graduate, comes with nearly 20 years in field of IT. Started his career in 1996, being Systems administrator and rose to his last position worked as Principal Architect. Vijay, worked for Datapro Information Technology Ltd, Inter University Center for Astronomy and Astrophysics, Mahindra British Telecom (now TechMahindra), Tech Mahindra, Bulldog Broadband UK, Cable&Wireless Worldwide (now part of Vodafone) UK, Sun Microsystems India Pvt, Target Corporation India Pvt. Ltd and Wipro Technologies. Throughout his experience, Vijay was engaged in the IT Infrastructure strategies, planning, design, implementation and operational support activities at various levels in Unix and Linux technologies.

Currently Vijay is working as an Independent consultant for Datacenter and Cloud technologies.

Acknowledgments

First and foremost, I would like to thank all my peers, colleagues, juniors and my bosses in past, who encouraged me to pen the skill I gained through my experience of more than 19 years in the IT infrastructure domain. It has taken a while to complete the book, but the idea has always been to ensure that the book helps those who are novice to clustering and would like to get a better understanding from "Concepts to implementation and configuration level."

Working in past organizations like Datapro Information Technology Ltd Pune, IUCAA Pune - India, Mahindra British Telecom (Now Tech Mahindra) – India and UK, Bulldog Broadband – UK, Cable & Wireless UK, Sun Microsystems India Pvt Ltd, Target Corporation India and Wipro Technologies India has been learning at every stage. Sun Microsystems exposed me to a vital opportunities on Sun Solaris Technologies which helped me in acquiring required skills sets.

I had multiple opportunities to implement local and geographic cluster in my past organizations. I had the privilege to work and interact with some great minds and highly skilled teams and individuals. With specific names, a big thanks to Divya Oberoi, (Faculty member at National Center for Radio Astrophysics - TIFR, Pune), Fiaz Mir (Strategy Architect – Vodafone, UK), Dominic Bundy (IT Cloud specialist), Guido Previde Massara (Owner and Director of FooBar consulting Limited), Satyajit Tripathi (Manager Oracle India Pvt Ltd), Anitha Iyer (Sr. Director, Software Engineering at Symantec, India), Poornima Srinivasan, IT Consultant and Leader, Target Corporation India Pvt Ltd, Sanjay Rekhi (Senior Technology Executive). Friends have always been technically associated with me. I would like to personally quote few individuals here, Shirshendu Bhattacharya (Program Manager, Google), Arijit Dey (Sr. Architect, Wipro), Rangarajan Vasudeva (Lead Engineer, Wipro Technologies), Mahatma Reddy (Sr Engineer) and Gurubalan T (Sr. Engineer, Oracle India).

Blessings of my parents (Dr J. D Upreti and Mrs Kamla Upreti), my elder brothers (Mr Ravindra Upreti and Mr Sanjay Upreti) and sisters (Smt Gayatri Joshi and Smt Savitri Pant) and all other relatives for their sustained encouragement and support has been a big moral boost. My wife Dr. Lata Upreti and son Aniruddha Upreti have been a great support for me, and helped me in best way they could in their own capacity while writing this book. A big thanks to a beautiful family for their support and encouragement.

The book could not have been completed by the support of my reviewer Mr. Hemachandran Namachivayam, Principle Engineer at Oracle Corporation India. His vast knowledge in Cluster technologies has been quite helpful in completing the book.

And finally the publishing of this book would not have been possible without the help of Mr. Celestin Suresh John and Ms. Prachi Mehta, who had been a dedicated resource from Apress. They were a continuous source of encouragement, and assisted me in getting the book published in time. Sincerely acknowledge your efforts and assistance.

Introduction

What Is This Book About?

The book is focused on understanding high availability concepts: Oracle Solaris Cluster and Veritas Cluster framework, installation and configuration with some examples of setting up applications as high available, and providing a cheat sheet on the list of commands used for setting up a cluster. The book assists with setting up clustering on VirtualBox-based virtual. Easy steps mentioned in the book will help readers to have a basic level understanding of high availability, cluster, and setting up cluster environments. A quick note on Oracle Solaris and Veritas Clusters:

> Oracle Solaris Cluster is a high availability software, originally created by Sun Microsystems and acquired by Oracle Corporations in 2010. Oracle Solaris Cluster helps in building high available environments using Active-Passive application failover. Oracle Solaris Cluster also comes with Disaster Recovery-based Geographic clustering functionality cross-site/geography using a high speed DWDM network backbone along with storage replication. The Oracle Solaris Cluster environment can be used for any kind of application and Database supported to be running in Oracle Solaris environments, having Stop/ Stop and Probe methods.

> Veritas Cluster software is High Availability Software provided by Veritas, which was later acquired by Symantec in 2005, known as Symantec Cluster. (https://www.symantec.com/en/in/cluster-server/), ensuring 24/7 high availability with minimal or no manual intervention. Likewise, any OS cluster solution providers, such as Symantec Cluster Server, also provides disaster recovery (DR) solutions. Veritas Cluster Server detects risks to application availability through monitoring triggers and ensures automated recovery of applications for high availability and disaster recovery. Veritas cluster also supports any kind of application that can be ported and configured under the given platform (e.g., Solaris, Linux, or Windows).

The book is aimed at providing elaborate steps on setting up virtual host-based lab clusters (Oracle Solaris and Veritas) on personal devices (Laptop or Desktop) for cluster installation, configuration, management, and administration. The book also covers some example functions of web- or java-based graphical user interface (GUI) for cluster management and administration.

Due to limitations of the Laptop/Desktop configuration, the setup is limited to only a two-node cluster build, although if configuration permits, you can add as many virtual hosts to the cluster using the steps mentioned below.

Who Will Get Help from the Book?

This book is targeted to anyone working in the IT Infrastructure domain with a basic understanding of the Unix/Solaris environment. Additionally the book will help engineers in IT Operations and support, who rarely get an opportunity to build live in OS clustered environments.

It is a single book that covers the basic high availability concepts, clustering framework, and components and installation and setup for both Oracle Solaris Cluster and Veritas Cluster. The easy steps provided here will surely help Systems Administrators and System Build Engineers to gain confidence in understanding availability and cluster build.

The easy writing as well as setup on the personal desktop/laptop will also help graduate students and those who would like to pursue careers in the field of IT Infrastructure domain. The real-life cluster setup simulated on the virtual environment is a starting point to gain a good level of cluster installation and configuration skills. The beginning of each chapter also helps readers understand the availability concepts for IT Infrastructure and Data Center.

How This Book Is Designed

The book is designed to first have a brief understanding of High Availability concepts and then elaborates on Oracle Solaris and Veritas Cluster framework, installation, and configuration steps, managing cluster resources using command line and GUI. The book also covers some more examples of cluster setup. The book ends with some frequently used command lines and their options for day-to-day cluster management.

Chapter 1: Availability Concepts The chapter covers the concepts of availability. It starts with the understanding of IT Infrastructure and Data Center, specific availability challenges, and how to address these challenges. It also discusses Operating System-level clustering concepts. And finally it covers how to understand the business value driven through availability.

Chapter 2: Cluster Introduction The chapter starts with a quick overview of cluster framework and then moves further on to Cluster Architecture. The chapter will detail Oracle and Veritas specific cluster frameworks.

Chapter 3: Cluster Build Preparations and Understanding VirtualBox The focus of this chapter is to describe preparation required for the cluster build. It details VirtualBox and its components. VirtualBox will be the virtual host solution as a part of a Lab exercise for setting up two-node clusters.

Chapter 4: Oracle Solaris Cluster Build This chapter is focused on the Oracle Cluster Build process, starting from planning to the cluster implementation. The chapter will cover prerequisites, installation, and configuration of two-node Oracle Solaris cluster environments built under VirtualBox.

Chapter 5: Setting Up Apache and NFS Cluster Data Services This chapter will cover adding two example applications – Apache and NFS – as a part of cluster failover services. The chapter will start with adding shared storages move further and with setting up metaset and mirroring of disks and then adding cluster resource groups and resources along with their dependencies.

Chapter 6: Veritas Clustering This chapter is about the Veritas Cluster and starts with the design phase of Veritas Cluster. The chapter then covers Veritas Cluster implementation, through cluster installation and setting up a Veritas Cluster framework.

Chapter 7: Setting Up Apache and NFS Services in Veritas Cluster Similar to Chapter 5 for setting up Apache and NFS applications in Oracle Solaris Cluster, this chapter also describes steps for bringing Apache and NFS applications under a cluster framework for high availability. Again, here it will first start with adding shared storage and configuring.

Chapter 8: Graphical User Interface for Cluster Management This chapter has information on Graphical User Interface as provided by both Oracle Solaris Cluster and Veritas Cluster. This chapter starts with initiating GUI, login, and then managing clusters through GUI. In addition to showing components of GUI, there are some examples of switching over cluster resource groups.

Chapter 9: Additional Examples – Cluster Configurations This chapter will have some more command-line examples of cluster configuration. It starts with steps for setting up Oracle Solaris Geographic Cluster. There are also examples of setting up NFS service using ZFS filesystems and zone clusters under Oracle Solaris Cluster build. And the last example in this chapter is about adding a customer build application to Veritas and Oracle Solaris clusters.

Chapter 10: Command-Line Cheat Sheet This is the last chapter of the book, covering some commonly used command lines for both Oracle Solaris Cluster and Veritas Cluster setup, administration, and other operational activities.

CHAPTER 1

■ ■ ■

Availability Concepts

Availability

Availability is the time that business services are operational. In other words, availability is a synonym of business continuity. And when it comes to IT Infrastructure, systems, site, or data center, availability reflects the span of time applications, servers, site, or any other infrastructure components that are up and running and providing value to the business.

The focus of this book is based on the IT Infrastructure and data center availability leading to business uptime.

IT Infrastructure availability ensures that its components are fault tolerant, resilient, and provide high availability and reliability within site and disaster recovery cross-site/data centers in order to minimize the impact of planned or unplanned outages. Reliability ensures systems have longer lives to be up and running, and redundancy helps ensure system reliability.

Expectations on high availability may vary depending upon the service level being adopted and agreed upon with the business stakeholders. And in terms of disaster recovery, the availability is the reflection of time to return to normal business services, either through failover of services to the disaster recovery site or through restoration from backup, ensuring minimal data loss and reduced time of recovery.

Availability Challenges

Having observed some major disasters in the IT Infrastructure and data center space, availability is a top priority for business continuity. We need to understand the challenges introduced due to the availability aspect of IT Infrastructure and/or data centers.

But before even starting to understand the challenges in managing and supporting IT Infrastructure specific to server availability, let's first understand the backbone of IT Infrastructure, which is a data center and its primary purpose.

> Data Center is a collection of server/computers connected using network and storage devices controlled by software and aims to provide seamless business functioning. A data center is the brain and also one of the sources of energy to drive the business faster with the least or no interruption.

> In the early age of data center design, there were computer rooms; the computers were built in a room dedicated to IT. With the rapid growth of IT requirements, risks on the data integrity and security, modularity, availability, and scalability challenges, the data centers were moved out of company premises to a dedicated site; and they kept network, security, and storage as different dedicated components of Data Center Management.

So what are the data center availability challenges? Here are some of the critical data center measures that lead to availability challenges.

At the very beginning, lack of planning for the selection of an IT site or data center site could have severe availability impact due to natural disasters such as floods, earthquakes, tsunamis, etc. Similarly unplanned floor design may lead to a disaster due to flood or any other water clogging.

Not having sufficient fire protection and policies is another big challenge to the availability and may lead to data center disasters. The next challenge is insufficient physical security, such as not having Photo Identity, absence of CCTV, not maintaining visitors' log registers, etc.

Hardware devices, such as Servers, Storages, and Network and their components installed with no redundancy will have an immediate impact on availability. Most of the traditional data centers suffer the disruption of services due to non-redundant devices.

Electrical power is one of the most critical parts of data center uptime. Not having dual power feeds, backup powers supplies, or green energy power sources are some of the critical areas of challenges for availability. Similarly, absence of temperature control in the data center will have a disastrous impact on running high-computing temperature-sensitive devices.

Unskilled or not, having the right level of skill and untrained technical resources are big contributors to risks on data center availability.

Not having monitoring solutions at different levels such as heating and cooling measurements of the data center to the monitoring of applications, servers, network- and storage-based devices will have direct impacts on the host availability. Also, having no defined and applied backup and restoration policy will have an impact on the host availability.

Absence of host security measures in terms of hardware and software security policies is another challenge to availability.

Addressing Availability Challenges

As discussed in the previous section, availability is the most important factor that ensures application and business uptime. To address the challenges posed to the data center availability, each of the above challenges, be it site selection, floor planning, fire safety, power supply redundancy, servers/network and storage-level redundancy, physical security, Operating System-level security, network security, resource skills, and monitoring solutions should be addressed and resolved.

When it comes to server availability, it reflects hardware redundancy and software-based high availability. In other words, redundant hardware components along with software-driven fault tolerant solutions ensure server availability. Figure 1-1 further gives detailed components impacting and contributing to the server availability.

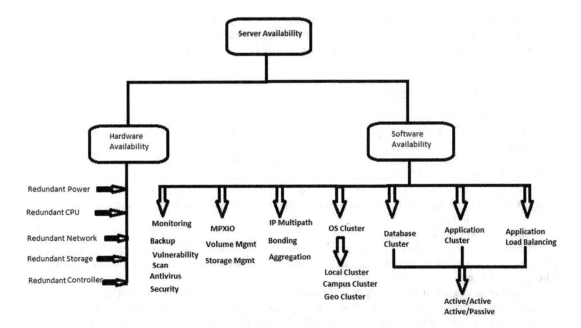

Figure 1-1. *High Availability Components*

As explained above, Server Availability is mainly covered as hardware and software availability. On hardware availability, introducing redundant hardware for critical components of the server will provide high resilience and increased availability.

The most critical part of addressing availability challenges is to ensure the server has redundant power points. Power supplies should be driven from two difference sources of power generators and with a minimal time to switch. Battery backup/generator power backups also ensure minimal or no server downtime.

The next important component for host availability is the CPU, and having more than one CPU can ensure, in the case of failure, that one of the processors that processes is failed over to a working CPU.

Next in the line addressing server availability challenges is to have redundant network components, both at switch level and server-level port redundancy. The network redundancy is later coupled with software-based network redundancy such as port aggregation or IP Multipathing or Interface Bonding to ensure network interface failures are handled well with very insignificant or no impact on the application availability.

Storage-based redundancy is achieved at two stages. One is at the local storage, by using either hardware- or software-based raid configuration; and second, using SAN- or NAS-based storage LUNs, which are configured for high availability. OS-based MPXIO software ensures the multipath.

On a larger scale for the data center (DC) availability, based on business availability requirements, data centers are classified and certified in four categories:

> Tier I – Single non-redundant distribution paths; 99.671% availability allows 28.817 hours of downtime.

> Tier II – Along with tier I capabilities, redundant site capacity, with 99.741% availability and allows 22.688 hours of downtime.

> Tier III – Along with tier II capabilities, Multiple distribution availability paths (dual powered), with 99.982% availability and allows 1.5768 hours of downtime.

> Tier IV – Along with tier III capabilities, HVAC systems are multipowered, with 99.995% availability and 26.28 minutes or .438 hours of unavailability.

And finally, when it comes to host monitoring (hardware, OS, and application), it should also be integrated with the event generators and events further categorized into different service levels based on the criticality of the event generated, ensuring minimum disruption to the services.

OS Clustering Concepts

Operating System cluster architecture is a solution driven by highly available and scalable systems ensuring application and business uptime, data integrity, and increased performance by performing concurrent processing.

Clustering improves the system's availability to end users, and overall tolerance to faults and component failures. In case of failure, a cluster in action ensures failed server applications are automatically shut down and switched over to the other servers. Typically the definition of cluster is merely a collection/ group of object, but on the server technology, clustering is further expanded to server availability and addressing fault tolerance.

Clustering is defined as below:

"Cluster analysis or clustering is the task of grouping a set of objects in such a way that objects in the same group (called a cluster) are more similar (in some sense or another) to each other than to those in other groups (clusters)." – *Wikipedia* definition

"Group of independent servers (usually in close proximity to one another) interconnected through a dedicated network to work as one centralized data processing resource. Clusters are capable of performing multiple complex instructions by distributing workload across all connected servers." – *Business Dictionary* (Read more: http://www.businessdictionary.com/definition/cluster.html#ixzz3dmQvJEdk)

OS-based cluster is classified based on the location of the cluster nodes installed. They are Local Cluster, Campus Cluster, Metropolitan Cluster, and Geographic Cluster.

> Local cluster is the cluster environment built in the same Data Center Site. In this configuration disks are shared across all cluster nodes for failover.

> Campus Cluster, also known as stretched cluster, is stretched across two or more Data Centers within the limited range of distance, and mirrored storages are visible across all other cluster nodes such as local cluster configuration.

> Metropolitan cluster setup with Metropolitan area, still limited by distances. The setup for Metropolitan cluster is similar to the one in Campus cluster, except that storage is set up for replication instead of disk mirroring, using Storage remote replication technologies. Metropolitan provides disaster recover in addition to the local high availability.

> Geographic cluster, which is ideally configured for a dedicated disaster recovery cluster configuration, is set up across two or more data centers geographically separated.

Local and campus clusters are set up with similar cluster configurations and using the same cluster software, although Metropolitan and Geographic clusters use a different software-based configuration, network configuration, and storage configuration (like replication True Copy, SRDF, etc.).

Business Value of Availability

Nonavailability of IT services has a direct impact on business value. Disruption to the business continuity impacts end users, client base, stakeholders, brand image, company's share value, and revenue growth. A highly available IT infrastructure and data center backbone of an enterprise caters to the bulk needs of customer requirements, reduces the time to respond to customers' needs, and helps in product automation – ultimately helping in revenue growth.

Below are some examples of incidents of data center disasters due to fire, flood, or lack of security that caused systems and services unavailability for hours and resulted in a heavy loss of revenues and a severe impact on the company's brand image.

On April 20, 2014, a fire broke out in in the Samsung SDS data center housed in the building. The fire caused users of Samsung devices users, including smartphones, tablets, and smart TVs, to lose access to data they may have been trying to retrieve. (`http://www.Data Centerknowledge.com/archives/2014/04/20/ data-center-fire-leads-outage-samsung-devices/`)

Heavy rain broke a ceiling panel in Datacom's (an Australian IT solutions company), colocation facility in 2010, destroying storage area networks, servers, and routers belonging to its customers. On September 9, 2009, an enormous flash flood hit Istanbul. Vodafone's data center was destroyed.

The addition of a single second adjustment applied to UT (Universal Time) due to Earth's rotation speed to the world's atomic clocks caused problems for a number of IT systems in 2012, when several popular web sites, including LinkedIn, Reddit, Mozilla, and The Pirate Bay, went down.

In 2007, NaviSite (now owned by Time Warner) was moving customer accounts from Alabanza's main data center in Baltimore to a facility in Andover, Massachusetts. They literally unplugged the servers, put them on a truck, and drove the servers for over 420 miles. Many web sites hosted by Alabanza were reportedly offline for as long as the drive and reinstallation work took to complete.

A few years ago there was a data center robbery in London. UK newspapers reported an "Ocean's Eleven"-type heist with the thieves taking more than $4 million of equipment.

Target Corporation, December 2013: 70 million customers' credit/debit card information was breached, amounting to a loss of about $162 million.

It is quite obvious that any impact on the availability of the data center components such as server, network, or storage will have a direct impact on the customer's business.

CHAPTER 2

■ ■ ■

Cluster Introduction: Architecture for Oracle Solaris Cluster and Veritas Cluster

Introduction to Cluster Framework

As defined in the previous chapter, clustering enables multiple servers to be treated as a part of single cluster of servers and provides high availability solutions to the application environment. Clustering can help in increased performance and ensures greater scalability and reduced costs through optimized utilization of participant servers. The backbone of cluster lies on the server, network, and storage capacities along with the operating system-level clustering software environment. A cluster framework ensures applications and/or database environments start with defined dependencies and ensures successful failover or failback initiated by monitoring triggers or through manual intervention. Cluster framework also ensures an easy scalability through addition or removal of servers, known as cluster nodes, to the cluster.

OS Clustering Architecture

A cluster architecture is a group of two or more computers/server/hosts/nodes built with fault tolerant components and connected using network, storage, and software components to make a single virtual or logical server, available anytime in either of the physical computer/server/hosts or nodes. On the other view, cluster framework is an architecture that allows systems to combine together as an aggregated host, a way of harnessing of multiple processors to work in parallel, sharing memory across multiple hosts So cluster is not just a solution to availability in the form of failover and fault tolerant services but also stretches to scalability and performance.

A high-level two-node cluster architecture is explained in Figure 2-1.

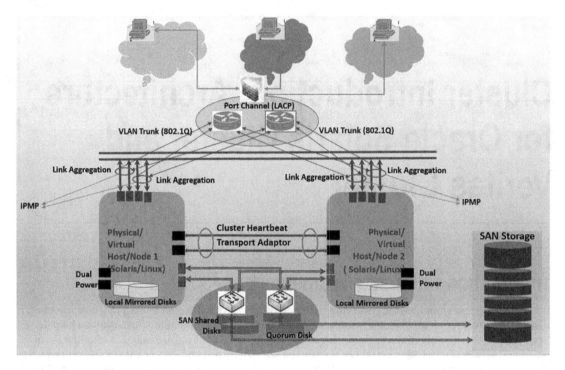

Figure 2-1. *Cluster Framework*

As shown in the above diagram, the basic design of a cluster framework consists of two or more cluster hosts/nodes – physical or virtual, Operating System, supported cluster software, network, and shared storage (SAN or NAS shared storage). The figure also shows some other aspects: redundancy design to support the cluster framework (like dual power supplies, Link Aggregation, and IPMP configuration).

Cluster Network

Network configurations should be set up with both server-level network card redundancy as well as having a redundant switch for failover. Network ports be configured to provide maximum redundancy allowing network survival due to the failure of the card at the server end or a failure of the switch.

A core component of cluster configuration is cluster heartbeat (transport interconnect). Cluster heartbeat plays a critical role for keeping a cluster alive. Heartbeat interconnects are used for pinging each cluster node, ensuring they are part of the cluster.

The other network component of cluster configuration is the core network (or company's internal network) that is used for communication between cluster resources (e.g., across applications or communications from application to database).

And the last component of the cluster network configuration is the communication to or from end users connecting from a public network to the back-end application under cluster configuration.

Redundant cluster network configuration is done differently for different kinds of configuration requirements. One of the configurations is to aggregate multiple network ports at the host level. The technology used for aggregating ports is either link aggregation (UNIX) or interface bonding (Linux) or NIC teaming. Link aggregation or interface bonding provides network redundancy/load balancing as well as providing combined bandwidth to the virtual network pipe created out of bonding. At the network configuration level, Port Channel – LACP will need to be configured to support the link aggregation configuration at the server end.

Additionally, IP Multipathing can be set up either on top of link aggregation or configured independently to further support the network redundancy via failover policies adopted (active/active or active/standby).

These will specifically be explained on the specific clustering framework (for Oracle Solaris Cluster or Veritas Cluster).

Cluster Storage

For the storage configuration, the cluster environment is set up by having both SAN fabric and host storage port-level redundancy. Cluster storage is a shared storage carved from SAN- or NAS-based redundant storage environments. Cluster storage LUNs (Logical Units), also known as multihome disks, are presented to all participant cluster nodes and made active/standby, based on which node is the active cluster node. Software MPXIO is used to create single virtual paths out of multiple redundant paths created out of SAN fabric and host storage ports. Ideally, disks pulled out of SAN storage are raid controlled and provide sufficient disk redundancy, although to have better resilient configuration, it's better to obtain storage from two separate storage appliances.

Quorum Device

Cluster uses quorum voting to prevent split brain and amnesia. Quorum determines the number of failures of node a cluster can sustain and for any further failure cluster must panic. Quorum disk is used for supporting the Cluster quorum.

Cluster Split Brain

Split brain occurs when cluster interconnects between cluster nodes break. In that case, each broken cluster node partitions to form a separate cluster and tries to bring up cluster services simultaneously and access the respective shared storage leading to data corruption. Additionally, it might duplicate network addresses, as each new partitioned clusters might own the logical hosts created as a part of the cluster.

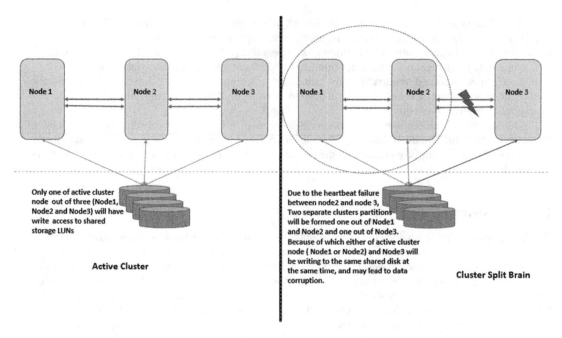

Figure 2-2. *Split Brain*

Quorum disk resolves this by ensuring a partition cluster with the majority of votes will be allowed to survive (like the above cluster made of Node1 and Node2) and other cluster partition (Node3) will be forced to panic and fence the node from disks to avoid data corruption.

Cluster Amnesia

As stated in Oracle Solaris documentation, "Amnesia is a failure mode in which a node starts with the stale cluster configuration information. This is a synchronization error due to the cluster configuration information not having been propagated to all of the nodes."

Cluster amnesia occurs when cluster nodes leave the cluster due to technical issues. Cluster uses the cluster configuration database to keep this updated across all cluster nodes. Although for the nodes going down due to technical reasons, it will not have an updated cluster repository. When all cluster nodes are restarted, the cluster with the latest configuration should be started first, meaning the cluster node brought down last should be brought up first. But if this is not done, the cluster itself will not know which cluster node contains the right cluster repository and may lead to a stale cluster configuration database.

Figure 2-3 below explains further the process of cluster amnesia.

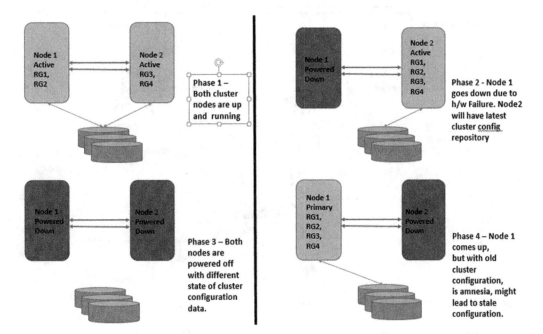

Figure 2-3. *Amnesia*

To avoid this, cluster quorum guarantees at the time of cluster reboot that it has at least one node (either quorum server or quorum disk) with the latest cluster configuration.

Oracle/Solaris Cluster Framework

Oracle Solaris Cluster design is the same as what is shown in Figure 2-1. Figure 2-4 shows a cluster design for an Oracle Solaris Cluster.

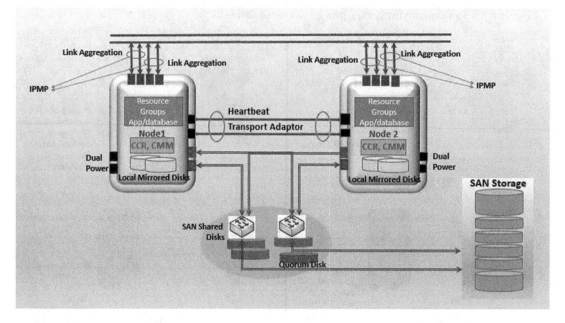

Figure 2-4. *A cluster design for an Oracle Solaris Cluster*

Oracle Solaris Cluster software has two components: Kernel and User Land.

Kernel land is the area that is controlled using OS kernel libraries and for setting up global file systems and devices, setting up network communications, the Sun Volume Manager for setting up multihome devices and for creating cluster configuration repositories, and managing cluster memberships and cluster communications.

User land is the area that is for user-controlled libraries and binaries for cluster command and libraries, and for setting up cluster resources and resource groups through the Resource Group Manager, making data services scalable and failover data services using the command line, etc.

Oracle Solaris Cluster Topologies

Cluster topology helps to understand the way shared devices are connected to cluster nodes in order to provide maximum availability.

There are three supported cluster topologies available for the Oracle Solaris cluster configuration, known as Clustered pairs, Pair+N and N+1 (Star), and N*N topologies.

In Cluster pairs topology, cluster nodes are configured in pair and storages are shared across paired cluster nodes, within the same cluster framework. This way the failover of the respective application will occur within the paired cluster nodes. An example of this configuration is when different types of applications (like application and database) are part of the same cluster administrative framework.

Pair+N topology means a pair of hosts are connected to shared storage and other hosts that are not directly connected to storages but uses cluster interconnects to access shared storage.

N+1 (Star) topology means a combination of primary hosts and one secondary/standby host. The secondary host should have a connection to all shared storages and have sufficient capacity to take the load of primary host in case of failure.

N*N, the most commonly used cluster topology, is configured by having each node connected to each shared storage, and the application can failover to either of the hosts available.

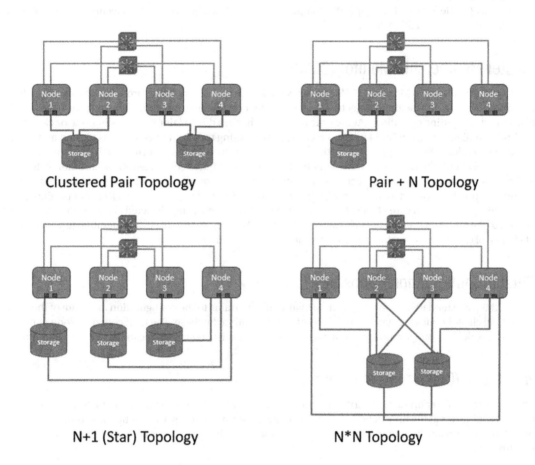

Figure 2-5.

Oracle Solaris Cluster Components

A critical component of the cluster design is the network configuration used at different layers. Each network layer serves the purpose of communication within cluster environments and outside the cluster. These network layers are **Public Network** – Network that the outside world or end user connects with the back-end host, typically web tier-based connectivity. **Core Network** – Company's internal network for communication (typically used for Application to DB connectivity), **Private Interconnect (Heartbeat connection)** – This is a heartbeat connection used only for intercommunications between hosts connected for availability polling. **Console network** – Host management console connection for remotely managing headless servers, and last, **Cluster Management Network** – Usually part of the console management network but optionally chosen to be part of a core network or separate dedicated network for cluster management.

The next components as parts of a cluster framework are shared disks. These disks can be shared as a part of SAN storage, or NAS storage, and they should be visible by all cluster nodes to ensure failover storage-based application services.

Further Oracle Solaris cluster-specific components are defined based on their specific cluster function to support the high availability feature.

Cluster Membership Monitor (CMM)

The Cluster Membership Monitor **(CMM) ensures** the health of a cluster node through active membership communicated via private interconnects. A critical cluster component protecting data integrity across distributed computing operations. At the time of cluster changes due to failures of cluster node or changes to cluster configuration, the CMM initiates reconfiguration using transport interconnects to send and receive status alerts. So basically, CMM is the core of cluster configuration ensuring persistent configuration. Further deeper into the technical understanding, CMM is a distributed set of agents that communicates and exchanges messages to perform consistent membership view on all nodes, driving synchronized reconfiguration in response to membership changes (nodes leaving or joining cluster), cluster partitioning (split brains, etc) is taken care of for safer reboot of cluster nodes, ensuring defected cluster nodes are cleanly left out of the cluster for repair, uses cluster heartbeats for keeping control of cluster membership and in case of change of cluster membership, it reinitiates the cluster configuration.

Cluster Configuration Repository

The CCR is a cluster database for storing information that pertains to the configuration and state of the cluster. All cluster nodes are synchronized for this configuration database. The CCR contains Node names, Disk Group, device configuration, current cluster status, and a list of nodes that can master each disk group.

Heartbeats/Cluster Interconnect

The core of the cluster uptime is heartbeat, which monitors cluster nodes ensuring reconfiguration of cluster repositories at the time of node joining or leaving the cluster group. Cluster heartbeats operate over dedicated private interconnects (cluster interconnects), helping seamless cluster configuration synchronization.

Cluster Membership

Every cluster node is assigned a cluster member id by assuring it to be part of cluster.

Quorum

The Cluster Membership Monitor (CMM) and quorum in combination assures, at most, one instance of the same cluster is operational at any time, at the time of broken cluster interconnect. Sun Cluster uses quorum voting to prevent split brain and amnesia.

As explained before, split brain means two nodes access the same device leading to data corruption so failure fencing is used to prevent split brain. Amnesia occurs when there is a change in cluster configuration while one of the nodes is down. When this node comes up, there will be an amnesia as to which is the primary cluster node, which keeps the correct cluster configuration data. If nodes are shut down one after the other, the last node leaving the cluster should be the first booting up in order to ensure CCR consistency.

Disk (I/O) Fencing

Helps preserve data integrity and non-cluster nodes are prevented from accessing and updating any shared disk/LUN. Or in other words, failure fencing protects the data on shared storage devices against undesired writes accessed by nodes that are no longer in the cluster and are connected to the shared disk.

In a two-node cluster, SCSI-2 reservation is used to fence a failed node and prevent it from writing to dual host-shared disks. For more than two nodes, SCSI-3 Persistence Group Reservation (PGR) provides fencing and helps shared disks' data consistency.

Fault Monitors

There are a number of monitors that are constantly monitoring the cluster and detecting faults; the cluster is monitoring applications, disks, network, etc. These are Data Service monitoring, Disk-Path monitoring, and IP Multipath monitoring respectively.

Cluster Resource Group and Resources

These are Cluster Application/Database or web services running as a part of cluster services for failover and/or load balancing. Cluster resources are components of Cluster Resource groups set up with dependencies. Some of the example cluster resources are NIC-based cluster resource, Floating IP-based cluster resource, HA Storage Cluster resource, and application/database-based cluster resources.

Data Services

A data service is the application cluster resources, like an Apache server or an Oracle database; the cluster will manage the resource and its dependencies, and it will be under the control of the Resource Group Manager (RGM). The RGM performs 1. Start and Stop the Data Service 2. Monitor the Data Service (faults, etc) and 3. Help in failing over the data services. Cluster resource groups and resources are configured with dependencies to ensure before the start of application necessary network and storage components are in place. Cluster resources are configured with start/stop and probe methods.

Cluster Daemons

Some of the core cluster daemons are listed below.

> **cluster** – System kernel process, the core of cluster daemon. This process cannot be killed because it is always in the kernel.

> **failfastd** – The failfast daemon allows the kernel to panic if certain essential daemons have stopped responding or failed.

> **cl_eventd** – This daemon registers and forwards cluster events (such as nodes entering and leaving the cluster).

> **qd_userd** – This daemon server is used for probing the health of Quorum devices.

> **rgmd** – This is the resource group manager daemon.

> **rpc.pmfd** – This is the process monitoring facility.

> **pnmd** – This is the public network management daemon for monitoring IPMP information.

cl_eventlogd – This daemon is used for logging logs cluster events into a binary log file.

cl_ccrad – This daemon helps in accessing CCR.

scdpmd – This daemon monitors the status of disk paths.

sc_zonesd – This daemon monitors the state of Solaris 10 non-global zones.

IP Multipathing

IPMP provides reliability, availability, and network performance for systems with multiple physical interfaces. IPMP keeps monitoring failed interface, allows to failover and failback network interfaces. In Oracle Solaris, two types of IPMP methods are used: Link-Based IPMP and Probe-Based IPMP. In Link-based IPMP, configuration mpathd daemon uses an interface driver to check the status of the interface and uses no TEST address for failure detection. Link-based IPMP is the default IPMP configuration. In Probe-based IPMP configuration, in.mpathd daemon sends out probes onto a TEST address to a target system on the same subnet. It uses a multicast address to probe the target system.

IPMP is configured with options as deprecated, failover, and standby. **Deprecated** is used when interface is used as a test address for IPMP (basically the interface is deprecated to be used only for test communication and not for any application data transfer). **Failover** option to ifconfig is used to make interface as failover or no failover when the interface fails. And the option **Standby** is used for the interface to be configured as standby.

Oracle Solaris IPMP involves in.mpathd daemon, /etc/default/mpathd configuration file and ifconfig command options for IPMP configuration.

The important parameters in mpathd configuration file are the following:

1. **FAILURE_DETECTION_TIME**: Time taken by mpathd to detect a NIC failure in ms (default value – 10 seconds)

2. **FAILBACK**: To enable or disable failback after the failed link becomes available (default value – yes)

3. **TRACK_INTERFACES_ONLY_WITH_GROUPS** – If turned on, interfaces configured as part of IPMP are only monitored (default value – yes)

Below are examples of **Probe-based** and **Link-based** IPMP configurations:

```
        Active interface(s):    e1000g0
                                e1000g1
Standby interface(s):  -
        Data IP addresse(s):    10.0.0.50
        Test IP addresse(s):    10.0.0.51
                                10.0.0.52
```

Active/Active configuration

To configure probe-based IPMP – command line

```
# ifconfig e1000g0 plumb 10.0.0.50 netmask + broadcast + group ipmp0 up addif 10.0.0.53
netmask + broadcast + deprecated -failover up
# ifconfig e1000g1 plumb 10.0.0.52 netmask + broadcast + deprecated -failover group
ipmp0 up
```

To configure probe-based IPMP – config file for permanent change

```
/etc/hostname.e1000g0:
10.0.0.50 netmask + broadcast + group ipmp0 up \
addif 10.0.0.51 netmask + broadcast + deprecated -failover up
/etc/hostname.e1000g1:
10.0.0.52 netmask + broadcast + deprecated -failover group ipmp0 up
```

Active/Standby configuration

To configure probe-based IPMP – command line

```
# ifconfig e1000g0 plumb 10.0.0.50 netmask + broadcast + group ipmp0 up addif 10.0.0.51
netmask + broadcast + deprecated -failover up
# ifconfig e1000g1 plumb 10.0.0.52 netmask + broadcast + deprecated -failover group
ipmp0 standby up
```

To configure probe-based IPMP – config file for permanent change

```
/etc/hostname.e1000g0:
10.0.0.50 netmask + broadcast + group ipmp0 up \
addif 10.0.0.51 netmask + broadcast + deprecated -failover up
/etc/hostname.e1000g1:
10.0.0.52 netmask + broadcast + deprecated -failover group ipmp0 up
```

Active/Active configuration

To configure Link-based IPMP – command line

```
# ifconfig e1000g0 plumb 10.0.0.50 netmask + broadcast + group ipmp0 up
# ifconfig e1000g1 plumb group ipmp0 up
```

To configure Link-based IPMP – config file for permanent change

```
/etc/hostname.e1000g0
10.0.0.50 netmask + broadcast + group ipmp0 up
/etc/hostname.e1000g1
group ipmp0 up
```

Active/Standby configuration

To configure Link-based IPMP – command line

```
# ifconfig e1000g0 plumb 10.0.0.50 netmask + broadcast + group ipmp0 up
# ifconfig e1000g1 plumb group ipmp0 standby up
```

To configure Link-based IPMP – config file for permanent change

```
/etc/hostname.e1000g0
10.0.0.50 netmask + broadcast + group ipmp0 up
/etc/hostname.e1000g1
group ipmp0 standby up
```

Link Aggregation

Link aggregation is a way to combine two or more interfaces to be combined as a single virtual interface. Link aggregation not only provides increased network bandwidth but also the network load balancing and high availability of interfaces as automatic reconfiguration.

Here is an example of setting up link aggregation:

For example, interfaces nxge0 and nxge1, the first unplumb interfaces (to bring them to unknown/ unconfigured state):

```
#ifconfig down unplumb nxge0
#ifconfig down unplumb nxge1
```

Create link aggregation without defining mode:

```
#dladm create-aggr -d nxge0 -d nxge1 1
Above command will create link aggregated interface as aggr0. To check the configuration
information of aggregation interface aggr1
# dladm show-aggr
key: 1 (0x0028)        policy: L4      address: 0:3:bc:e8:7d:f4 (auto)
device       address            speed          duplex  link    state
nxge0        0:3:bc:e8:7d:f4    10000  Mbps    full    up      standby
nxge1        0:3:bc:e8:7d:f5    10000  Mbps    full    up      standby
And finally plumb and configure interface as below
ifconfig aggr1 plumb
# ifconfig aggr0
Aggr0: flags=1000842<BROADCAST,RUNNING,MULTICAST,IPv4> mtu 1500 index 8
inet 0.0.0.0 netmask 0
ether 0:3:bc:e8:7d:f4

# ifconfig aggr1 192.168.100.1/24 broadcast + up
# ifconfig aggr1
Aggr0: flags=1000843<UP,BROADCAST,RUNNING,MULTICAST,IPv4> mtu 1500 index 8
inet 192.168.100.1 netmask ffffff00 broadcast 192.168.100.255
ether 0:3:bc:e8:7d:f4
```

MPXIO

MPXIO is a software used for creating a single virtual path out of multiple HBA PATHs for storage devices, as a part of storage redundancy. To configure MXPIO, cluster nodes need to have /kernel/drv/scsi_vchi, /kernel/drv/fp.conf, and /kernel/drv/qlc.conf files need to be updated with MXPIO to be set to disable.

Recommended Quorum Configuration

To avoid cluster split brain and amnesia, each cluster node is assigned a cluster vote. For a cluster to survive, it typically has as best practice n-1 quorum devices (n represents total number of cluster nodes) for majority voting wins: **in other words, quorum device votes should always be less be less than the number of nodes**. So far a two-node cluster or at least one quorum device (either a quorum disk or quorum server) should be added.

Two-node cluster configurations will require one quorum device to allow at least two quorum votes available at the time of failure of one cluster node.

More than two-node clusters usually doesn't require a quorum as a cluster can survive failure of one cluster node. Although, on the flip side, to restart the cluster at some point, it will need a majority of votes. Here are some examples of configuring quorum devices for more than two-node clusters.

For three-node clusters, where all three nodes are active cluster nodes, two quorum devices can be shared across three cluster nodes at a time. So this will assure a minimum of three votes required for a quorum. The other possible configuration for a three-node cluster could be where one node is used as standby cluster node. In that case, each one of the two quorum devices can be presented to one active and standby node to ensure that the minimum-required three quorum votes are available.

Similarly for a four-node cluster configuration, they should be configured in pairs to allow one node failure from each pair, which means adding two additional quorum devices. So the minimum vote (quorum vote) should always be 4, with a total vote count as 6.

The following illustration represents a different quorum configuration as explained above.

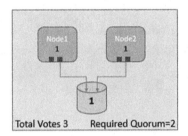

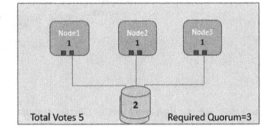

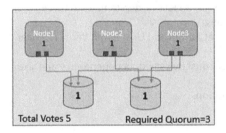

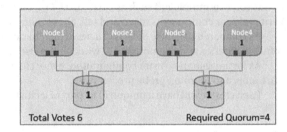

Figure 2-6. *A different quorum configuration*

Veritas Clustering Framework

A Veritas cluster framework also goes with the similar lines of generic cluster configuration as explained in Figure 2-1, except a few components, such as Veritas cluster, does not depend on Quorum Disk configuration. Veritas Cluster does not require an IPMP or Link Aggregation configuration. An IPMP Link Aggregation configured at an Oracle Solaris OS layer needs additional configuration from Veritas Cluster configuration.

Veritas cluster does have its own terminologies and components used for setting up Veritas cluster environments. Veritas cluster framework requires Cluster Nodes, Veritas Cluster Software, and Network and Storage configuration on a very high-level configuration planning. A basic high-level Veritas Cluster design is illustrated in Figure 2-7.

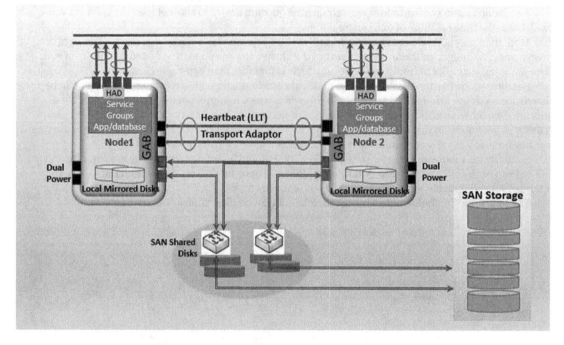

Figure 2-7. *A basic high-level Veritas Cluster design*

As it appears on Figure 2-4, apart from the generic configuration explained before for the Cluster build, it uses some terminologies such as GAB, HAD, LLT, and Service groups. So let's understand what these Veritas cluster components mean and talk about their functionalities.

As compared to Oracle Solaris Cluster, which has components at Kernel and User Land, Veritas Cluster software binaries and daemons are at work on the User Land.

As for any generic cluster configuration, every cluster resource must be set with a dependency and with start, stop, and monitor/probe procedures.

Each cluster will have a unique id as part of a cluster configuration.

Veritas Cluster Components

Service Group

Typical Service groups in Veritas Cluster are synonyms to Cluster Resource Groups explained before, which is a grouping of cluster resources along with resource dependencies. A single cluster node/host may have multiple service groups (based on the workload it can take) targeting different client requests. VCS keeps monitoring the state of the cluster resources and resource groups and, in case of failure, fails them over to other available cluster nodes as part of that service group. This is known as cluster failover service.

Cluster service groups are further classified as Failover Service Groups, Parallel Service Groups, and Hybrid Service groups. In Failover service groups, the specific service group will be online one node at a time. With Parallel service groups, they run parallel on all specific nodes being part of the service group. To understand Hybrid service groups, let's first have a quick view of System Zones. System Zone attributes enable setup of a group of nodes for the initial service group failover decision. So a Hybrid service group is a combination of both Failover and Parallel Service Groups, set up for replicated data clusters. So within a system zone it will behave like a failover and across system zones, it will work in parallel.

Veritas Cluster Service Group is a special cluster resource group that is used for managing cluster resources required by VCS components. The group contains resources for Cluster Manager (Web Console), Cluster Notifications, and Wide Area Connecter (WAC).

Switchover and Failover

Switchover is when cluster resources are orderly shut down on one node and brought up in the similar order of start on the node; whereas for failover, when the orderly shutdown of application resources is not possible, it's started in the orderly manner on the other node.

Cluster Resource

Cluster resources are entities made up of hardware- and software-based application components. Cluster resources are set up with the dependencies to ensure an orderly start and stop of application components. Cluster resources are set with the Type, such as NIC, IP, HA Storage, Application, etc. As mentioned before, in most of the cluster service group configurations, NIC, floating IP, and Shared storage resources play critical roles for application resources to start. In other words, for starting an application, it should start with the virtual IP address (to connect to the application) and share storage, where application/database is installed.

Agents in VCS

VCS agents are cluster processes that control the behavior of cluster resource, such as online, offline, cleaning, information, or monitoring of cluster resources. Each cluster resource type will have a specific cluster agent. At the start, the agent obtains the resource properties and other information from VCS.

Agents are classified as Bundled (part of default VCS build), Enterprise (third party controlled and licensed), and Custom Agents (manually developed for in-house applications).

High Availability Daemons (HAD)

High Availability Daemon, also known as VCS engine, runs on each system and ensures the cluster is behaving as per the cluster configuration, cascading information when a node joins or leaves the cluster, responding to the cluster commands issued to act upon, and taking corrective action when something fails. The daemon/engine uses agents to monitor and manage cluster resources.

HostMonitor Daemon

VCS HostMonitor daemon is used for monitoring CPU and Swap utilization. It reports to the engine log if the threshold has been reached and accordingly HAD initiates action. VCS engine creates VCShm cluster resource of type HostMonitor under VCShmg service group.

Group Membership Service (GAB)/Atomic Broadcast

GAB is responsible for cluster membership and cluster communications. GAB ensures the cluster integrity by updating cluster membership using heartbeat (LLT) status from each node. It sends and receives information to and from each cluster node on the running configuration changes or state. It guarantees the broadcast communication across each cluster node. Communication across one or more network channels is called regular membership; across private communication links it is called Jeopardy membership; and if the HAD daemon dies but the node is alive is called Daemon Down Node Alive (DDNA).

Low Latency Transport (LLT)

LLT is a private heartbeat communication across cluster nodes. These are dedicated IP stack or virtual private connections for dedicated cluster communication. LLT also distributes network load across private interconnects to allow maximum throughput and fault tolerant communication.

I/O Fencing Module

I/O fencing is a quorum-type configuration under VCS and ensures only one cluster survives when the private interconnect communications are lost. I/O fencing is also clubbed with SCSI-3 persistent reservation to avoid data corruption due to split brain and amnesia.

Cluster Management Console/CLI

This is a web based or Java console management console to configure and operate cluster. It also helps in viewing a cluster configuration hierarchy. The command-line interface of VCS is an alternate way to manage and administer a VCS environment.

Veritas Cluster Topologies

Cluster topologies are dependent on the number of cluster nodes configured for redundancy and availability. Basically the models are based on active/active or active/standby also known as Symmetric and Asymmetric configuration.

Active/Active configuration requires that all cluster nodes are having service groups up and running and at the time of failure of one cluster node, and its service groups' failover to other active cluster nodes. Although for this kind of configuration there has to be sufficient resource capacity (CPU/Memory/Swap) available for the cluster to failover. N-to-N is and Active/Active configuration means that all participant nodes will share the service groups and at the time of failure of one node, its service group/s should be failing over to other active node.

Active/Passive configuration has one of the nodes on standby mode to failover cluster services. This is an easy and reliable configuration in terms of application availability, although the side effect is underutilization of resource capacity available.

In N-to-1 configuration, an additional node is configured as a redundant/standby node (like for two-node cluster) to allow the failover of one or more cluster nodes going down and failing over their service groups to the standby host. For this kind of configuration there has to be sufficient capacity on standby node to run application services moved off failed nodes. Second, during failback, all the respective cluster service groups should be brought back to their original nodes.

In N+1 configuration, which is similar to have additional standby nodes, this standby node should only be used for failure of one node. As soon the failed node comes back online, that will serve as the standby node for any future failure.

■ ■ ■

## CHAPTER 3

Cluster Build Preparations and Understanding VirtualBox

Preparation for the Cluster Builds

So far we understand two cluster solutions, Oracle Solaris Cluster and Veritas Cluster, as a part of cluster build. We also learned the theoretical background of high-level cluster architecture and cluster components. Moving forward, let's start preparing for the cluster build process. The purpose of this book is to simulate the real-life cluster build as a part of a virtual environment and walk through cluster build and configuration steps. As a pre-cluster build, be prepared with having a decently configured Laptop or Desktop, Host Virtualization software (VirtualBox), Operating system (Solaris 10), Network Configuration, Storage configuration (for shared storage configuration), Cluster Software (Oracle Solaris Cluster or Veritas Cluster) before starting with Installation and configuration of cluster build and setup.

Basic configuration based on the above requirements – those for setting the virtual host clustered environments as a tested configuration for the purpose of writing this book are below, although this should work with the latest versions of VirtualBox, Solaris OS and Sun Cluster, and Veritas Cluster software.

Table 3-1.

Hardware	Desktop/Laptop with below configuration	
	Operating System	Windows 7 OS
	RAM	6 GB RAM
	CPU	Quad core CPU (2.56GHz)
	OS Disk	Drive has sufficient space to host 2 Solaris Hosts of 20GB each (Min 40GB free space). (D:\Shared-Data)
	Shared Disks	Min 20GB of Disk Space (Virtual Drives to be set up for shared disks)
Software	**Virtual Box**	`http://dlc-cdn.sun.com/VirtualBox/4.3.20/`
	Virtual Host Operating System	Solaris 10 1/13 u11 as VirtualBox Template
	OS Download Link	`http://www.oracle.com/technetwork/server-storage/solaris11/vmtemplates-vmVirtualBox-1949721.html`
	Oracle Solaris Cluster	Oracle Solaris Cluster 3.3 U2
	Cluster Download Link	`http://www.oracle.com/technetwork/server-storage/solaris-cluster/downloads/index.html`
	Veritas Cluster	Veritas Cluster Server 6.1 (Storage Foundation and High Availability Solaris 6.0.1 for Solaris X64
	Download Link	`https://www4.symantec.com/Vrt/offer?a_id=24928`
		(You must have SymAccount Login to access the download page)

Introduction to VirtualBox

So far the discussion has been around the generic availability challenges, but now we move further on the cluster build across virtual hosts being set up under VirtualBox. From here on the further steps are based on the clustering across virtual environments created under VirtualBox.

The setup will be a simulation of real-world cluster builds, both in terms of virtual networking and virtual storage configuration. Any further steps and information followed through will be completely based on the virtual environment. On a very high level, the steps will be starting with installing VirtualBox, setting up of Solaris-based virtual hosts under VirtualBox, and then followed by installing and configuring Solaris Cluster software and/or Veritas Cluster Software.

Oracle **VM VirtualBox** (formerly **Sun VirtualBox, Sun xVM VirtualBox,** and **Innotek VirtualBox**) is a hypervisor for x86 computers from Oracle Corporation. Developed initially by Innotek GmbH, it was acquired by Sun Microsystems in 2008, which was in turn acquired by Oracle in 2010. (`https://en.wikipedia.org/wiki/VirtualBox`).

VirtualBox core package is available as free software under GNU General Public License (GPL V2) since December 2010. VirtualBox extension pack comes with additional support of USB 2.0; Remote Desktop Support; and Preboot Execution Environment (PXE boot), which is used under PUEL licensing for personal use, educational purposes, or free evaluation.

VirtualBox supports hosting Linux, Windows, and Solaris (X86)-based guest environments. VirtualBox also supports both 32-bit and 64-bit-based environments. It allows us to import and export virtual host appliances.

VirtualBox Components

Some of the core components of the VirtualBox are System, Display, Storage, and Networking configuration as far as setting up virtual host environments is concerned. Below is a quick look at these components and their functions.

System

This section of VirtualBox describes Base memory (memory required to run a virtual host environment), Boot order, Chipset, Pointing device (mouse), and Extended features like Enable I/O APIC, Enable EFI, or Hardware Clock in UTC time.

Next in this section comes a Processor, it and allows us to select the number of virtual processors. Set the Execution Cap and using Extended features (Enable/Disable PAE/NX).

The last option is using the Acceleration for Paravirtualization Interface (None/Default/Legacy/ Minimal/Hyper-V or KVM).

Display

This option is for the selection of screen requirements, such as Video Memory, Monitor Counts, Scale factor, and Acceleration (Enable/Disable 3D Acceleration and Enable/Disable 2D Video Acceleration).

The next option is to configure Remote Display, and by default this is disabled.

The last option in this is to Enable/Disable Video Capture, which is by default disabled.

Storage

VirtualBox support storage configuration for SATA, IDE, SCSI, SAS, iSCSI, disk controllers. It also supports the import of ISO, DVD, or floppy devices.

Networking

VirtualBox supports to configure network adaptors in these ways:

> **Not Attached** – Network adaptor is there but not connected.
>
> **NAT** – Network Address Translation, used for preventing external network directly accessing internal communications. Used for connecting to Internet from the guest host, although outside world will not be able to connect to internal guests.
>
> **NAT network**
>
> **Bridged Network** – For the bridged adaptor, the guest networking directly uses a physical adaptor and uses same IP addressing as in the physical adaptor, either using DHCP or Fixed address. This treats the guest network as having direct access to Internet.
>
> **Internal Network** – For internal networking across guest hosts. No access to public or application network; only used for communication across hosts such as heartbeat connection.

Host only network – This is a kind of loop back address, which doesn't require having a physical adaptor/interface, used for communication across a set of guest hosts (virtual hosts).

Generic networking – Not often used, it basically uses the default networking driver.

VirtualBox allows exporting and importing VDI environments as a part of backup and restore services. Virtual Box also allows us to create a clone of environments to reduce the efforts of rebuilding hosts.

VirtualBox hosts can be grouped in for the ease of management of virtual hosts by giving a name to the group. In our setup we will be using the names Sun Cluster Demo or Veritas Cluster Demo group consisting of two virtual hosts.

Detailed FAQs on VirtualBox is available at `https://www.VirtualBox.org/manual/ch12.html`

Installation of VirtualBox

Installation of Virtual Box goes through a few easy steps, starting from downloading the software to executing the downloaded installation binary.

- Download the VirtualBox from the `http://download.VirtualBox.org/VirtualBox/4.3.20/VirtualBox-4.3.20-96997-Win.exe`

- Double-Click on the file downloaded to start the installation

- Click below Next to continue for installation

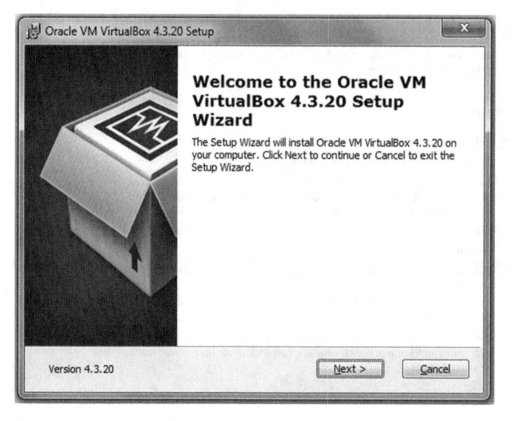

Select default location or choose the location where you want the VirtualBox software to be installed and click **Next** to continue.

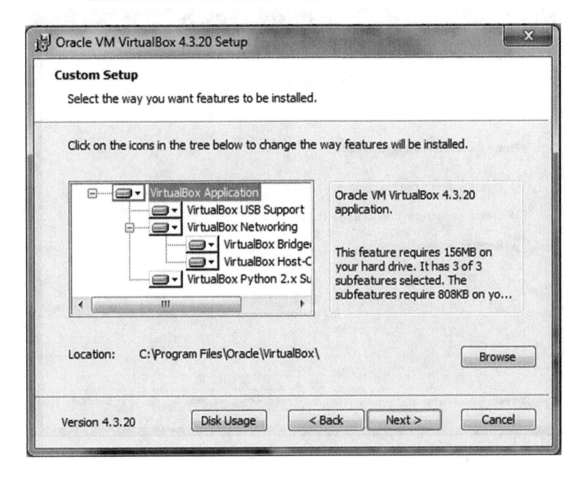

1. Choose the default selection and click on next to continue.

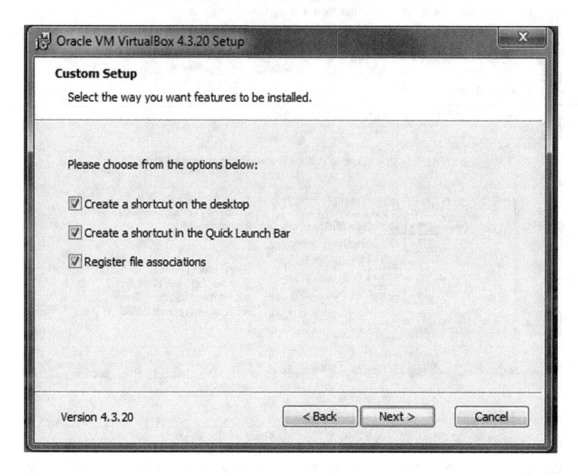

2. Click yes on the warning messages to continue with the installation.

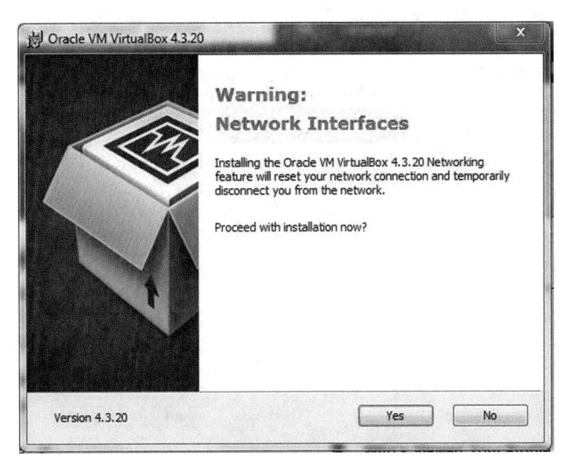

3. And finally click Install to start the installation of VirtualBox.

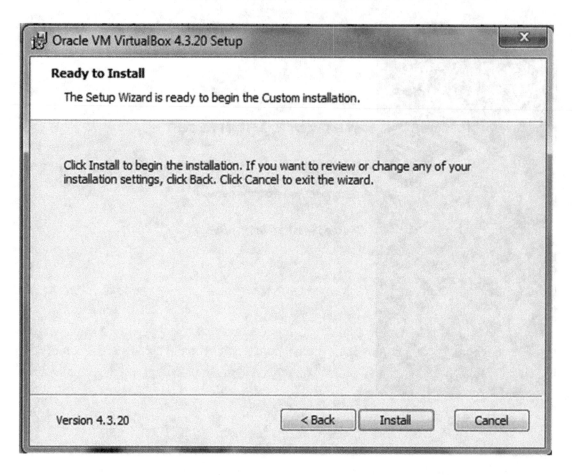

4. Installation of VirtualBox will start as below.

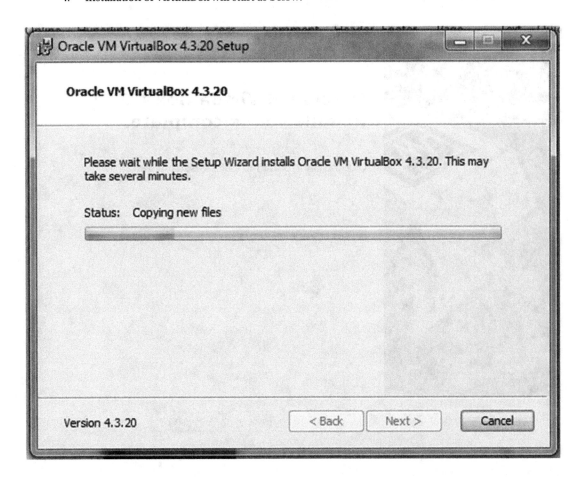

5. And finally click on Finish to complete the installation.

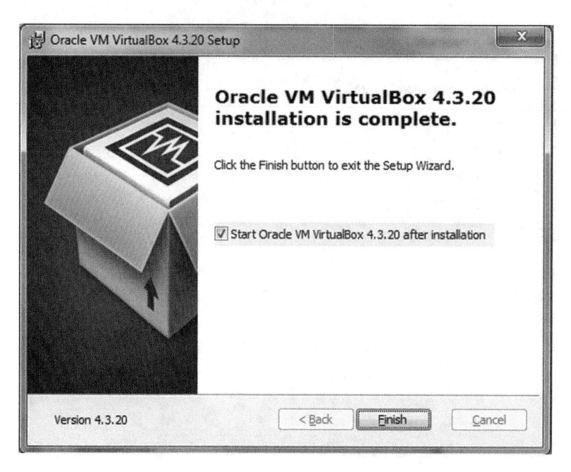

6. Post installation completion, the below screen will appear (this can be invoked by selecting VirtualBox from the "All Programs" of Windows).

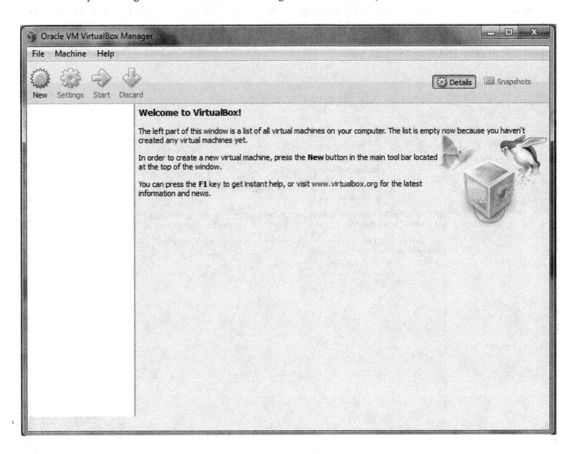

Setting Up Solaris 10 OS Hosts Under VirtualBox

Locate the downloaded image of **Oracle VM Templates for Oracle VM VirtualBox for Oracle Solaris 10**, as described in the Preparation for cluster build.

Start VirtualBox software and click on File and select "Import Appliance" (or alternatively type Ctrl+I) to import the template image as downloaded.

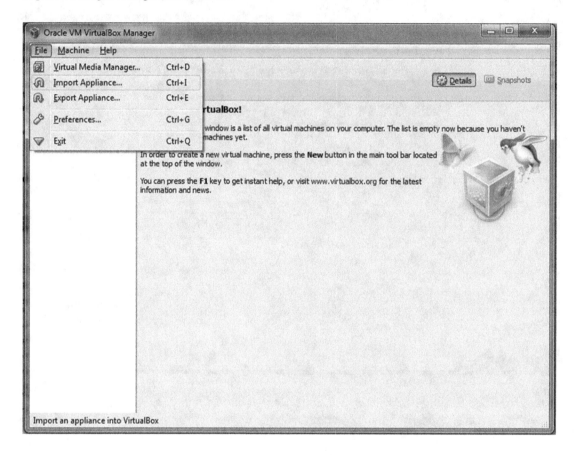

Click on the right-hand folder sign and select the location of the downloaded Solaris 10 OVM file (Solaris10_1-13_VM.ovm). Click Next to continue.

Click on Import to import the Solaris 10 image. Keep the defaults configuration as set below. We will make the necessary changes at later stages for each of the components as and where they are needed.

Import of the OVM file will start as follows. Wait for the installation to get completed.

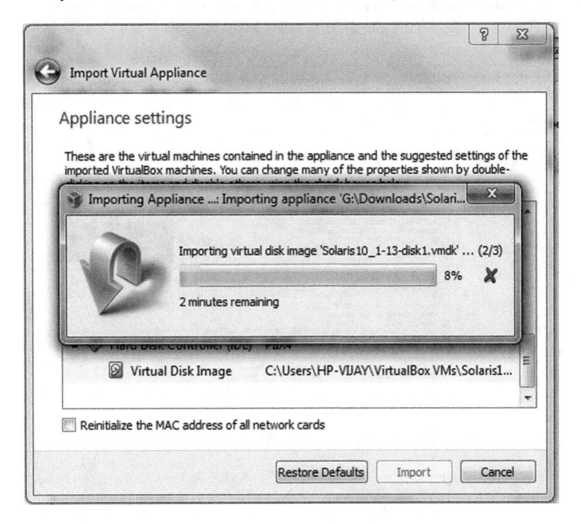

Once the import process is complete, the following screen will appear. This will show details of the Solaris 10 virtual host in VirtualBox created by import image. As you see below, the virtual host has been configured with default 1.5GB RAM and a network interface and default storage is IDE primary master for native OS.

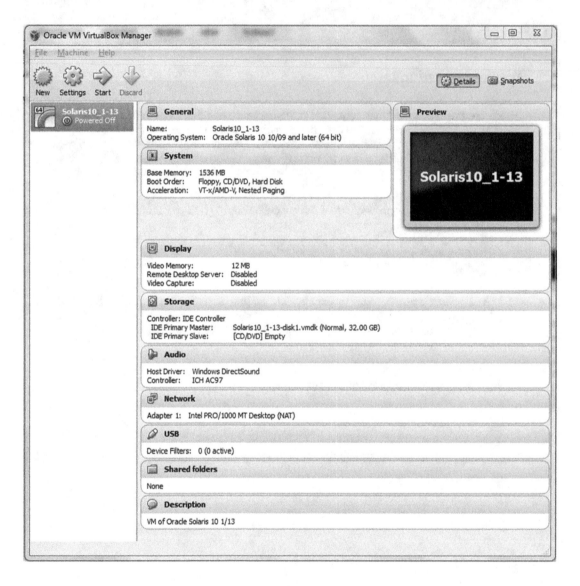

The above setup is for the default Solaris 10 at an unconfigured stage. To start the Solaris 10 configuration follow through the steps of configuration below. First select the virtual host and right-click and select start (or double-click on the host) to start the virtual host.

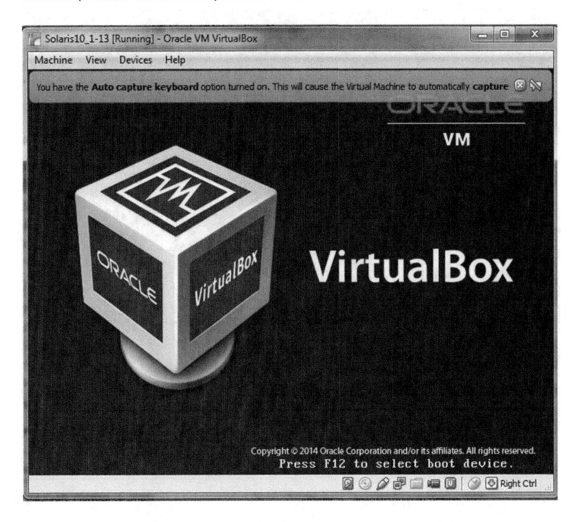

Select the default "Oracle Solaris 10 1/13 S10x_u11wos_24a X86" to continue with the host configuration.

The next step is to select the Keyboard Type (choose the language that suites your region and keyboard). As in the below example it has been chosen as U.S.-English language.

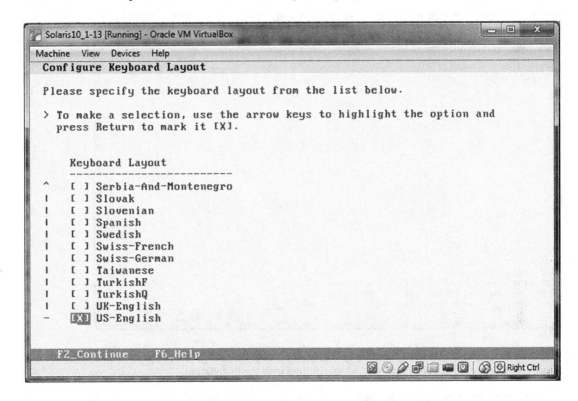

Press Esc+2 to continue with the installation. As a next default action, it creates default rsa and dsa key pairs for communication, followed by network interface configuration.

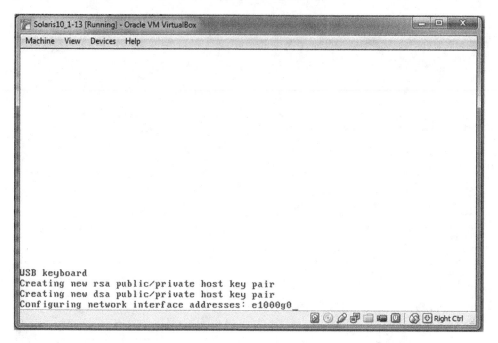

Once the physical network adaptor/interface (e.g., e1000g0) is configured, proceed further with the network configuration as below. Press Esc+2 to continue with the installation.

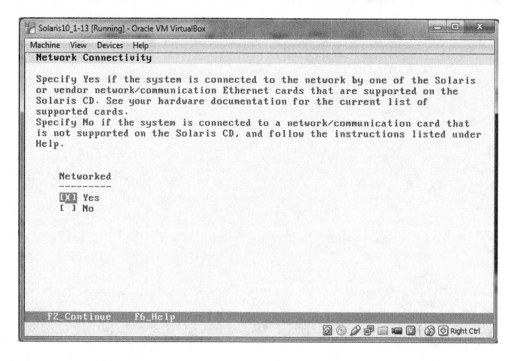

Set the default network configuration as static IP instead of DHCP. Press Esc+2 to continue with the installation.

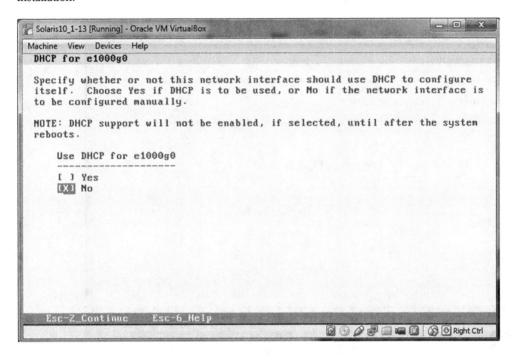

Give a name to the host; here we will use the host name as first cluster node as demo-clus1. Once the name is typed, Press Esc+2 to continue with the installation.

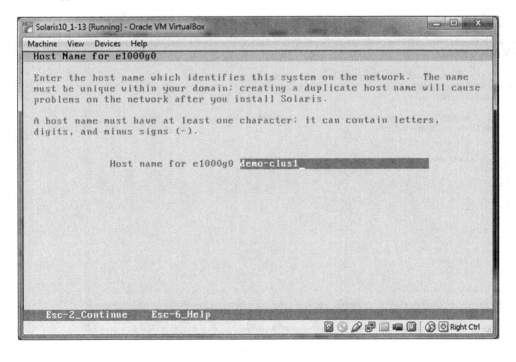

Next is to set the IP address for the interface selected in the previous step (as seen below). Once having typed the IP address, Press Esc+2 to continue with the installation.

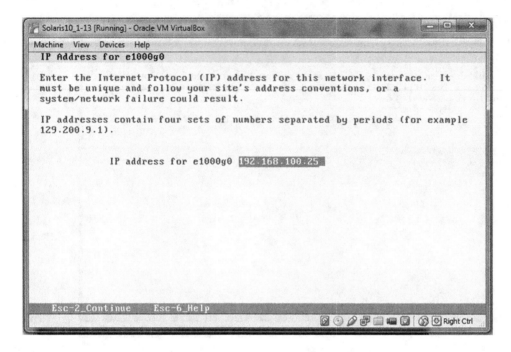

Once the IP addresses are set, it's time to set the subnet of the IP configuration below. Select Yes for the host to be part of the subnet and Press Esc+2 to continue with the installation.

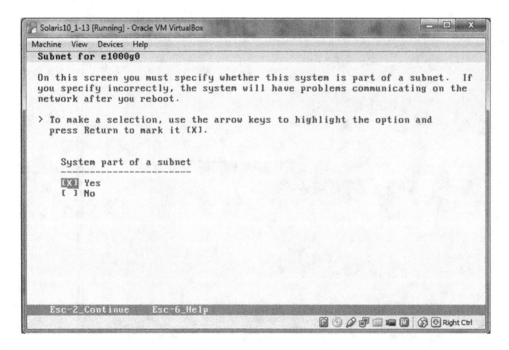

Select the netmask (for the clustering requirements and simplicity of configuration); let's set this to 255.255.255.0. Once the netmask has been typed, Press Esc+2 to continue with the installation.

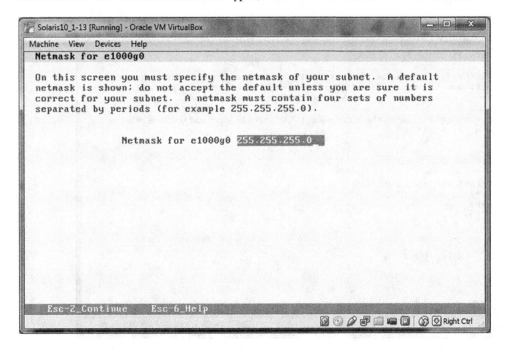

Next in the phase of OS configuration, select if IPV6 is to be enabled and for the required configuration let's leave this as not configured. Once selected **No** for Enable IPV6 for e1000g0, Press Esc+2 to continue with the installation.

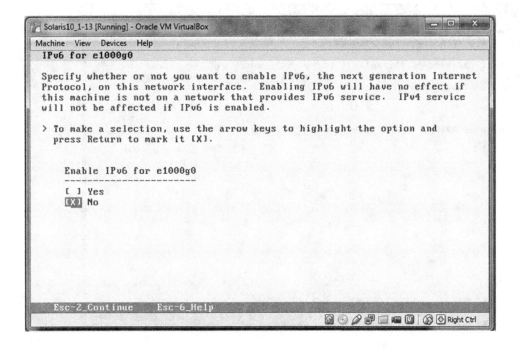

As a next step to the Solaris 10 configuration, set the default gateway IP address. Once selected "Specify one," and then Press Esc+2 to continue with the installation.

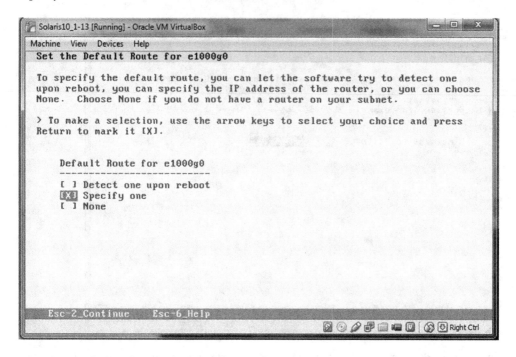

Provide the default gateway IP address; and as an example it has been set to 192.168.100.1 as below. Once having typed the name, Press Esc+2 to continue with the installation.

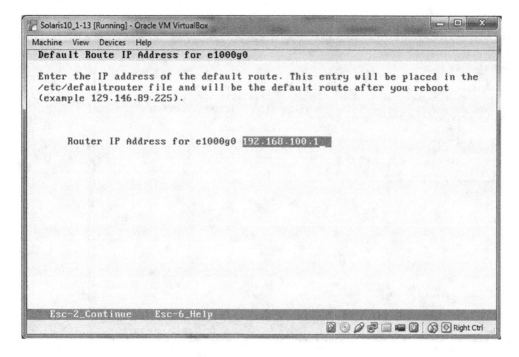

Finally, once the network configuration information is provided, confirm the configuration (or use Esc+4 Key if you wish to make changes to the chosen configuration). Press Esc+2 to continue with the configuration of Solaris 10 environment.

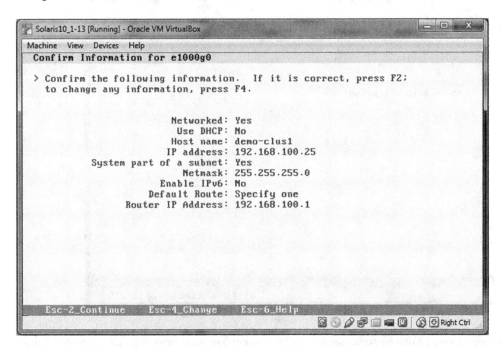

Once the network configuration is completed, select No at this stage for no Kerberos security configuration. If need be this can be set at the later stage post-cluster builds.

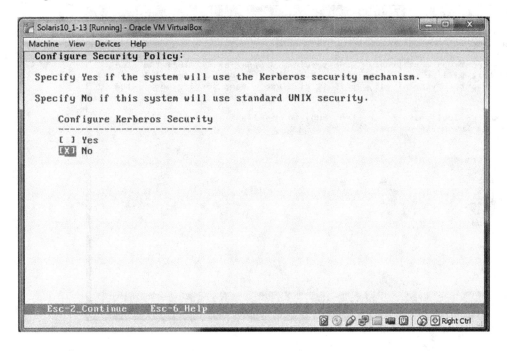

Once Kerberos security has been selected, Press Esc+2 to continue with the installation.

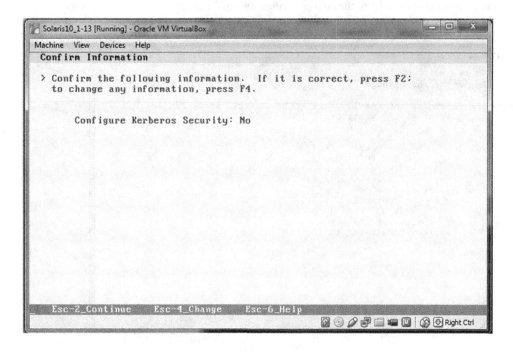

Unless needed, select None for Name services to ease the configuration process for cluster builds at the later stage. Once chosen **None**, Press Esc+2 to continue with the installation.

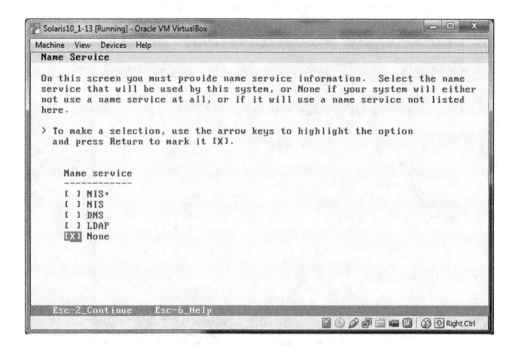

Once selecting Name service as None, Press Esc+2 to continue with the installation.

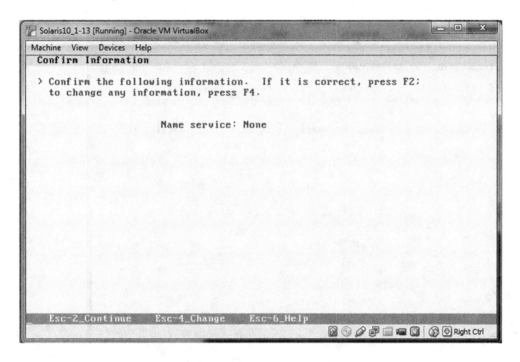

For the NFS4 Domain Name configuration, use the default NFSV4 domain derived by the system. Once selecting the NFSv4 Domain Configuration, Press Esc+2 to continue with the installation.

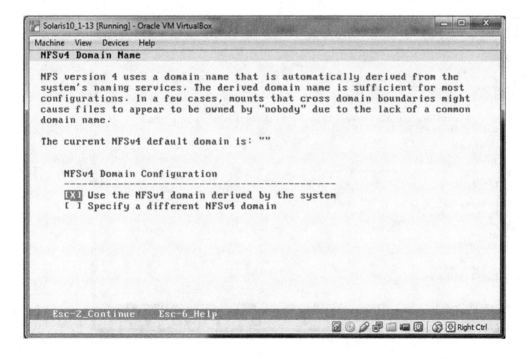

Confirm the information for NFSv4 Domain configuration by Pressing Esc+2 to continue with the configuration.

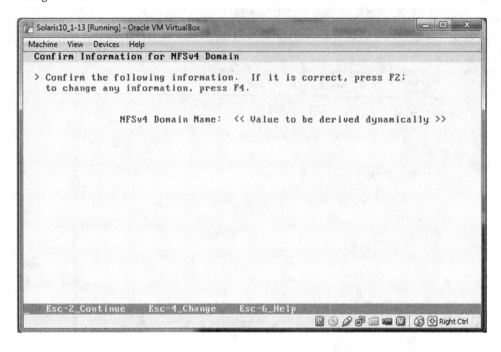

As for the final few steps, select the Time Zone. The below example is set to Asia (although you choose the Continents and Oceans of the area you would like to have configuration set to). Once having chosen the Continents and Oceans, Press Esc+2 to continue with the installation.

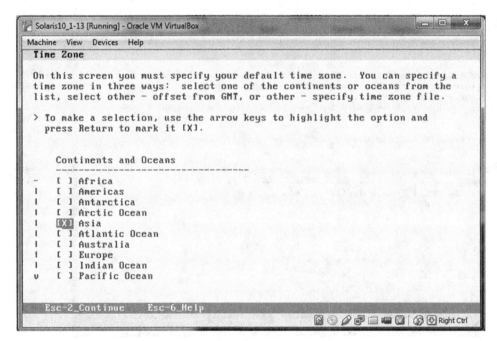

Select the Country or Region (as an example India is chosen). Once selecting the Country and Region, Press Esc+2 to continue with the installation.

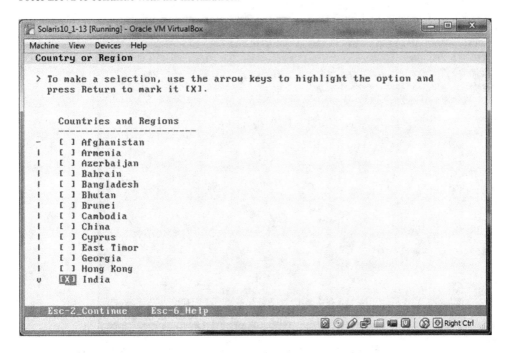

Once selecting country and region, the default date and time will be chosen as a default configuration. You might see the Warning message for the Time of Day, which can be ignored at this stage of Solaris 10 virtual host builds.

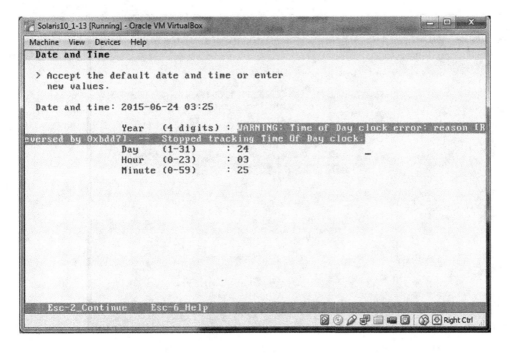

Before making a final decision on Time Zone and Date and Time, reconfirm the same and by Pressing Esc+2 to continue with the installation.

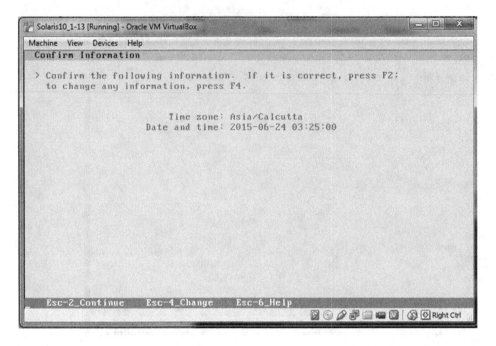

And as a final step to Oracle Solaris 10 configuration, set up the root password for the virtual host. Set the password of your choice. Make sure password is set as per the password policy ensuring password is safe and secure. Once having typed the password, Press Esc+2 to continue with the installation.

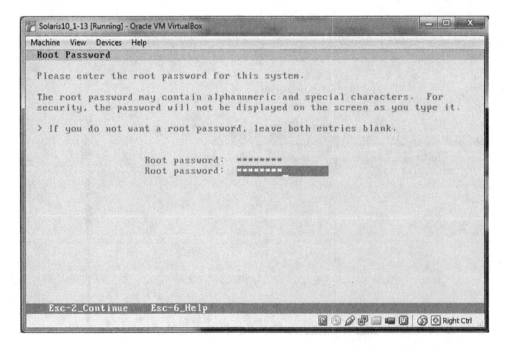

And that finishes the Oracle Solaris 10 configuration. With all the above steps completed, the system will now reboot by itself to make the new configuration information updated.

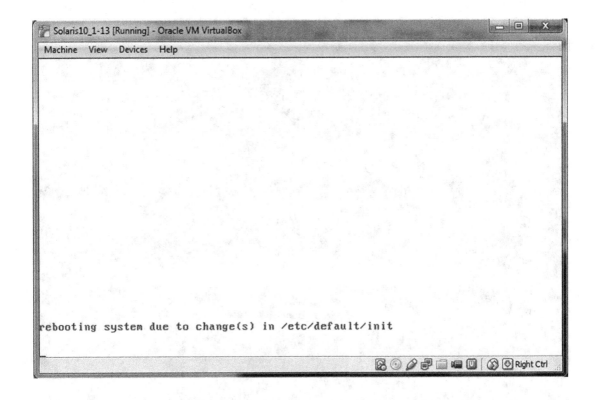

And post-reboot the host should come back with the screen below for the user to log in to the host. And this completes the Oracle Solaris 10 host build process.

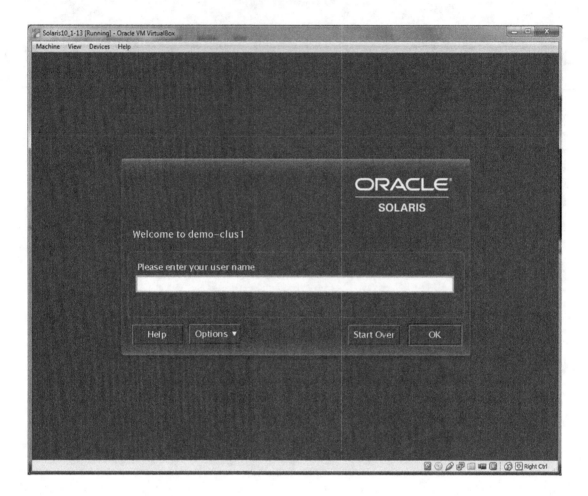

Log in to the VirtualBox console by typing root login and password as set before and the screen below will appear. Right-click on the workspace and start the terminal to open the command terminal to be used for further cluster build processes.

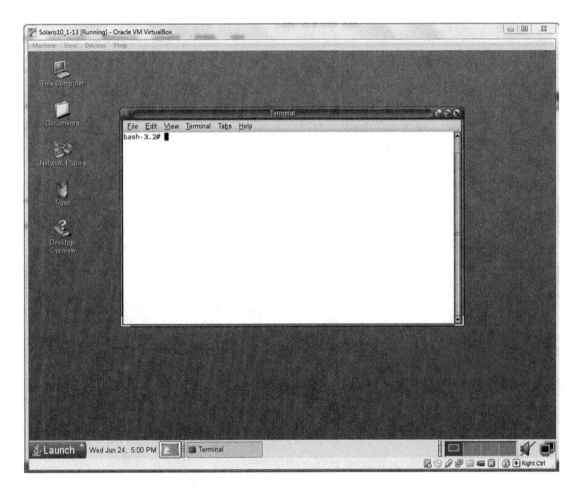

So far the above steps are needed for setting up Oracle Solaris 10 OS virtual host. As the cluster builds it will require two virtual hosts and another configuration for network and storage. This will be discussed in the next chapter on the configuration required for OS cluster builds. This will include configuring the virtual host, installing the cluster binary, and cloning the virtual host as an ease-of-cluster build process.

■ ■ ■

## CHAPTER 4

Oracle Solaris Cluster Build

The focus of this chapter is to help build Oracle Solaris Cluster environments on personal laptops or desktops. These steps will be for a simulated cluster environment, although we will cover all steps required for the cluster build with some limitations and restrictions. To begin with the cluster build, keep the build plan ready with all required information.

Oracle Solaris Cluster Planning

Oracle cluster planning involves multiple phases of activities starting from design phase to hardware procurement to network configuration to storage configuration, installing and configuring cluster components, configuring Cluster resource groups and resources, and finally testing and verification of failover services.

Oracle Solaris Cluster Planning	
High-Level Cluster Design	High-Level Cluster design, Decision on Cluster Topology, Cost Estimation.
Hardware Planning	Servers, PCI Cards, CPU, Memory, Storage, Network, Power
	Rack Mount
	Cabling, Patching.
Cluster software planning	Prerequisite for cluster build (Licensing)
	Cluster Name
	Software versions compatibility
	OS and software patches
Network Planning	Port configuration for Channel Port and Trunking, Firewall port access
	List of FQDN hostnames for each subnet
	Network Subnet for public, core and private network
	Floating IP DNS names required by applications/Databases
	Quorum Server (Optional)
	NTP configuration
	IP Multipathing Configuration

(*continued*)

Oracle Solaris Cluster Planning	
Storage planning	Dedicated and Multihome disks (Storage LUNs), NAS drive, etc.
	Disk Layouts, Filesystem Layout
	Quorum device (Quorum disk or Quorum Server)
Cluster Data Services planning	Number of Cluster nodes
	Cluster Resource Name/s
	Cluster Resource Dependencies
	Cluster resource VIP (Virtual floating IP), with FQDN name
	Cluster resource group names
	Cluster group dependencies
Switchover testing	Testing cases resource group for failover and verifying application availability
	Failover cluster resource group

This list of planning information will help in small, large, or enterprise-scale cluster builds, as a part of installation and configuration tasks. For the purpose of simulated cluster build environments, we may not be required to follow all the steps, but we will walk through each step as a part of the process in general.

High-level Cluster Design

As a first step toward cluster build, prepare a high architecture diagram. High-level designs should be comprised based on respective application/business requirements and solution designs. The high-level cluster design should cover the server's layout, network connections diagram, and storage design. High-level designs should be approved by both approved application owners and the infrastructure architect before signing off to the next level of low-level design.

For the cluster build, using virtual hosts, illustrated below, is high-level design.

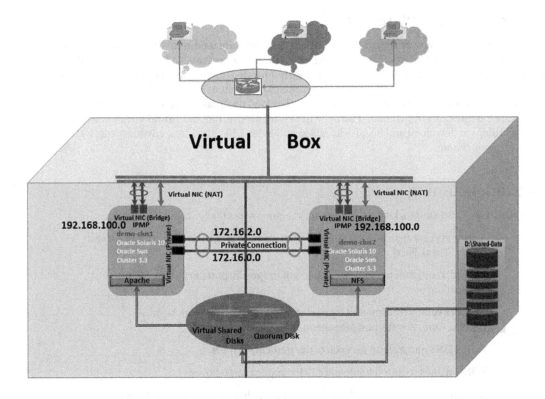

Figure 4-1.

The topology adopted here is for the two-node cluster along with shared virtual disks. As per the design, there will be four interfaces configured, out of which two interfaces as bridge interface used for application communication and will be set up as IPMP for failover, and the remaining two interfaces will be configured for the private interconnect (Heartbeat). Oracle Solaris Cluster selects the default subnet for the configuration of private interfaces. In parallel to cluster design, also define the cost implication of cluster implementation.

Hardware Planning

Once the design is reviewed by respective architects, it's time to procure hardware. Hardware planning involves planning for the right kind of server in terms of capacity (CPU and memory) and other configuration components such as HBA and PCI cards. The choice of the right kind of hardware should be based on the workload, performance, and redundancy requirements. Additionally, procurement of network devices such as switches, router, or firewall or using existing hardware capacity, cabling, and patching are other important parts of hardware planning.

Once hardware is procured, be prepared with rack mount, powers, cabling, and patching plans in place.

For the purpose of writing this book, two virtual hosts under Virtual Box environment are required to have Desktop/Laptop with the necessary configuration (Min Quad Core CPU and 6 GB RAM) as stated in Table 3.1 under "Preparation for the Cluster Build."

Cluster Software Planning

Keep all the required software for cluster build ready. The software requirement is already listed in Table 3-1 under "Preparation for the Cluster Build" along with compatible versions and patches. In addition to this software, also have required application software with start/stop and probe methods ready. Make sure software is acquired with necessary licenses to ensure the agreement for use of the product.

For purpose-stated VirtualBox setup, we will be working on Apache and NFS as two cluster services. Make sure the software is downloaded with the necessary license. (Solaris 10 and VirtualBox do not require licenses.) Steps to download and install VirtualBox and Solaris 10 virtual host environments were explained in the previous chapter.

Network Planning

As per the High-Level Design, keep all the network requirements ready. These will include:

> Switch Port configuration to support IPMP, Link Aggregation (Port Channel), and VLAN (Trunk Port).

> Firewall requirement to allow connection to specific ports to connect to the application.

> Network subnet information for each communication network layer (Public, Core, Private, and Management/console).

> FQDN DNS name setup for each of the participant hosts.

> FQDN names required for floating IP for application failover.

> If quorum server is planned instead of quorum disk, then FQDN configuration.

> Decide on ports configured for IPMP (IP Multipathing) and decide the IPMP configuration-type Link based or Probe based.

> Decide on the ports configured as Link aggregated port and submit switchport – Port Channel configuration request.

> Decide on the VLAN configuration for the specific network ports and submit the Trunk Port configuration request.

FQDN IP Address Planning

For the purpose of the stated setup, make sure VirtualBox is configured with the required network interfaces and keep the hostname and IP addresses list handy for further configuration as shown below.

Cluster Hosts	IP Address	Name
Cluster nodes	192.168.100.25	demo-host1
	192.168.100.26	demo-host2
Sun Cluster HA for Apache logical hostname	192.168.100.35	web-lh
Sun Cluster HA for NFS logical hostname	192.168.100.45	nfs-lh
Cluster Name	demo-clus	

Quorum Server

Quorum server is an alternate way of setting up a quorum as a replacement to a quorum device. This is the typical procedure.

Storage Planning

Storage planning is the most critical part of the cluster configuration. As a part of planning, keep the requirements ready.

To decide on local host storage capacity as well as storage from SAN or NAS device.

Mark the list of storage LUNs pointing to multiple hosts and which storage LUN should point to which cluster node.

To decide on storage LUN, based on IOPS and nature of read and write.

To decide on storage replication if required.

Mapping of NAS device (if used), pointing to specific host and specified permissions.

Decide on the number of quorum devices based on the number of hosts.

To decide on layout of filesystem of storage LUN.

Decide the disks used for creating mirrored disks and metasets.

For the purpose of Virtual Host cluster builds, only the shared disks used by application and one quorum device will be required. Below is the list of disk configurations that will be used for each Data Service visible through both cluster hosts.

Apache:	D:\Shared-Disks\sdisk1
	D:\Shared-Disks\sdisk2
NFS:	D:\Shared-Disks\sdisk3
	D:\Shared-Disks\sdisk4
Quorum:	D:\Shared-Disks\Qdisk

Cluster Data Service/Resource Group and Resource

Before setting up cluster environments, be ready with the information on the following:

List of cluster resource groups.

List of cluster resources.

Dependencies of cluster resource groups and resources.

Timeout, failover, failback, etc., configuration parameters.

Cluster start/stop and probe scripts required to start, stop, or probing required cluster services.

For the purpose of VirtualHost cluster build, Apache and NFS applications will be used. They will be set up with below names, types and dependencies.

Apache Data Service

Resource Group web-rg

Resource web-lh – Logical Host resource for Apache (VIP for apache failover).

apache-rs – Apache resource for running apache binaries.

webstore-rs – Apache datastore for keeping DocumentRoot (Index.html).

Resource Type SUNW.apache

Dependencies For Apache web service (apache-rs) to run,

First floating IP should be configured (web-lh).

And webstore-rs should be in place to invoke apache service. So the dependencies are apache-rs depends on web-lh and webstore-rs.

NFS Data Service

Resource Group nfs-rg

Resource nfs-lh – Logical Host resource for NFS

nfs-res – NFS resource to start NFS services.

Resource Type SUNW.nfs

Dependencies nfs-res will be dependent on nfs-lh

Failover Test Plans

Keep the failover test plans ready to ensure application starts up and shuts down cleanly. It also successfully fails over within participating cluster nodes.

Oracle Solaris Cluster Implementation
VirtualBox Network Configuration for Oracle Solaris Cluster Hosts

As a first step toward the cluster implementation, start with configuring networking components of virtual environments. The networking configuration includes the steps of two interfaces configured as Bridge network and two interfaces for Private heartbeat connections. As for the example cluster (Apache and NFS), there is no need for two layers of network communication inside the virtual hosts, so avoid the setup of Host Only Adaptor. From the knowledge point of view, the NAT as well as Host Only Adaptor are also configured.

As a first step toward the network configuration, Click on **File ➤ Preferences ➤ Network ➤ NAT Networks**

Click on the **+ sign at the right to** add NAT Network virtual interface. The default name of the network will be chosen as NatNetwork.

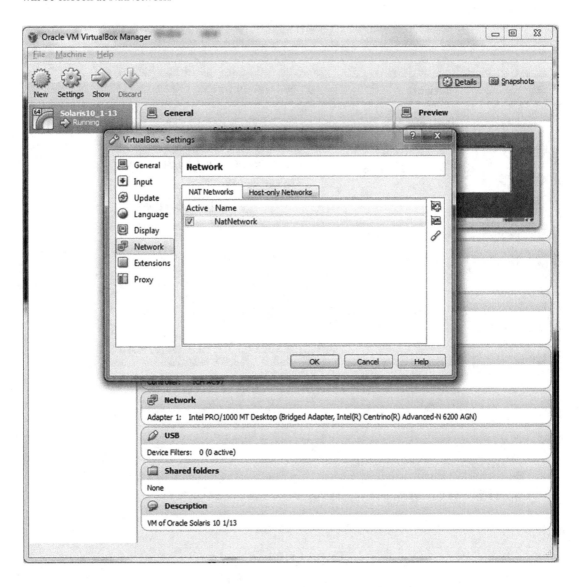

Double-Click on the NatNetwork and assign IP network for DHCP as below. You can choose to have a choice of IP Network selection, although keep a note of this information prior to the selection of each layer of network subnets.

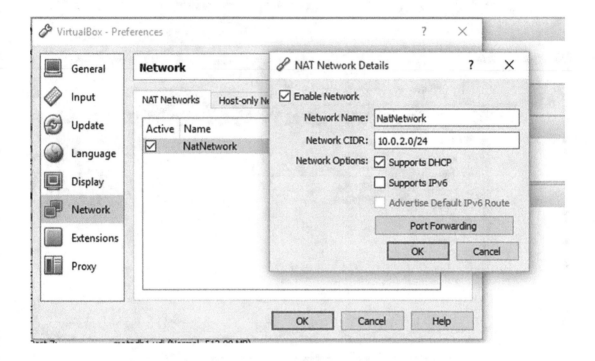

Next, select Host-only-Networks and click on + sign for adding Host only Ethernet Adapter.

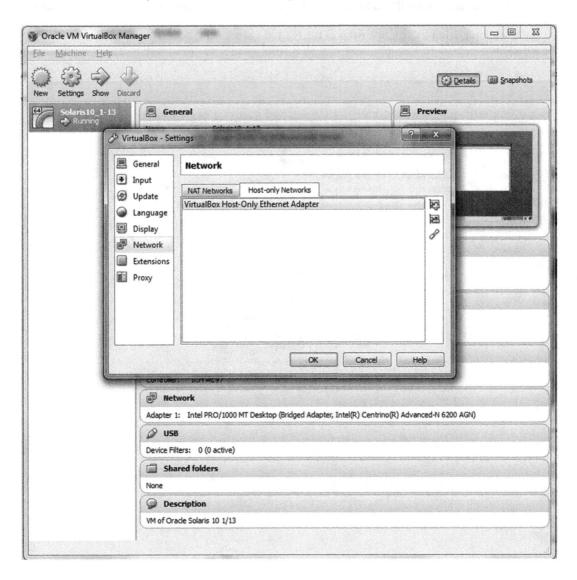

Set the IPV4 Address and Network subnet for the network configuration. Set a fixed IP address for the Host Only Adaptor as the Static IP will be configured as the host for host IP addresses as a part of application IP configuration.

In the example below let's configure this as 192.168.100.1 as a starting address and use subnet 255.255.255.0.

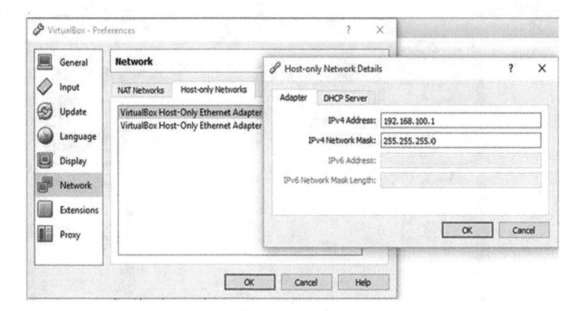

Add another Host-only Adaptor with a different IP subnet as below.

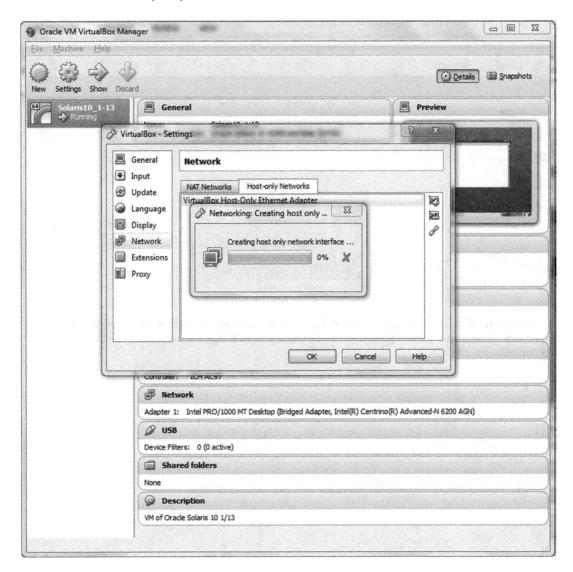

With the starting address as 192.168.20.1 and using the subnet 255.255.255.0.

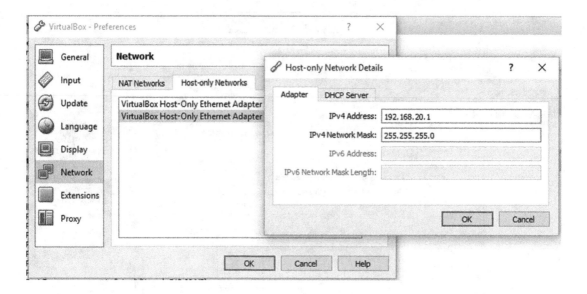

Once VirtualBox Ethernet adaptors are set up, let's now configure virtual host interfaces. We will be required to configure hosts with first two interfaces configured as Bridge and remaining two interfaces as Internal Network.

To configure interfaces, the first virtual interface is to be configured as Bridge Interface. For this purpose first select the virtual host (**Solaris10_1-13**), and click on **Settings** and then click on **Network** and select **Adapter 1**. Here click on **"Enable Network Adapter"**, and select Bridged Adapter by clicking option in front of **"Attached to"**. Make sure the **Advance** option under **"Cable Connected"** is chosen.

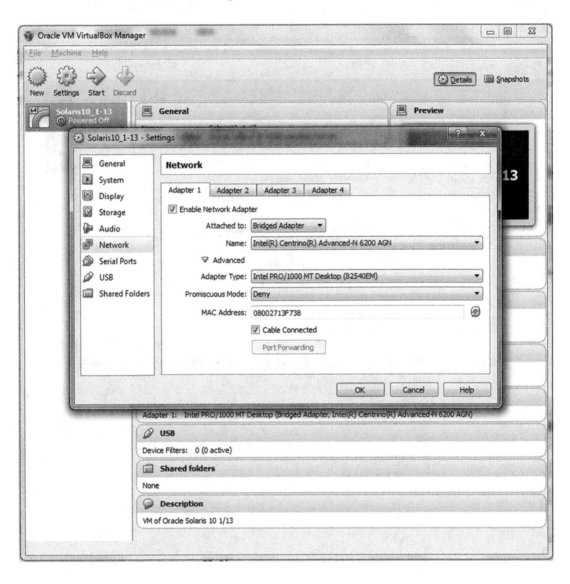

Configure the Adapter 2 the same as Adapter 1.

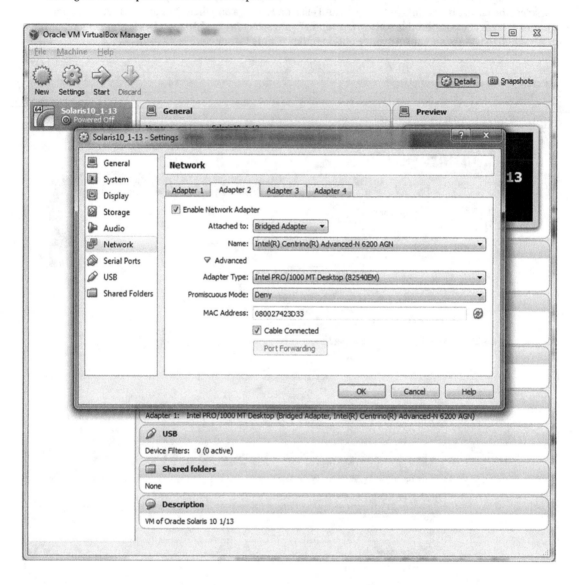

Third and fourth adapters are to be set up as Internal Network and to be used for Private Connection. Configure private interfaces as below.

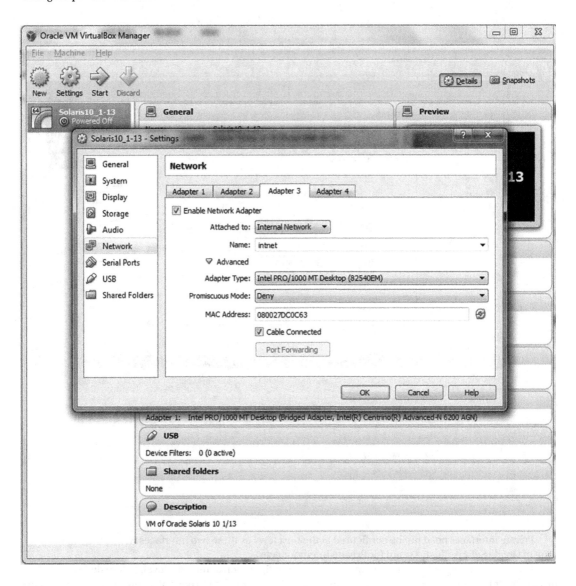

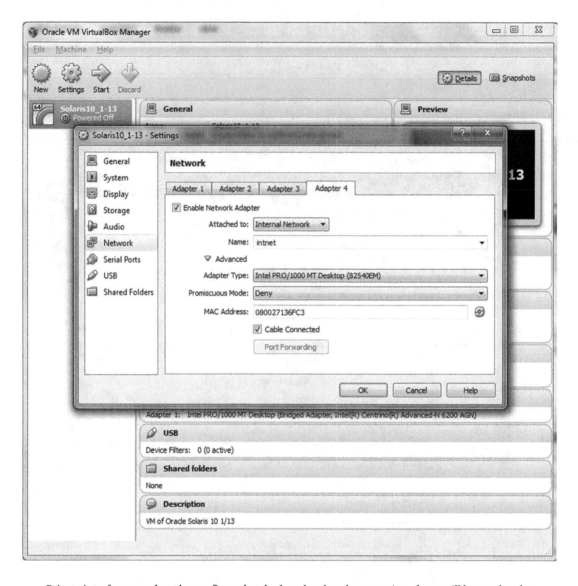

Private interfaces need not be configured at the host level as these two interfaces will be used at the time of Oracle Solaris Cluster setup for Private Interconnects.

For the time being, we will not set up the network configuration at the host level. Before that we will install the Oracle Solaris Cluster Software ("Not Setup"). This is for the purpose of cloning this virtual host to create another cluster node with the similar configuration and cluster binaries.

Installation of Oracle Solaris Cluster Software

Transfer Oracle Solaris Cluster software to the host using ftp or sftp method of file transfer and copy them to /opt/cluster directory (make sure /opt/cluster directory is created before transferring file to the host).

Once file transferred, log in to the virtual host as root (at VirtualHost console), and unzip the files as

```
#cd /opt/cluster; unzip solaris-cluster-3_3u2-ga-x86.zip
#cd /opt/cluster/Solaris_x86
```

And Run installer at the command prompt

```
#./installer
```

The above command invokes GUI to start installing the Oracle Solaris Cluster Software. Click on **Next** to continue with the installation process.

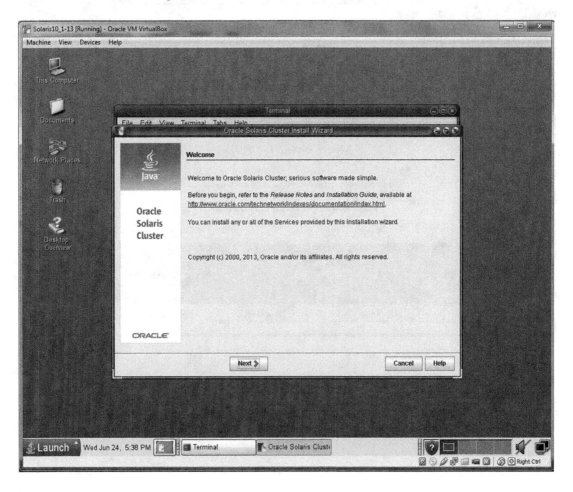

At the next screen on selecting software components, choose Options as Oracle Solaris Cluster 3.3u2, Oracle Solaris Cluster Manager, and Oracle Solaris Cluster Agents 3.3u2.

Options Oracle Solaris Cluster Geographic Edition 3.3 u2 is for installing Oracle Geographic Cluster setup, which is out of the scope of the book. For VirtualHost setup High Availability Session Store is also not required. As we will be using quorum disk setup, Quorum Server configuration is also not needed.

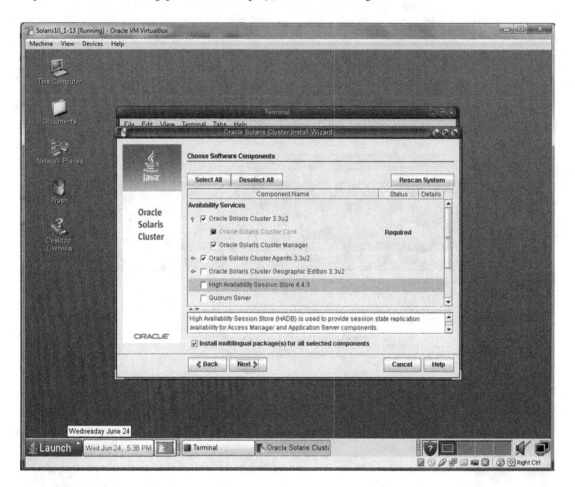

The next screen will first verify prerequisites for the installation of the software such as disk space, memory, swap space, Operating System Patches, and Operating System Resources as below.

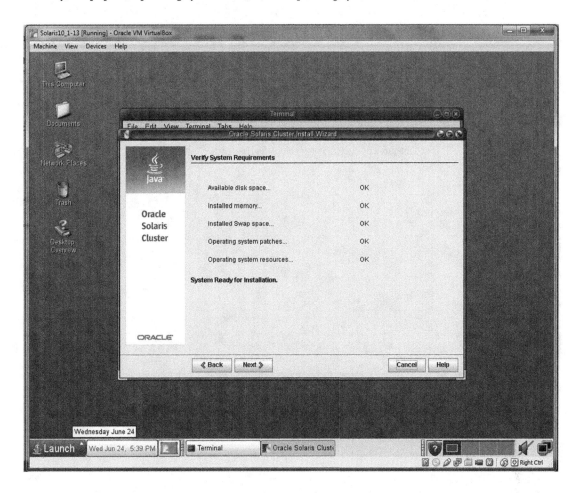

Post verification, click **"Next"** to continue with the installation. Now the screen will ask for the configuration type and choose option to configure later and click **"Next"** to continue.

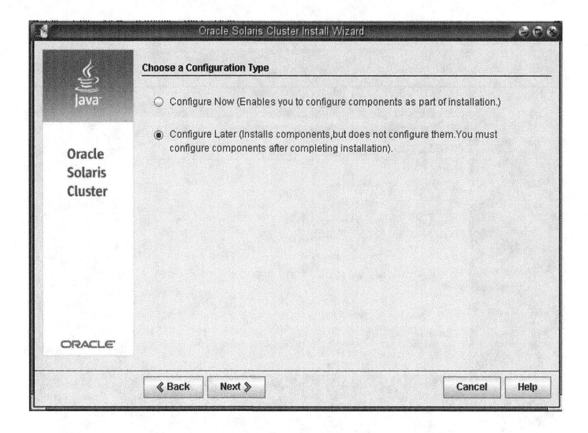

Click on **"Next"** to continue, the last confirmation on the installation will appear, and click **"Next"** to continue with the installation.

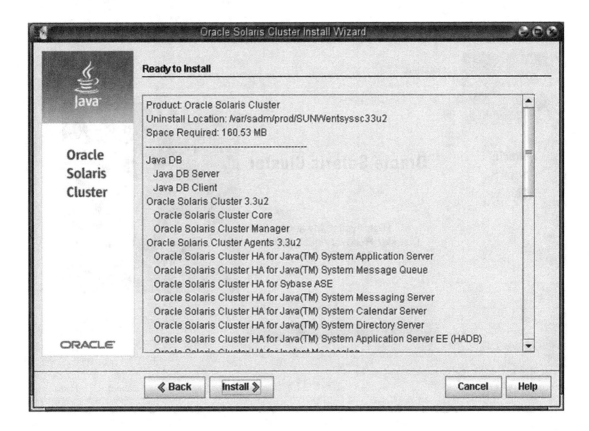

Installation of the software will now start and you should see below a progress bar as the installation progresses.

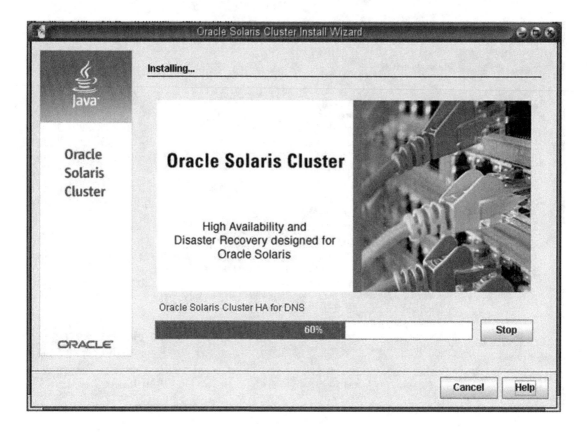

Post installation is complete, and the screen below will appear for the verification of installation. It's best to have a look at the installation log for any error during installation.

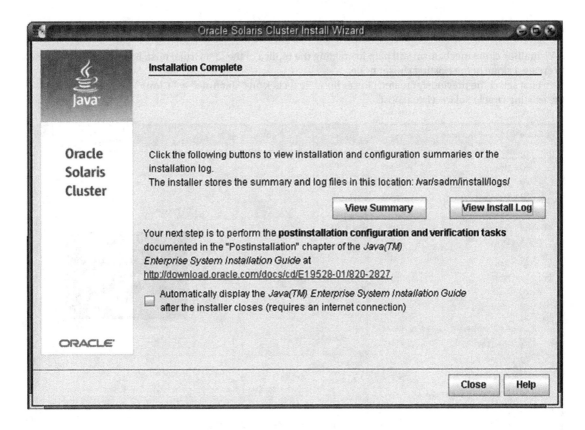

This completes the Oracle Solaris Cluster Installation. At the next step we will create a clone of this host to set up another cluster node.

Cloning and building second cluster node

A VirtualBox clone mechanism will help in creating the replica of the first virtual host. Follow the steps below to create a clone of the existing cluster node.

First select the previously created cluster host. Next click on **"Machine"** ➤ **"Clone"** to create a clone of the existing Oracle Solaris virtual host.

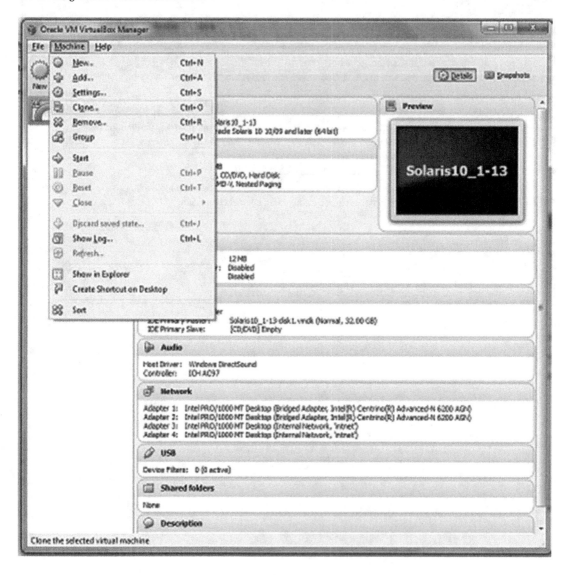

A default cluster clone name will be given (leave the name as is, as we can change this name later on). Click on **"Next"** to continue with the cloning process.

Select the clone type. As we will be setting up a dedicated cluster node, select **"Full done"** and select **"Next"** to continue.

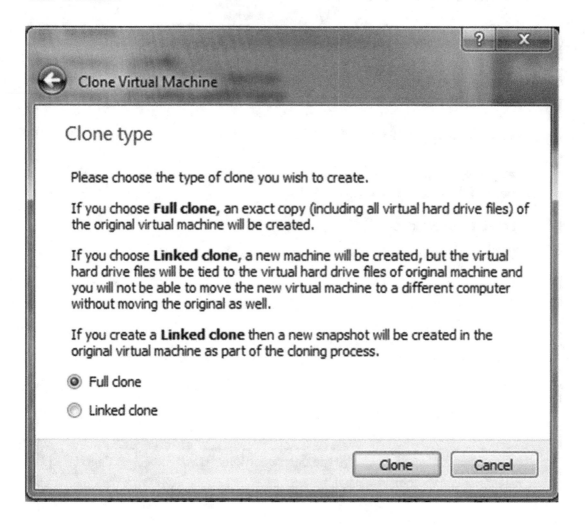

Cloning will now start. Wait for the cloning to be completed. Once cloning completes, close the window and you should be able to see another virtual host created as Solaris10_1_13.

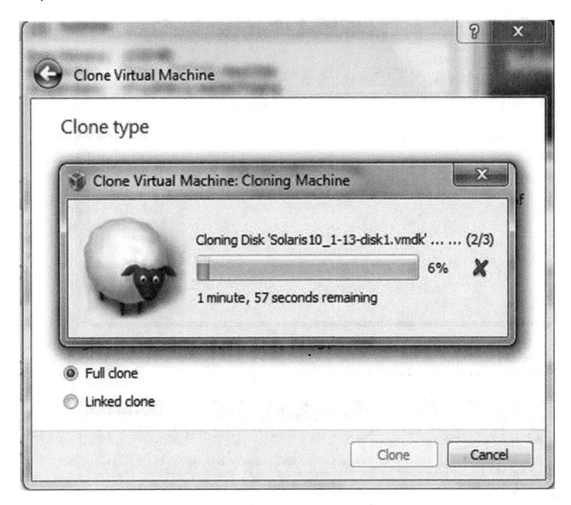

Once a clone is created, start the newly created host. Once the host is booted, log in to the host as root and run sys-unconfig command to unconfigure the existing network configuration parameters as below.

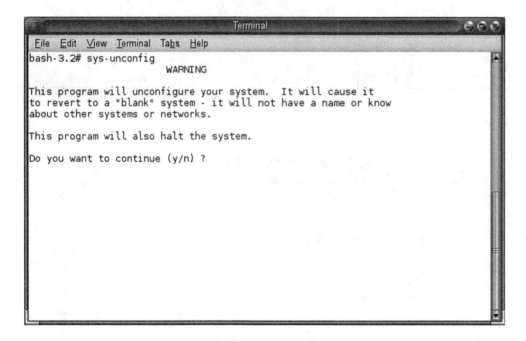

Select y to continue with the node reconfiguration process and follow the steps below. Select **Networked** as **Yes** and press **"Esc+2"** keys to continue.

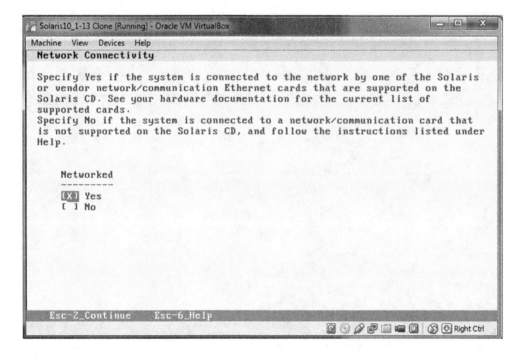

For the time being, let's configure interface e1000g0 interface only, as the remaining configuration will be done later on. Select this interface and press **"Esc+2"** to continue.

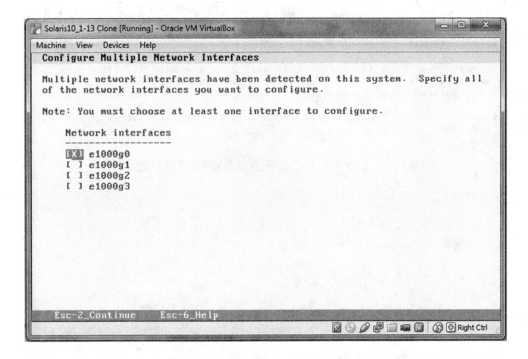

Choose "No" to DHCP for the interface e1000g0 and press **Esc+2** to continue.

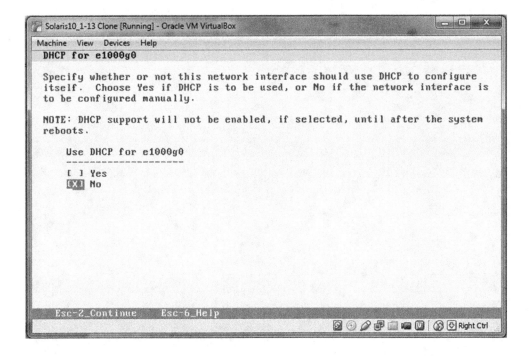

Give the name to the second cluster node as **demo-clus2** and press **"Esc+2"** to continue.

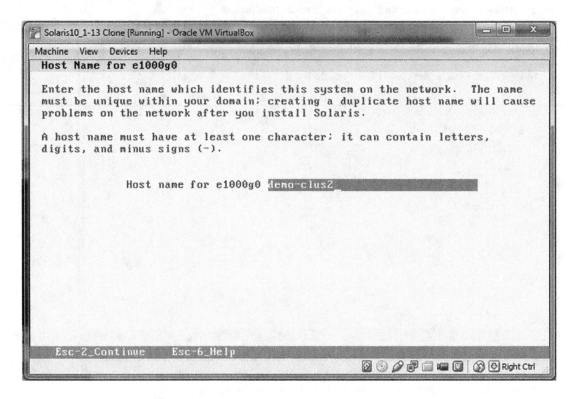

Now assign an IP address (as below, 192.168.100.26) to the host and press **"Esc+2"** to continue.

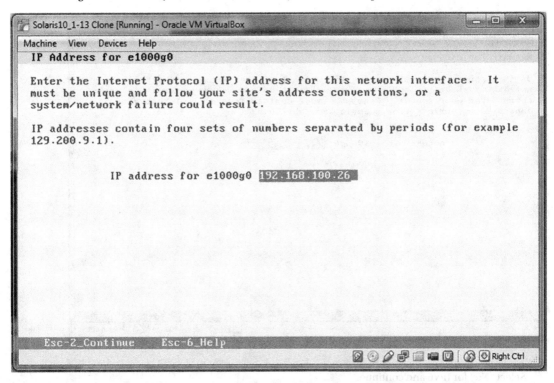

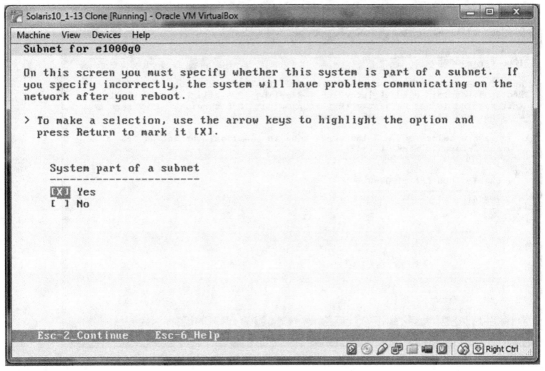

Set the netmask as 255.255.255.0 and press **Esc+2** to continue.

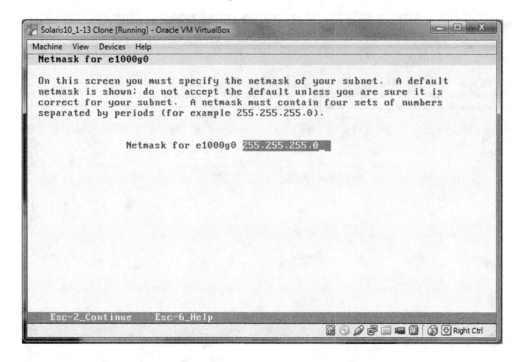

Select **"No"** for IPV6 and continue.

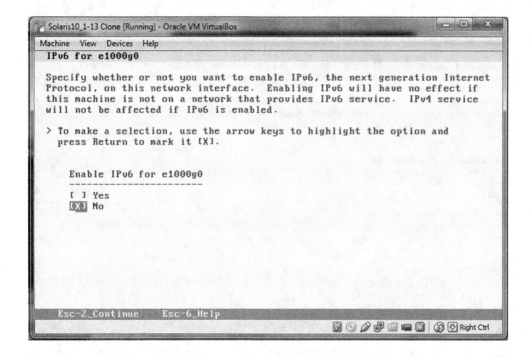

Select **"Specify one"** for setting default route for e1000g0 interface.

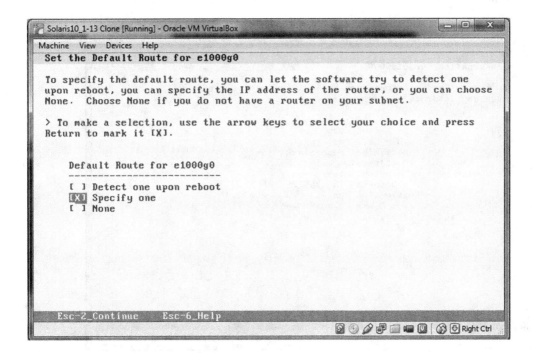

Assign default route IP address as 192.168.100.1.

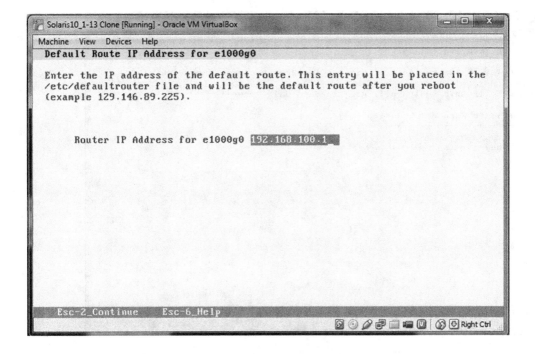

Verify information before continuing to commit the configuration. If all appears fine as below, press **"Esc+2"** to continue.

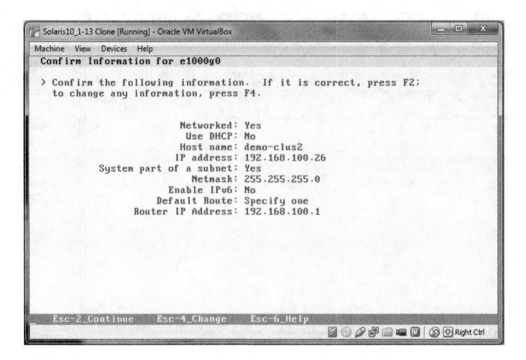

Select **"No"** for Kerberos Security policy and press **"Esc+2"** to continue.

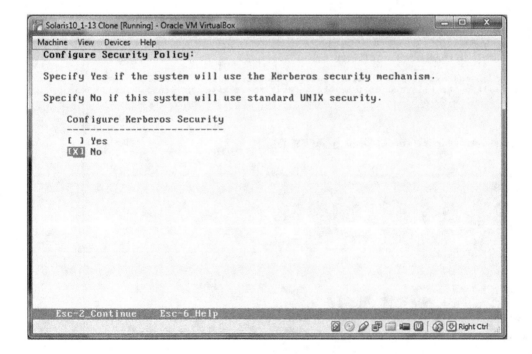

To confirm press **"Esc+2"** to continue.

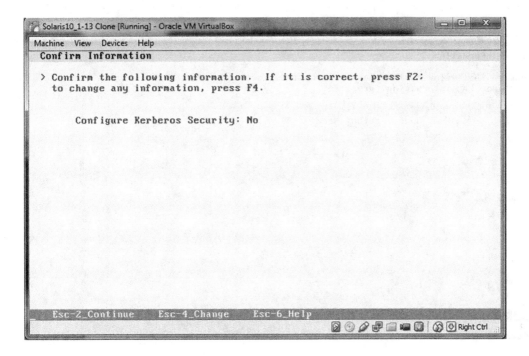

Select **"None"** for no name service, and press **"Esc+2"** to continue.

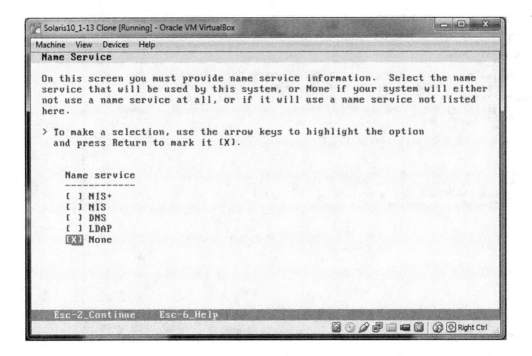

Confirm the Name Service as None and press **"Esc+2"** to continue.

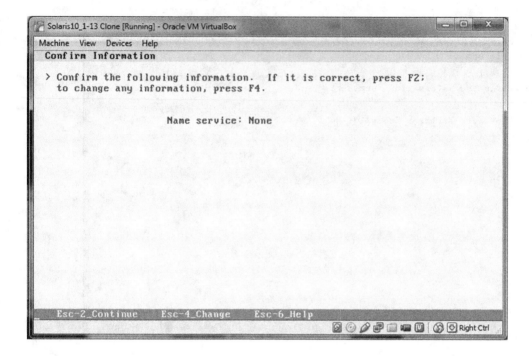

Select **"Use the NFSv4 domain derived by the system"** and press **"Esc+2"** to continue.

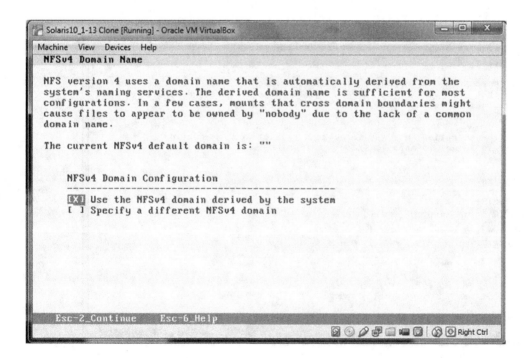

Select "Asia" as time zone and press **"Esc+2"** to continue.

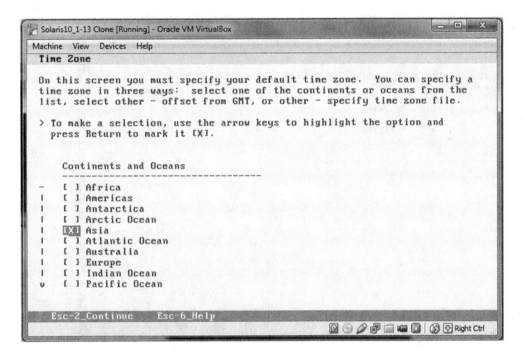

Select your country (select "India") and press **"Esc+2"** to continue.

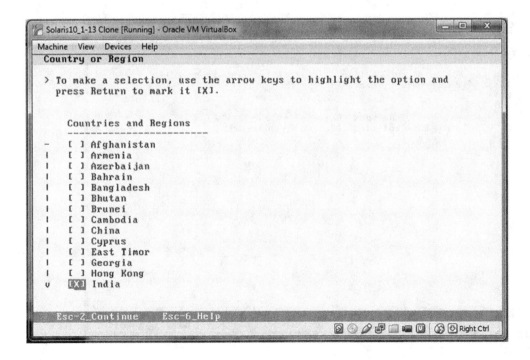

System date and time will be automatically selected and press **"Esc+2"** to continue.

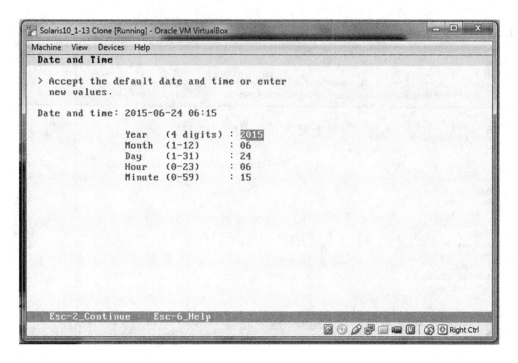

Confirm the time zone and press **"Esc+2"** to continue.

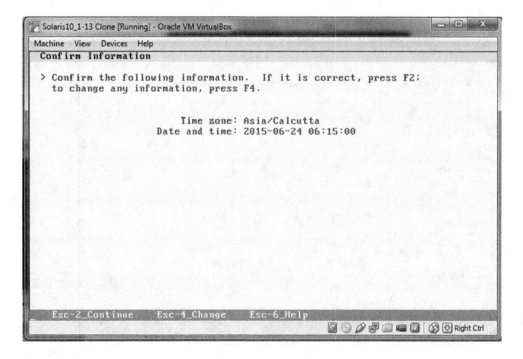

And finally set the root password and press **"Esc+2"** to continue.

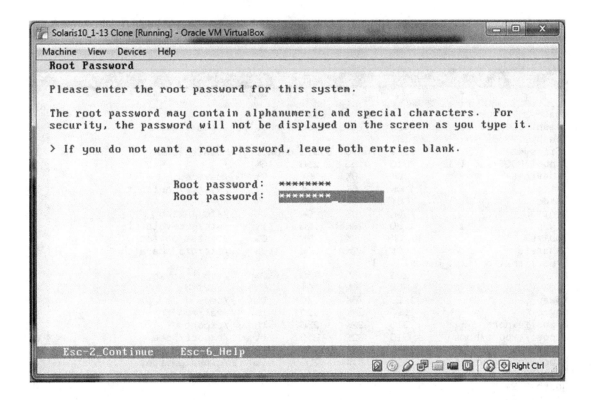

Once the host reconfiguration process is complete as above, bring up both cluster nodes.

Prerequisite configuration for cluster setup

Before we start proceeding with the cluster setup process, hosts must be preconfigured with some required configuration parameters. These are setting up /globaldecies directory, passwordless root access across cluster nodes, update /etc/hosts file with all participant nodes, floating IPs, private hosts and any other communication IP addresses, RPC and TCP wrappers configuration, IPMP configuration and shared storage (drives here) device setup. So let's explain and set up each configuration one by one.

Setup /Globaldevices Directory

As the default OS is built using ZFS, do not manually create /globaldevices directory using mkdir command for the global device repositories. Rather, follow these steps:

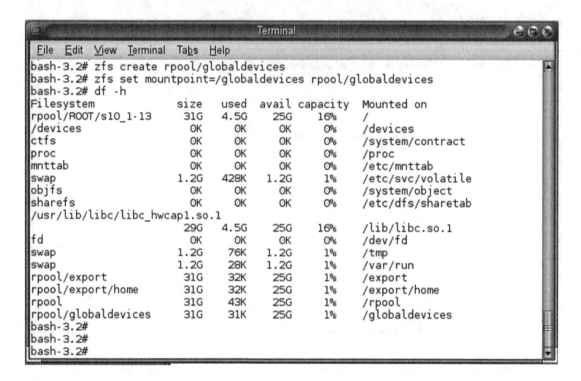

Passwordless Root Access Across Cluster Nodes for SSH

Next on the Oracle Solaris Cluster prerequisite step, set up passwordless root access across cluster nodes. This will help me cluster the configuration build process.

For this, first generate an rsa authentication-based public key and then transfer them across to other nodes. It's the same way from other node transfer keys to this node. To generate the rsa key, run the command:

#ssh-keygen –t rsa and follow default to generate security key. (Leave the pass phrase as blank.)

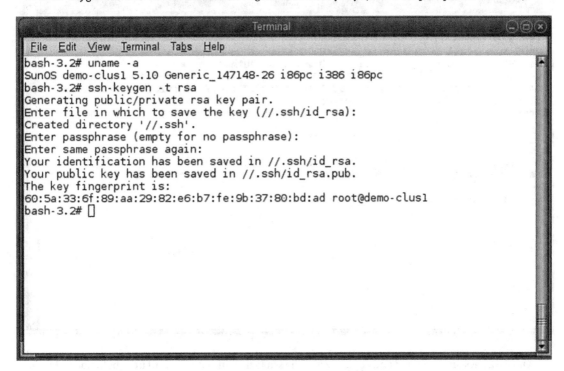

Next, id_rsa.pub key generated under the directory /.ssh needs to be remotely copied to other cluster node as authorized_keys under the same /.ssh directory.

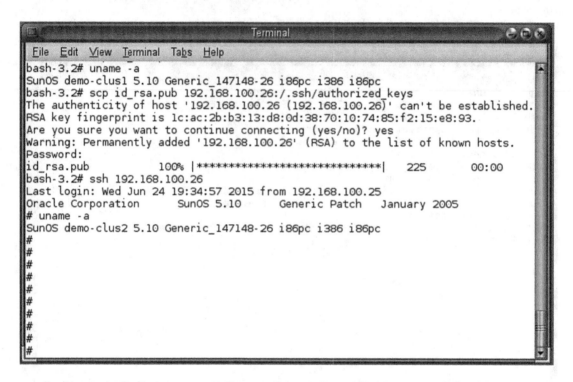

```
bash-3.2# uname -a
SunOS demo-clus1 5.10 Generic_147148-26 i86pc i386 i86pc
bash-3.2# scp id_rsa.pub 192.168.100.26:/.ssh/authorized_keys
The authenticity of host '192.168.100.26 (192.168.100.26)' can't be established.
RSA key fingerprint is 1c:ac:2b:b3:13:d8:0d:38:70:10:74:85:f2:15:e8:93.
Are you sure you want to continue connecting (yes/no)? yes
Warning: Permanently added '192.168.100.26' (RSA) to the list of known hosts.
Password:
id_rsa.pub              100% |*****************************|   225        00:00
bash-3.2# ssh 192.168.100.26
Last login: Wed Jun 24 19:34:57 2015 from 192.168.100.25
Oracle Corporation      SunOS 5.10       Generic Patch   January 2005
# uname -a
SunOS demo-clus2 5.10 Generic_147148-26 i86pc i386 i86pc
#
#
#
#
#
#
#
#
#
```

Once rsa keys are generated and copied, verify the ssh login without password from both nodes. Just in case ssh login as root is not permitted, follow these steps:

#vi /etc/ssh/sshd_config

Look for the word PermitRootLogin, RSAAuthentication, and PubkeyAuthentication and change option no to yes as below:

PermitRootLogin yes
RSAAuthentication yes
PubkeyAuthentication yes

And save the file. Restart ssh service:

svcadm restart ssh

Update /etc/hosts file

Next as a prerequisite, update /etc/hosts file with the IP addresses for both cluster nodes and virtual IP addresses to be used for cluster build as below:

```
Terminal
File  Edit  View  Terminal  Tabs  Help
#
# Internet host table
#
127.0.0.1        localhost
::1      localhost
192.168.100.25  demo-clus1          loghost
192.168.100.26  demo-clus2

192.168.100.35  web-vip
192.168.100.45  nfs-vip
~
~
~
~
~
~
~
~
~
~
~
"/etc/hosts" 10 lines, 172 characters
```

Updating ntp.conf

NTP is used for synchronizing the time. For setting up clusters, ensure all the cluster nodes are synchronized with each other. Any difference in time may have a severe impact on the cluster availability as their configurations are likely to get out of sync.

RPC and TCP Wrappers Configuration

Ensure below OS configurations parameters are in place on both cluster nodes as root login.

```
demo-clus1# svccfg -s network/rpc/bind setprop config/local_only=false
```

or alternatively using:

```
demo-clus1# svccfg
svc:> select network/rpc/bind
svc:/network/rpc/bind> setprop config/local_only=false
svc:/network/rpc/bind> quit
demo-clus1# svcadm refresh network/rpc/bind:default
```

```
demo-clus1# svcprop network/rpc/bind:default | grep local_only
demo-clus1# svccfg -s rpc/bind setprop config/enable_tcpwrappers = false
demo-clus1# svcadm refresh rpc/bind
demo-clus1# svcadm restart rpc/bind
```

```
# bash
bash-3.2# cacaoadm enable
bash-3.2# uname -a
SunOS demo-clus1 5.10 Generic_147148-26 i86pc i386 i86pc
bash-3.2# svccfg -s rpc/bind setprop config/enable_tcpwrappers=false
bash-3.2# svcadm refresh rpc/bind
bash-3.2# svcadm restart rpc/bind
bash-3.2# svccfg -s system/webconsole setprop options/tcp_listen=true
bash-3.2# svcadm refresh svc:/system/webconsole:console
bash-3.2# eeprom local-mac-address?=true
bash-3.2# svcs multi-user-server
STATE          STIME    FMRI
online          9:22:58 svc:/milestone/multi-user-server:default
bash-3.2# █
```

local-mac-address setting to true is not needed for X86 environments (but will be required to be set in SPARC Architecture-based systems only).

IPMP Configuration

As explained before, IPMP (IP Multipathing) allows cluster interfaces failover within a very short period from failed interface to other active interfaces. The setup for IPMP setup for Public Interface needs to be configured for Link Based as below:

#vi /etc/hostname.e10000g0

Insert the line on the above file as:

demo-clus1 group sc-ipmp0 netmask + broadcast + up
addif 192.168.100.10 netmask + broadcast + deprecated –failover up
#vi /etc/hostname.e1000g1

Insert below line for IPMP configuration as:

192.168.100.30 netmask + broadcast + deprecated –failover group sc-ipmp0 up

Save the file and reboot the host. Files should look like this and ifconfig – a should return value as below:

```
bash-3.2# uname -a
SunOS demo-clus1 5.10 Generic_147148-26 i86pc i386 i86pc
bash-3.2# cat /etc/hostname.e1000g0
demo-clus1 group sc-ipmp0 netmask + broadcast + up
addif 192.168.100.10 netmask + broadcast + deprecated -failover up
bash-3.2# cat /etc/hostname.e1000g1
192.168.100.30 netmask + broadcast + deprecated -failover group sc-ipmp0 up
bash-3.2#
```

```
bash-3.2# ifconfig -a
lo0: flags=2001000849<UP,LOOPBACK,RUNNING,MULTICAST,IPv4,VIRTUAL> mtu 8232 index
 1
        inet 127.0.0.1 netmask ff000000
e1000g0: flags=89000842<BROADCAST,RUNNING,MULTICAST,IPv4,NOFAILOVER,OFFLINE> mtu
 0 index 2
        inet 0.0.0.0 netmask 0
        groupname sc-ipmp0
        ether 8:0:27:13:f7:38
e1000g0:1: flags=89040842<BROADCAST,RUNNING,MULTICAST,DEPRECATED,IPv4,NOFAILOVER
,OFFLINE> mtu 1500 index 2
        inet 192.168.100.10 netmask ffffff00 broadcast 192.168.100.255
e1000g1: flags=9040843<UP,BROADCAST,RUNNING,MULTICAST,DEPRECATED,IPv4,NOFAILOVER
> mtu 1500 index 3
        inet 192.168.100.30 netmask ffffff00 broadcast 192.168.100.255
        groupname sc-ipmp0
        ether 8:0:27:42:3d:33
e1000g1:1: flags=1000843<UP,BROADCAST,RUNNING,MULTICAST,IPv4> mtu 1500 index 3
        inet 192.168.100.25 netmask ffffff00 broadcast 192.168.100.255
bash-3.2#
```

Configure the demo-clus2 node as mentioned below.

```
bash-3.2# uname -a
SunOS demo-clus2 5.10 Generic_147148-26 i86pc i386 i86pc
bash-3.2# cat /etc/hostname.e1000g0
demo-clus2 group sc-ipmp0 netmask + broadcast + up
addif 192.168.100.20 netmask + broadcast + deprecated -failover up
bash-3.2# cat /etc/hostname.e1000g1
192.168.100.31 netmask + broadcast + deprecated -failover group sc-ipmp0 up
bash-3.2# ▮
```

```
bash-3.2# ifconfig -a
lo0: flags=2001000849<UP,LOOPBACK,RUNNING,MULTICAST,IPv4,VIRTUAL> mtu 8232 index
 1
        inet 127.0.0.1 netmask ff000000
e1000g0: flags=89000842<BROADCAST,RUNNING,MULTICAST,IPv4,NOFAILOVER,OFFLINE> mtu
 0 index 2
        inet 0.0.0.0 netmask 0
        groupname sc-ipmp0
        ether 8:0:27:8e:14:e8
e1000g0:1: flags=89040842<BROADCAST,RUNNING,MULTICAST,DEPRECATED,IPv4,NOFAILOVER
,OFFLINE> mtu 1500 index 2
        inet 192.168.100.20 netmask ffffff00 broadcast 192.168.100.255
e1000g1: flags=9040843<UP,BROADCAST,RUNNING,MULTICAST,DEPRECATED,IPv4,NOFAILOVER
> mtu 1500 index 3
        inet 192.168.100.31 netmask ffffff00 broadcast 192.168.100.255
        groupname sc-ipmp0
        ether 8:0:27:4d:f4:b9
e1000g1:1: flags=1000843<UP,BROADCAST,RUNNING,MULTICAST,IPv4> mtu 1500 index 3
        inet 192.168.100.26 netmask ffffff00 broadcast 192.168.100.255
bash-3.2#
```

Now let's give a user-friendly name to both cluster nodes as mentioned in VirtualBox. Shut down both cluster nodes. Select the specific host and click on Settings as below.

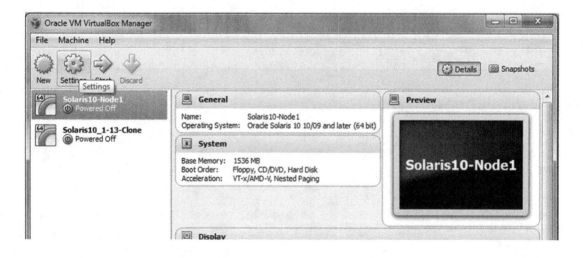

Rename the virtual host.

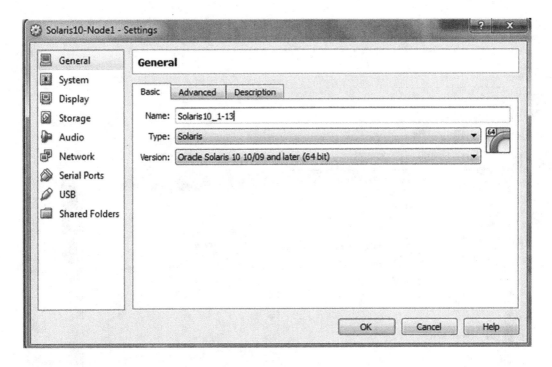

Repeat the same for other cluster nodes and change the hostname.

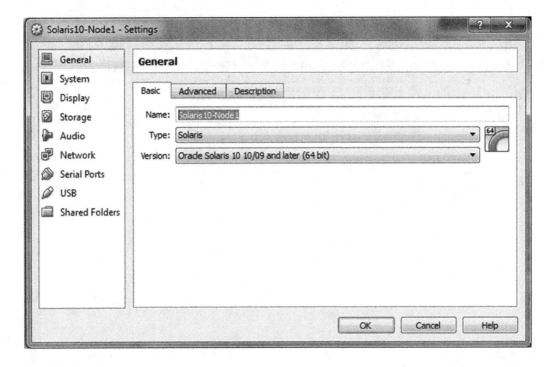

Shared Storage Device Configuration

For the purpose of VirtualBox-based Cluster configuration for Oracle Solaris cluster, to set up the shared storage drives first create SATA controller and dedicate the disks to the given SATA controller.

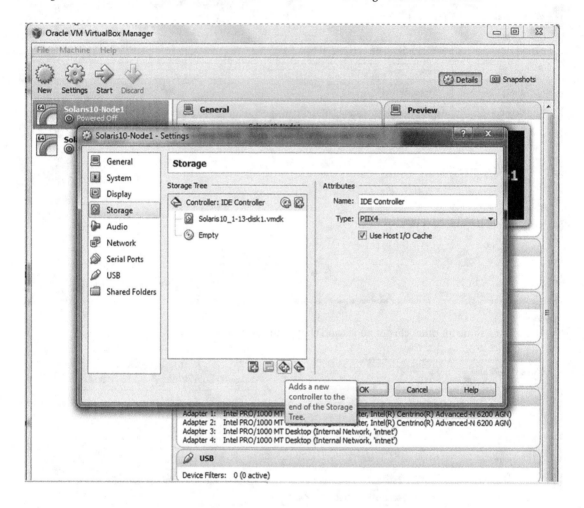

Click on the + sign and select the SATA controller and click OK to add SATA controller.

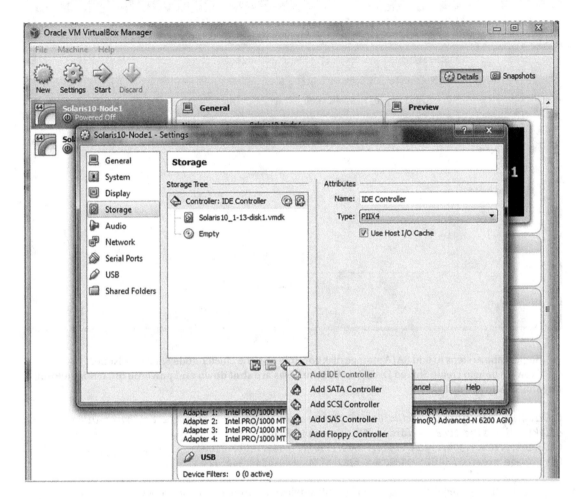

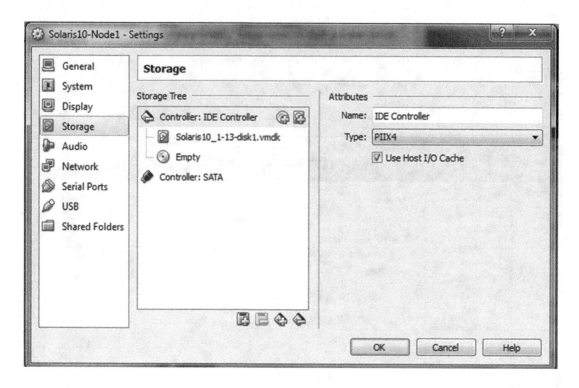

Repeat above steps to add SATA storage disk controller on the cluster node Solaris10-Node2.

Now it's time to create Shared Disks **(make sure hosts are shut down and powered off, before adding any shared storage disks)**.

```
C:\Program Files\Oracle\VirtualBox>VBoxManage.exe createhd --filename D:\Shared-Disks\
sdisk1.vdi --size 2048  --format VDI --variant Fixed
0%...10%...20%...30%...40%...50%...60%...70%...80%...90%...100%
Disk image created. UUID: 98890ae9-f7a2-4f34-9ed9-48dfc3d06929
```

Create other shared disks used by apache, nfs services, Quorum disk or any other purpose later on.

```
C:\Program Files\Oracle\VirtualBox>VBoxManage.exe createhd --filename D:\Shared-Disks\
sdisk2.vdi --size 2048 --format VDI --variant Fixed
C:\Program Files\Oracle\VirtualBox>VBoxManage.exe createhd --filename D:\Shared-Disks\
sdisk3.vdi --size 2048 --format VDI --variant Fixed
C:\Program Files\Oracle\VirtualBox>VBoxManage.exe createhd --filename D:\Shared-Disks\
sdisk3.vdi --size 2048 --format VDI --variant Fixed
C:\Program Files\Oracle\VirtualBox>VBoxManage.exe createhd --filename D:\Shared-Disks\
sdisk5.vdi --size 2048 --format VDI --variant Fixed
C:\Program Files\Oracle\VirtualBox>VBoxManage.exe createhd --filename D:\Shared-Disks\
sdisk6.vdi --size 2048 --format VDI --variant Fixed
```

```
C:\Program Files\Oracle\VirtualBox>VBoxManage.exe createhd --filename D:\Shared-
Disks\sdisk1.vdi --size 2048 --format VDI --variant Fixed
0%...10%...20%...30%...40%...50%...60%...70%...80%...90%...100%
Disk image created. UUID: 3645faa6-acb5-4fb3-88d0-8330de61d7d7

C:\Program Files\Oracle\VirtualBox>VBoxManage.exe createhd --filename D:\Shared-
Disks\sdisk1.vdi --size 2048 --format VDI --variant Fixed
0%...10%...20%...30%...40%...50%...60%...70%...80%...90%...100%
Disk image created. UUID: 5194f84a-f8b0-4c5c-afa0-4a432010229e

C:\Program Files\Oracle\VirtualBox>VBoxManage.exe createhd --filename D:\Shared-
Disks\sdisk2.vdi --size 2048 --format VDI --variant Fixed
0%...10%...20%...30%...40%...50%...60%...70%...80%...90%...100%
Disk image created. UUID: 97a52f9c-6ef3-46ca-8365-1b21454e11af

C:\Program Files\Oracle\VirtualBox>VBoxManage.exe createhd --filename D:\Shared-
Disks\sdisk3.vdi --size 2048 --format VDI --variant Fixed
0%...10%...20%...30%...40%...50%...60%...70%...80%...90%...100%
Disk image created. UUID: 373f5931-61b5-4db9-be90-1802d64c3220

C:\Program Files\Oracle\VirtualBox>VBoxManage.exe createhd --filename D:\Shared-
Disks\sdisk4.vdi --size 2048 --format VDI --variant Fixed
0%...10%...20%...30%...40%...50%...60%...70%...80%...90%...100%
Disk image created. UUID: 0f029f90-53ad-48a7-9053-22367baaa6c3

C:\Program Files\Oracle\VirtualBox>VBoxManage.exe createhd --filename D:\Shared-
Disks\sdisk5.vdi --size 2048 --format VDI --variant Fixed
0%...10%...20%...30%...40%...50%...60%...70%...80%...90%...100%
Disk image created. UUID: 7413d526-a525-40a7-be4d-3fc6cc68e617

C:\Program Files\Oracle\VirtualBox>VBoxManage.exe createhd --filename D:\Shared-
Disks\sdisk6.vdi --size 2048 --format VDI --variant Fixed
0%...10%...20%...30%...40%...50%...60%...70%...80%...90%...100%
Disk image created. UUID: f2083b50-0890-4c06-8f1d-34dc2c8e1f00

C:\Program Files\Oracle\VirtualBox>
```

Next mark these disks as **SATA shared** using these commands:

VBoxManage.exe storageattach Solaris10-Node1 --storagectl "SATA" --port 1 --device 0 --type
hdd --medium D:\Shared-Disks\sdisk1.vdi --mtype shareable
VBoxManage.exe storageattach Solaris10-Node1 --storagectl "SATA" --port 2 --device 0 --type
hdd --medium D:\Shared-Disks\sdisk2.vdi --mtype shareable
VBoxManage.exe storageattach Solaris10-Node1 --storagectl "SATA" --port 3 --device 0 --type
hdd --medium D:\Shared-Disks\sdisk3.vdi --mtype shareable
VBoxManage.exe storageattach Solaris10-Node1 --storagectl "SATA" --port 4 --device 0 --type
hdd --medium D:\Shared-Disks\sdisk4.vdi --mtype shareable
VBoxManage.exe storageattach Solaris10-Node1 --storagectl "SATA" --port 5 --device 0 --type
hdd --medium D:\Shared-Disks\sdisk5.vdi --mtype shareable
VBoxManage.exe storageattach Solaris10-Node1 --storagectl "SATA" --port 6 --device 0 --type
hdd --medium D:\Shared-Disks\sdisk6.vdi --mtype shareable

```
Command Prompt                                                    [─] [□] [ ⅩⅩ ]

C:\Program Files\Oracle\VirtualBox>VBoxManage.exe storageattach Solaris10-Node1
--storagectl "SATA"  --port 1 --device 0 --type hdd --medium D:\Shared-Disks\sdi
sk1.vdi --mtype shareable

C:\Program Files\Oracle\VirtualBox>VBoxManage.exe storageattach Solaris10-Node1
--storagectl "SATA"  --port 2 --device 0 --type hdd --medium D:\Shared-Disks\sdi
sk2.vdi --mtype shareable

C:\Program Files\Oracle\VirtualBox>VBoxManage.exe storageattach Solaris10-Node1
--storagectl "SATA"  --port 3 --device 0 --type hdd --medium D:\Shared-Disks\sdi
sk3.vdi --mtype shareable

C:\Program Files\Oracle\VirtualBox>VBoxManage.exe storageattach Solaris10-Node1
--storagectl "SATA"  --port 4 --device 0 --type hdd --medium D:\Shared-Disks\sdi
sk4.vdi --mtype shareable

C:\Program Files\Oracle\VirtualBox>VBoxManage.exe storageattach Solaris10-Node1
--storagectl "SATA"  --port 5 --device 0 --type hdd --medium D:\Shared-Disks\sdi
sk5.vdi --mtype shareable

C:\Program Files\Oracle\VirtualBox>VBoxManage.exe storageattach Solaris10-Node1
--storagectl "SATA"  --port 6 --device 0 --type hdd --medium D:\Shared-Disks\sdi
sk6.vdi --mtype shareable
```

Repeat above steps for Solaris-Node2 virtual host as shown below:

```
Command Prompt                                                    [─] [□] [ Ⅹ ]

C:\Program Files\Oracle\VirtualBox>VBoxManage.exe storageattach Solaris10-Node2
--storagectl "SATA" --port 1 --device 0 --type hdd --medium D:\Shared-Disks\sdis
k1.vdi --mtype shareable

C:\Program Files\Oracle\VirtualBox>VBoxManage.exe storageattach Solaris10-Node2
--storagectl "SATA" --port 2 --device 0 --type hdd --medium D:\Shared-Disks\sdis
k2.vdi --mtype shareable

C:\Program Files\Oracle\VirtualBox>VBoxManage.exe storageattach Solaris10-Node2
--storagectl "SATA" --port 3 --device 0 --type hdd --medium D:\Shared-Disks\sdis
k3.vdi --mtype shareable

C:\Program Files\Oracle\VirtualBox>VBoxManage.exe storageattach Solaris10-Node2
--storagectl "SATA" --port 4 --device 0 --type hdd --medium D:\Shared-Disks\sdis
k4.vdi --mtype shareable

C:\Program Files\Oracle\VirtualBox>VBoxManage.exe storageattach Solaris10-Node2
--storagectl "SATA" --port 5 --device 0 --type hdd --medium D:\Shared-Disks\sdis
k5.vdi --mtype shareable

C:\Program Files\Oracle\VirtualBox>VBoxManage.exe storageattach Solaris10-Node2
--storagectl "SATA" --port 6 --device 0 --type hdd --medium D:\Shared-Disks\sdis
k6.vdi --mtype shareable
```

Add the Quorum disk as well to the SATA Controller and assign the port for both virtual hosts:

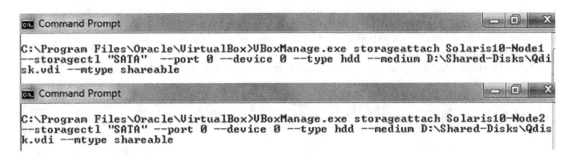

Finally, make the all disks as shareable to both hosts.

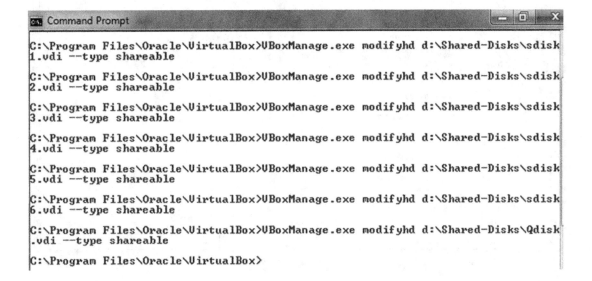

Boot hosts and run below commands to update device tree and did devices databases:

devfsadm –C (Update device create) and

scdidadm –r (Refresh did device tree). Once disks are added the VirtualBox screen should look like the one below.

Set Up Local Disks

The next task is to add two disks of 512MB to be used for metadb. These will not be shared, as each metadb will be local to its host. For this, shut down both nodes and then select the virtual host Solaris10-Node1 and then click on Settings and click on as below to add a new disk. Instead of using the command line as above, we will use GUI to create new disks.

Select Controller:SATA (by clicking on it) and click on left + sign as below to add a new disk:

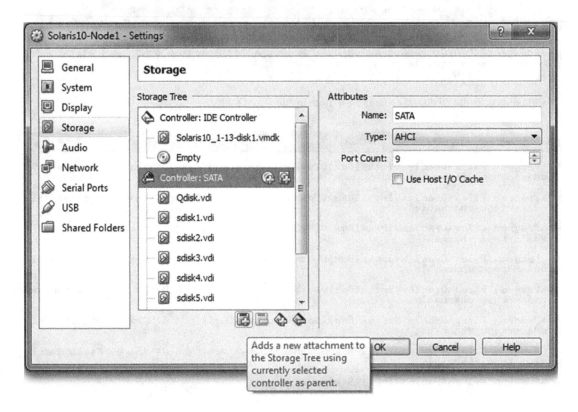

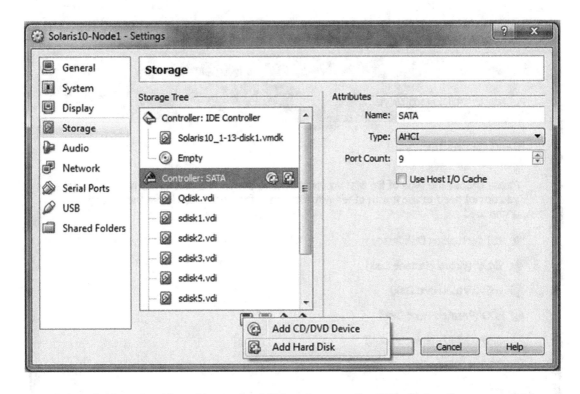

Click on "Add Hard Disk" to add a new hard disk under controller SATA. Click on "create new disk."

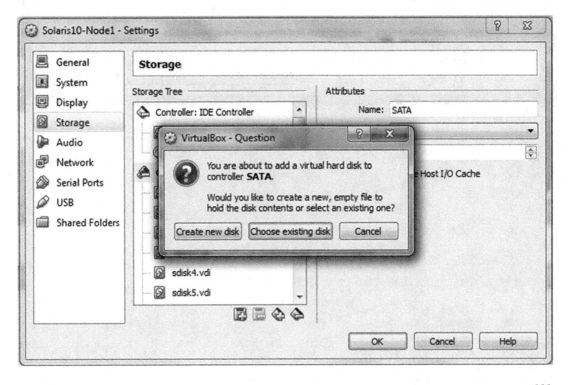

Select VDI as below and Click Next button to continue.

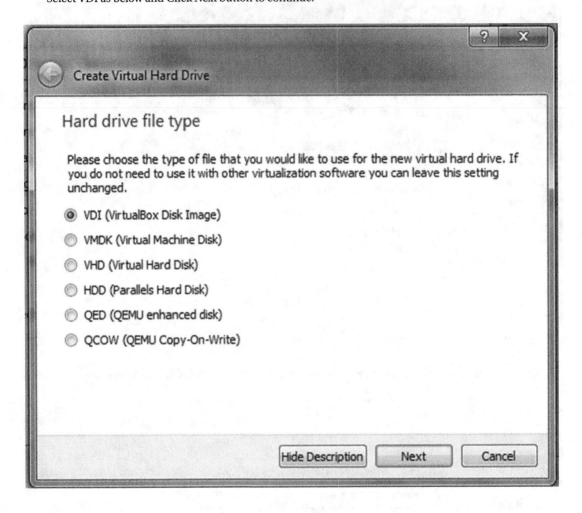

Select Fixed size as below.

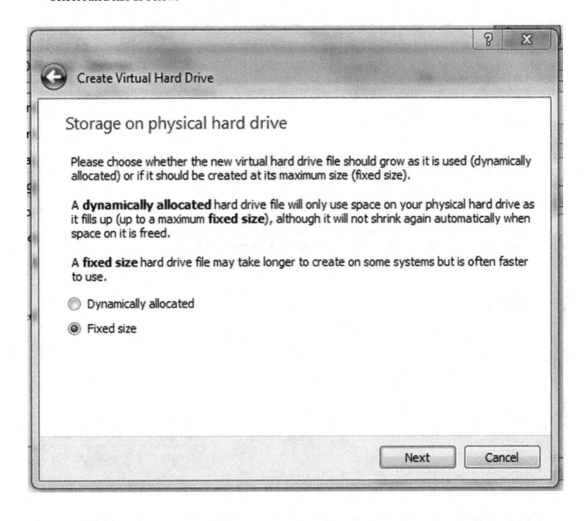

Give the name of the disk as metadb1 and allocate a size of 512MB.

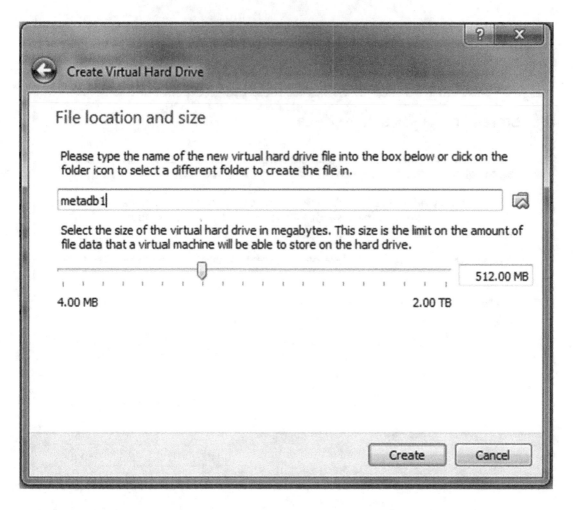

Click on create to create a new disk. Repeat above steps for create another disk as metadb2 of 512 on the virtual host Solaris10-Node1. Create metadb11 and metadb12 disks on host Solaris10-Node2 as mentioned in the steps above.

This completes VirtualBox-based storage and network configuration and the screen should look like those below. Verify each component as in the screen below and ensure all the configurations are placed correctly as described.

Once the configurations for both hosts are verified, power on both virtual hosts and log in. At the login prompt, run the commands below to check the disks using the format command. Run the format options below to configure newly created disks.

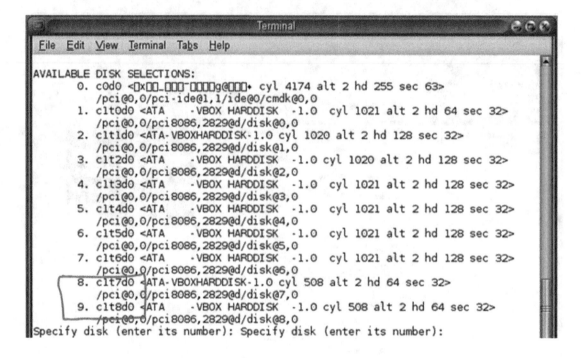

By default all the assigned disks (shared or local) will be in an unconfigured state. Follow these steps to configure them.

Select disk 0 -> fdisk -> y -> type -> 0 -> p -> p (This will help in configuring disks).

Press q to quit and land on disk partition window.

Repeat this step to remaining disks 1–9 as below.

      1 -> <Enter> -> <Enter> -> 0 -> 0 ->

      Press q to quit and land on disk partition window.

      2 -> <Enter> -> <Enter> -> 0 -> 0 ->

      Press q to quit and land on disk partition window.

      3 -> <Enter> -> <Enter> -> 0 -> 0 ->

      Press q to quit and land on disk partition window.

      4 -> <Enter> -> <Enter> -> 0 -> 0 ->

      Press q to quit and land on disk partition window.

      5 -> <Enter> -> <Enter> -> 0 -> 0 ->

      Press q to quit and land on disk partition window.

6 -> <Enter> -> <Enter> -> 0 -> 0 ->

Press q to quit and land on disk partition window.

7 -> <Enter> -> <Enter> -> 0 -> 0 ->

Press q to quit and land on disk partition window.

8 -> <Enter> -> <Enter> -> 0 -> 0 ->

Press q to quit and land on disk partition window.

9 -> <Enter> -> <Enter> -> 0 -> 0 ->

Finally press q and q to come out of partition window and back to the command prompt.

Set Up metadb for Metaset Creation

Once all disks are configured, we will use slice 2 of disks 8 and 9 to create metadb using the following commands:

metadb -af -c 3 -f c1t7d0s2

metadb -a -c3 c1t8d0s2

Verify metab state by running metadb command as shown below.

```
Terminal
File  Edit  View  Terminal  Tabs  Help
bash-3.2# metadb
        flags              first blk        block count
    a m  pc luo        16               8192          /dev/dsk/c1t7d0s2
    a    pc luo        8208             8192          /dev/dsk/c1t7d0s2
    a    pc luo        16400            8192          /dev/dsk/c1t7d0s2
    a    pc luo        16               8192          /dev/dsk/c1t8d0s2
    a    pc luo        8208             8192          /dev/dsk/c1t8d0s2
    a    pc luo        16400            8192          /dev/dsk/c1t8d0s2
bash-3.2#
```

Set up the Oracle Solaris Cluster software binary path to PATH environment variable under the root login's .profile file to run cluster commands without giving complete paths to the software binaries.

```
#vi /.profile
#Shift+G (to go to the end of the file)
        i (to start typing into the .profile file)
        PATH=$PATH:/usr/sbin:/usr/openwin/bin:/usr/cluster/bin
        export PATH
```

and it should appear as:

```
PATH=$PATH:/usr/cluster/bin
export PATH
MANPATH=$MANPATH:/usr/cluster/man
export MANPATH
```

As a last step to the prerequisite, make sure interfaces e1000g0 and e1000g1 are online but e1000g2 and e1000g3 are at an unknown state.

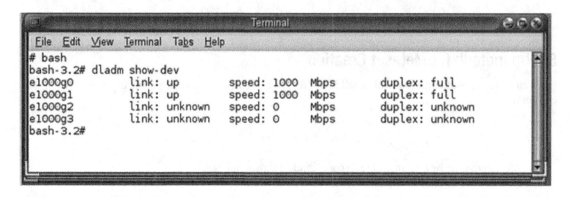

Oracle Solaris Cluster Setup

So before we start with cluster setup, we have completed the necessary prerequisite steps to ensure a smooth and seamless setup of the cluster framework. Now it's time to install Sun Cluster on both nodes.

Run scinstall for Cluster Installation and Configuration

To start with Oracle Solaris Cluster setup, run the command:

#scsinstall

This screen will appear:

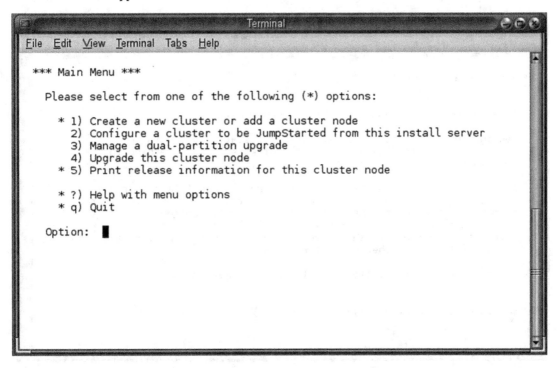

Select Option 1 to create a new cluster.

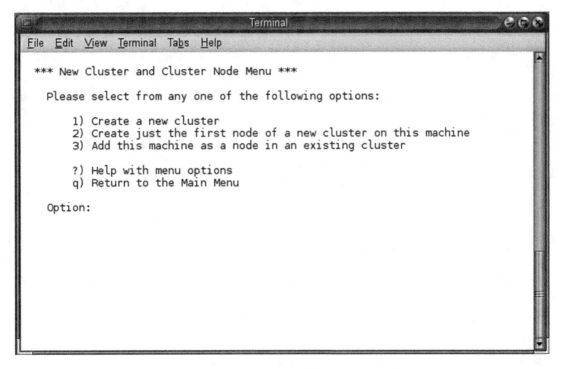

Select default yes to continue with the cluster build.

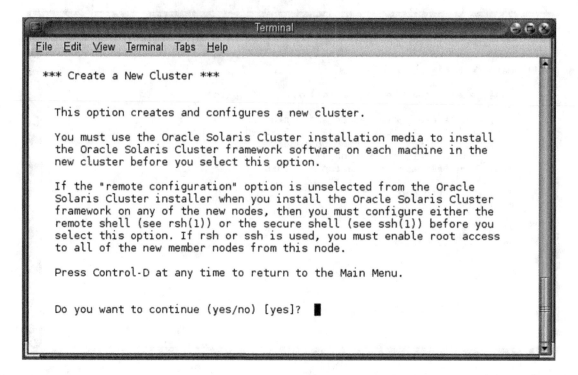

Select Custom for the cluster configuration. Custom cluster configuration will help disabling global fencing as we are using SATA disks here.

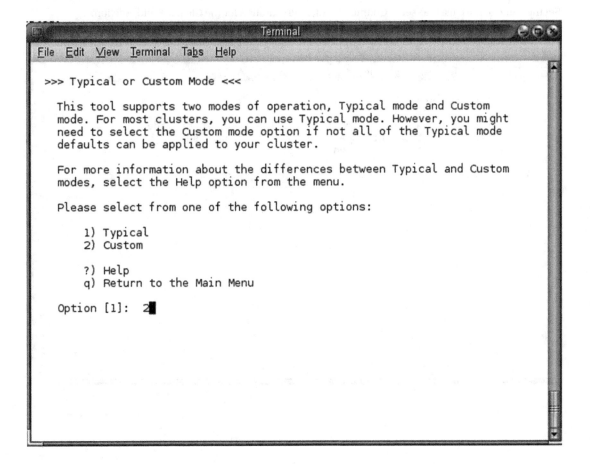

Set Cluster Name

Set the name of the cluster as set in Chapter 3 under "Preparation for the Cluster Build" section.

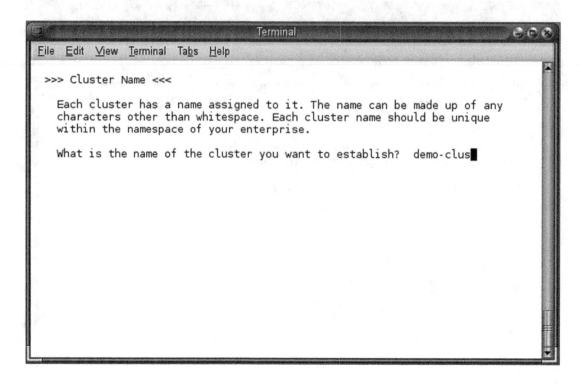

Add Cluster Nodes

Once a cluster name is set, it's time to add cluster nodes as demo-clus1 and demo-clus2.

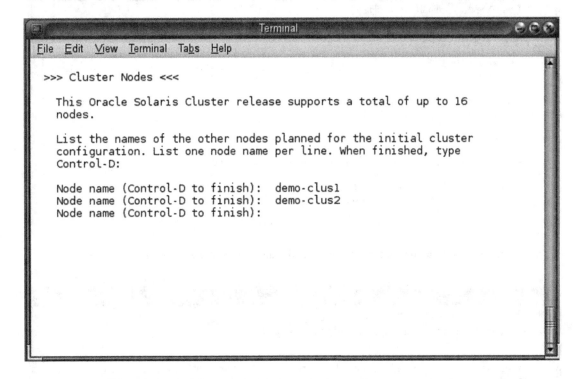

Type Ctrl+D to confirm these two hosts.

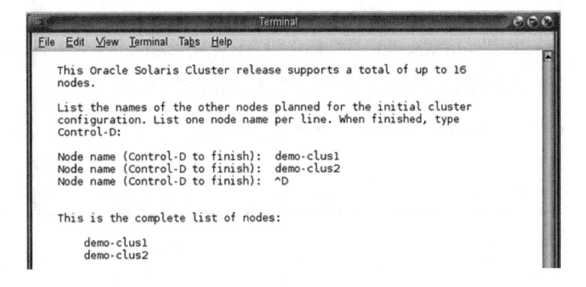

Verify below by selecting default yes by confirming.

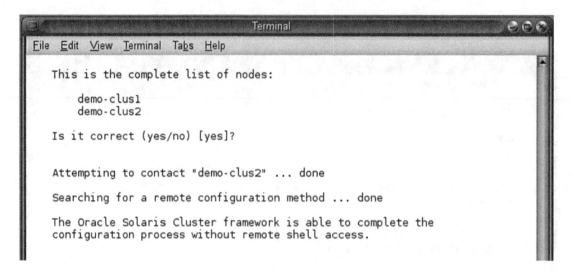

Next is to set DES authentication, as part of the authentication requests to add cluster nodes.

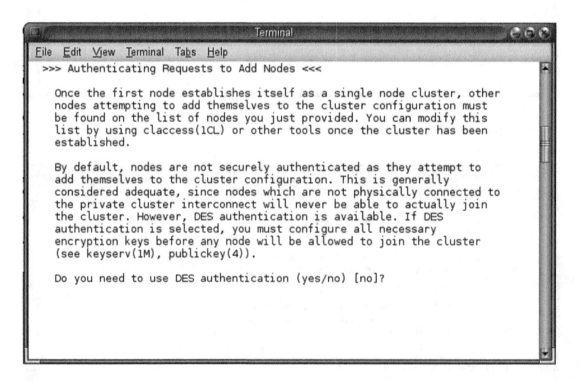

Add Transport Adapters

Now let's configure private interconnects (heartbeat interfaces).

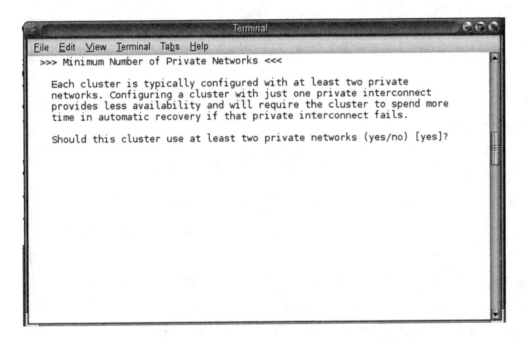

Here there is no switch involved for this configuration, so select no to Point-to-Point as below.

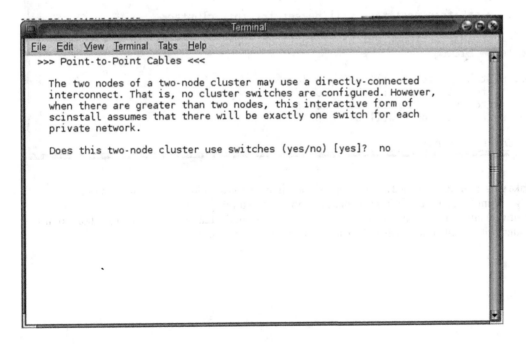

Select the transport adapters as e1000g2 and e1000g3.

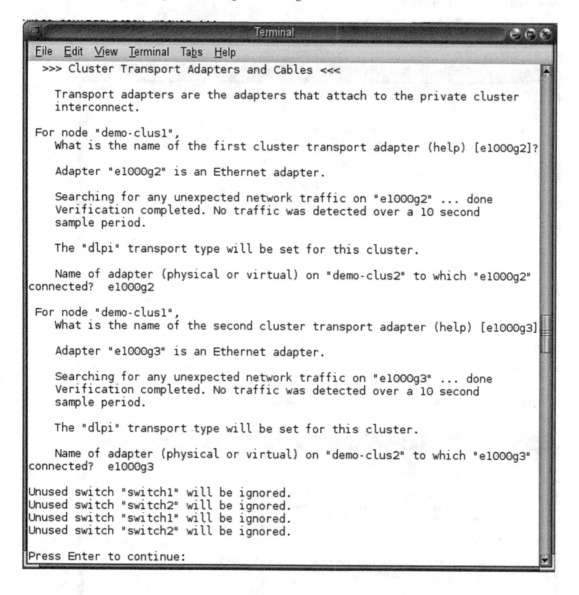

Make sure interfaces e1000g2 and e1000g3 are not in use, so as mentioned at the planning stage, unconfigure/unplumb these interfaces to make sure there is no traffic passing through these interfaces. Ideally, private interconnects should be dedicated cross cables (in the real-life server configuration), or if used under switch configuration, then dedicated vlan for private communication.

The next screen will show the Network Address for the Cluster Transport.

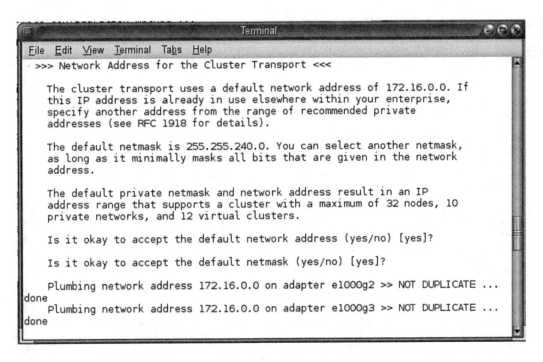

As mentioned before, the purpose of choosing Custom option is to turn off global fencing. So write yes for turning off global fencing.

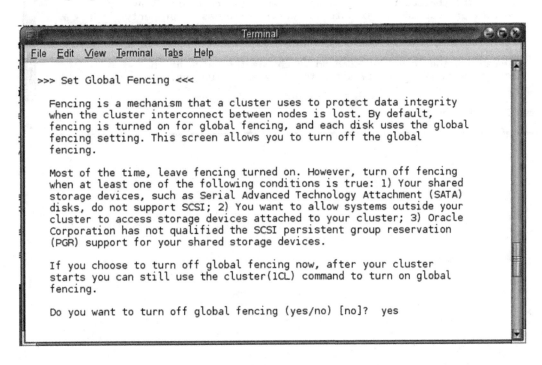

Press Enter to continue for the default resource security configuration as shown here.

```
>>> Resource Security Configuration <<<

    The execution of a cluster resource is controlled by the setting of a
    global cluster property called resource_security. When the cluster is
    booted, this property is set to SECURE.

    Resource methods such as Start and Validate always run as root. If
    resource_security is set to SECURE and the resource method executable
    file has non-root ownership or group or world write permissions,
    execution of the resource method fails at run time and an error is
    returned.

    Resource types that declare the Application_user resource property
    perform additional checks on the executable file ownership and
    permissions of application programs. If the resource_security property
    is set to SECURE and the application program executable is not owned
    by root or by the configured Application_user of that resource, or the
    executable has group or world write permissions, execution of the
    application program fails at run time and an error is returned.

    Resource types that declare the Application_user property execute
    application programs according to the setting of the resource_security
    cluster property. If resource_security is set to SECURE, the
    application user will be the value of the Application_user resource
    property; however, if there is no Application_user property, or it is
    unset or empty, the application user will be the owner of the
    application program executable file. The resource will attempt to
    execute the application program as the application user; however a
    non-root process cannot execute as root (regardless of property
    settings and file ownership) and will execute programs as the
    effective non-root user ID.

    You can use the "clsetup" command to change the value of the
    resource_security property after the cluster is running.


Press Enter to continue:
```

Configure Quorum Device

The next screen is to configure a quorum device. At this stage let's not configure but add a quorum disk post cluster host configuration. Choose yes to disable automatic quorum device selection.

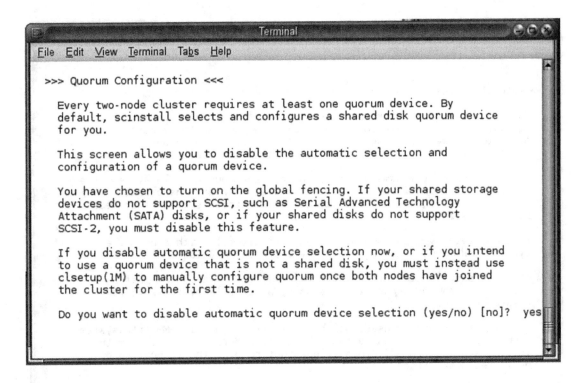

Global Device File System

At this stage, the global device file system will be set up. This is used for holding cluster node device information. Here a lofi file system will be used for setting up the global filesystem as below.

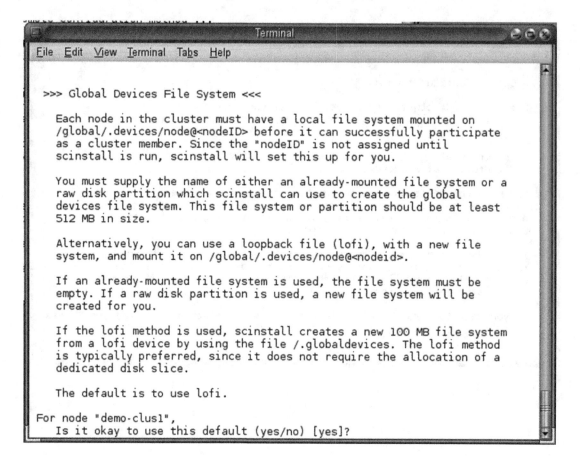

```
>>> Global Devices File System <<<

Each node in the cluster must have a local file system mounted on
/global/.devices/node@<nodeID> before it can successfully participate
as a cluster member. Since the "nodeID" is not assigned until
scinstall is run, scinstall will set this up for you.

You must supply the name of either an already-mounted file system or a
raw disk partition which scinstall can use to create the global
devices file system. This file system or partition should be at least
512 MB in size.

Alternatively, you can use a loopback file (lofi), with a new file
system, and mount it on /global/.devices/node@<nodeid>.

If an already-mounted file system is used, the file system must be
empty. If a raw disk partition is used, a new file system will be
created for you.

If the lofi method is used, scinstall creates a new 100 MB file system
from a lofi device by using the file /.globaldevices. The lofi method
is typically preferred, since it does not require the allocation of a
dedicated disk slice.

The default is to use lofi.

For node "demo-clus1",
    Is it okay to use this default (yes/no) [yes]?
```

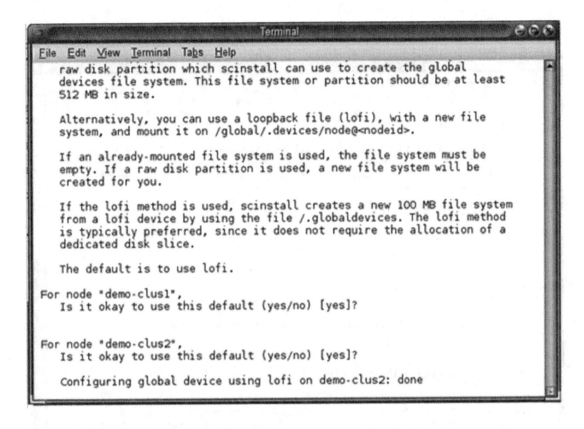

Confirm Cluster New Cluster Build

And finally select default yes to continue with the cluster node creation.

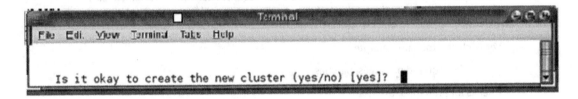

And select default no to continue with cluster setup.

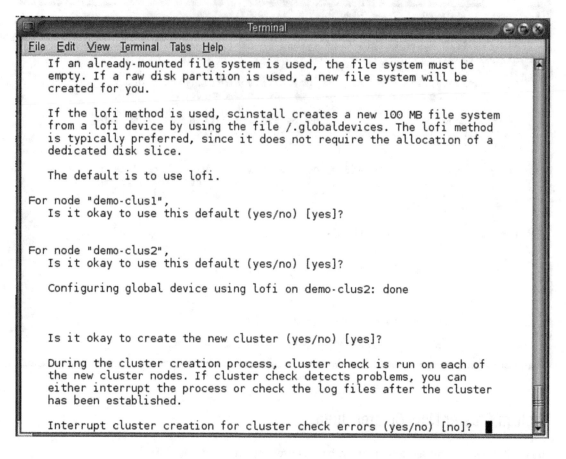

```
                                    Terminal
 File  Edit  View  Terminal  Tabs  Help
   If an already-mounted file system is used, the file system must be
   empty. If a raw disk partition is used, a new file system will be
   created for you.

   If the lofi method is used, scinstall creates a new 100 MB file system
   from a lofi device by using the file /.globaldevices. The lofi method
   is typically preferred, since it does not require the allocation of a
   dedicated disk slice.

   The default is to use lofi.

 For node "demo-clus1",
   Is it okay to use this default (yes/no) [yes]?


 For node "demo-clus2",
   Is it okay to use this default (yes/no) [yes]?

   Configuring global device using lofi on demo-clus2: done



   Is it okay to create the new cluster (yes/no) [yes]?

   During the cluster creation process, cluster check is run on each of
   the new cluster nodes. If cluster check detects problems, you can
   either interrupt the process or check the log files after the cluster
   has been established.

   Interrupt cluster creation for cluster check errors (yes/no) [no]? █
```

The next step will be cluster creation process, which will begin cluster configuration checks.

Post verification, the cluster build process will begin. The activity will run in the background with the following steps:

Verify cluster transport adapters

Checks for required packages, patches

Checks for prerequisites

Once the cluster checks are successfully completed, cluster nodes will be configured as per the configuration accepted in the previous section. Cluster nodes will be rebooted one by one after successful configuration of cluster nodes.

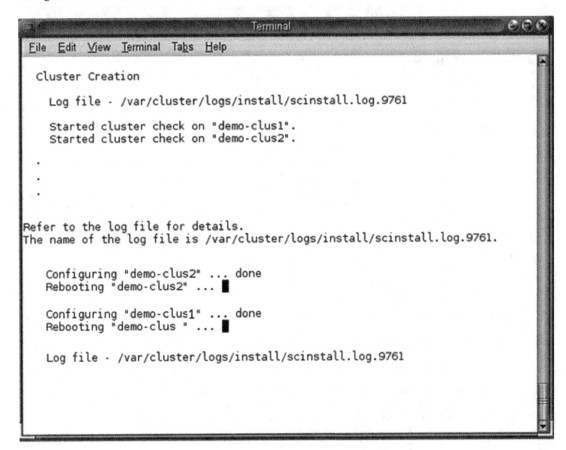

Check for errors and if there are any critical errors, fix them before proceeding. Here is the quick snapshot of the node rebooting in cluster nodes.

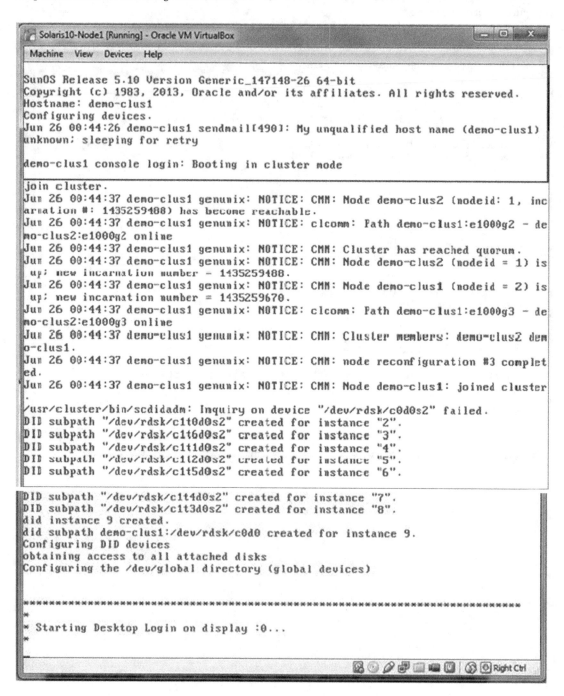

Verify Cluster Framework Configuration

Once cluster configuration is completed, it's time to check and verify cluster configuration. Make sure none of the cluster states are in failure or offline.

For this purpose, only two of the critical cluster states will be verified.

One is ensuring both cluster nodes are up and online.

```
bash-3.2# clnode status

=== Cluster Nodes ===

--- Node Status ---

Node Name                                      Status
---------                                      ------
demo-clus2                                     Online
demo-clus1                                     Online

bash-3.2#
```

And second, checking private interconnect status (heartbeat connection status)

```
bash-3.2# clintr status

=== Cluster Transport Paths ===

Endpoint1               Endpoint2               Status
---------               ---------               ------
demo-clus2:e1000g3      demo-clus1:e1000g3      Path online
demo-clus2:e1000g2      demo-clus1:e1000g2      Path online

bash-3.2# █
```

Run the command 'cluster status' and ensure nothing is set to Faulted state. So far no cluster resource groups are created, so the cluster status will have some blank information.

```
bash-3.2# cluster status | more

=== Cluster Nodes ===

--- Node Status ---

Node Name                               Status
---------                               ------
demo-clus2                              Online
demo-clus1                              Online

=== Cluster Transport Paths ===

Endpoint1               Endpoint2               Status
---------               ---------               ------
demo-clus2:e1000g3      demo-clus1:e1000g3      Path online
demo-clus2:e1000g2      demo-clus1:e1000g2      Path online

=== Cluster Quorum ===

--- Quorum Votes Summary from (latest node reconfiguration) ---

            Needed    Present   Possible
            ------    -------   --------
            1         1         1

--- Quorum Votes by Node (current status) ---

Node Name        Present      Possible     Status
---------        -------      --------     ------
demo-clus2       1            1            Online
demo-clus1       0            0            Online

=== Cluster Device Groups ===

--- Device Group Status ---

Device Group Name      Primary       Secondary     Status
-----------------      -------       ---------     ------


--- Spare, Inactive, and In Transition Nodes ---

Device Group Name    Spare Nodes    Inactive Nodes    In Transistion Nodes
-----------------    -----------    --------------    --------------------


--- Multi-owner Device Group Status ---

Device Group Name          Node Name          Status
-----------------          ---------          ------

=== Cluster Resource Groups ===

Group Name        Node Name        Suspended      State
----------        ---------        ---------      -----

=== Cluster Resources ===

Resource Name        Node Name        State      Status Message
-------------        ---------        -----      --------------
```

```
=== Cluster DID Devices ===

Device Instance            Node                Status
----------------           ----                -------
/dev/did/rdsk/d1           demo-clus2          Ok

/dev/did/rdsk/d2           demo-clus1          Ok
                           demo-clus2          Ok

/dev/did/rdsk/d3           demo-clus1          Ok
                           demo-clus2          Ok

/dev/did/rdsk/d4           demo-clus1          Ok
                           demo-clus2          Ok

/dev/did/rdsk/d5           demo-clus1          Ok
                           demo-clus2          Ok

/dev/did/rdsk/d6           demo-clus1          Ok
                           demo-clus2          Ok

/dev/did/rdsk/d7           demo-clus1          Ok
                           demo-clus2          Ok

/dev/did/rdsk/d8           demo-clus1          Ok
                           demo-clus2          Ok

/dev/did/rdsk/d9           demo-clus1          Ok

=== Zone Clusters ===

--- Zone Cluster Status ---

Name      Node Name     Zone Host Name      Status     Zone Status
----      ---------     --------------      ------     -----------
```

Cluster will be at the installmode to allow further cluster configuration. Check and verify the status as below:

```
# cluster show -t global | grep installmode
    installmode:                              enabled
```

Adding Quorum Disk

Next is to run clsetup (scsetup) command to add quorum disk as marked before

#clsetup:

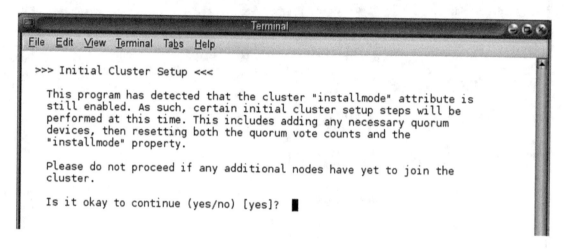

Press Enter key to continue with default yes.

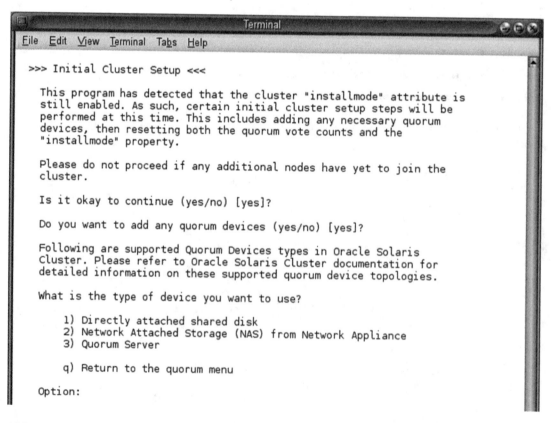

Select 1 to choose DAS disk as the quorum device.

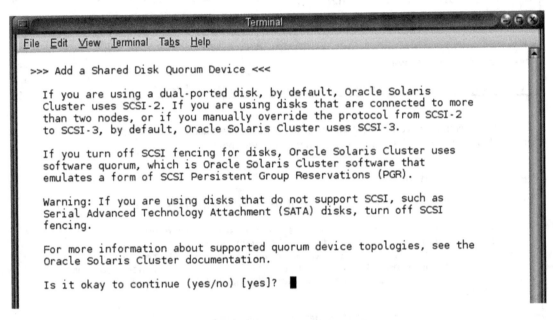

To know the quorum disk that was assigned before (1GB), run the format command to find out the disk, and then **cldevice** (or **scdidadm** –L) command to check the connected DID device.

Add the quorum disk **d2** and continue.

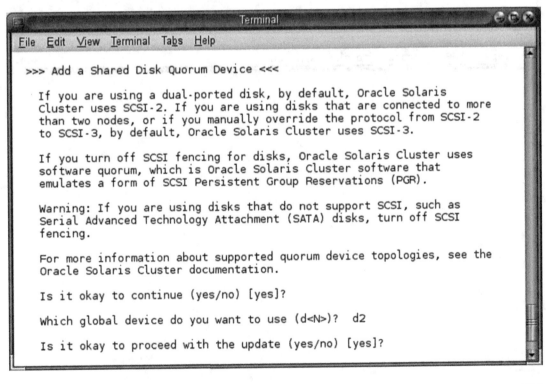

```
/usr/cluster/bin/clquorum add d2

    Command completed successfully.

Press Enter to continue:

    Do you want to add another quorum device (yes/no) [yes]?   no
```

And finally, confirm to come out of the installmode and make cluster active in order to make it operational for adding new cluster resources and resource groups.

```
Press Enter to continue:

    Do you want to add another quorum device (yes/no) [yes]?   no

    Once the "installmode" property has been reset, this program will skip
    "Initial Cluster Setup" each time it is run again in the future.
    However, quorum devices can always be added to the cluster using the
    regular menu options. Resetting this property fully activates quorum
    settings and is necessary for the normal and safe operation of the
    cluster.

    Is it okay to reset "installmode" (yes/no) [yes]?

/usr/cluster/bin/clquorum reset
/usr/cluster/bin/claccess deny-all

    Cluster initialization is complete.

    Type ENTER to proceed to the main menu:
```

Check the quorum status.

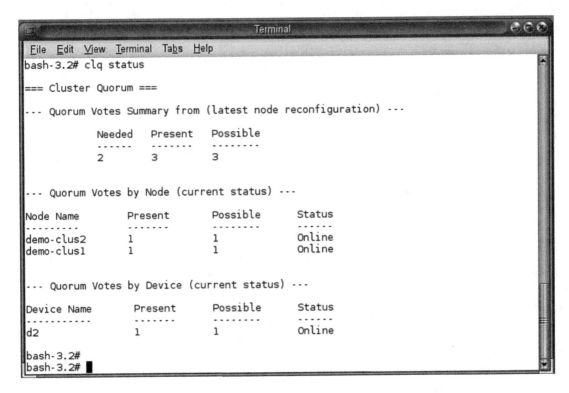

```
bash-3.2# clq status

=== Cluster Quorum ===

--- Quorum Votes Summary from (latest node reconfiguration) ---

            Needed    Present    Possible
            ......    .......    ........
            2         3          3


--- Quorum Votes by Node (current status) ---

Node Name        Present        Possible        Status
.........        .......        ........        ......
demo-clus2       1              1               Online
demo-clus1       1              1               Online


--- Quorum Votes by Device (current status) ---

Device Name      Present        Possible        Status
...........      .......        ........        ......
d2               1              1               Online

bash-3.2#
bash-3.2#
```

Run Generic Tests to Verify Cluster Framework

Just to verify clusters, bring down one cluster node, and other cluster node should be up and running (as quorum disk add to required quorum vote) and vice versa for the other cluster node.

And this completes the cluster framework installation and configuration.

In the next chapter we will setup metadevices, configure disks, and create cluster resource groups and cluster resources.

Accessing Oracle Solaris Cluster GUI

Once Oracle Solaris Cluster is installed, it can alternatively be accessed and managed using Web GUI as below: https://<IP Address of the Cluster Host>:6789. Access the GUI using the root password to gain complete access to the cluster for management and administration.

Veritas Cluster GUI is accessible as web GUI or Java Console (Java Cluster Manager).

■ ■ ■

## CHAPTER 5

Setting Up Apache and NFS Cluster Data Services

Now it's time to set up example cluster resource group and underline cluster resources. For purposes of this book, we will set up Apache and NFS as Data Services.

As a part of Apache cluster resource, set up the following list of activities to be performed:

Setting up Apache Cluster resource environment

Add shared storages to be used by Apache

Verify shared storages allocated for Apache

Mirror specified storage shared disks for Apache

Create metaset out of shared storage disks for Apache

Register Data Service Apache

Create resource group for Apache

Create cluster resources for Apache

Bring Apache Cluster resource group online

Test & verify start/stop and failover testing of Apache Cluster Services

Setting Up Apache Cluster Resource Environment

For setting up Apache Data services, Apache cluster resource group, resource, floating hostname are already planned. Apache usually comes as a part of default Solaris 10 build and is installed under /usr/apache2 and configured under /etc/apache2 and documents set under /var/apache/htdcos directories. You will also find previous versions of apache installed under /usr/apache, configured under /etc/apache, and documents set under /var/apache directory.

In case default Apache is not installed as a part of system build, download and install Apache software either from http://www.apache.org or http://www.sunfreeware.com. Installation of Apache is not within the scope of this book.

Also make sure that the shared disks are available to be used by Apache for DocumentRoot configuration: in other words, location where Index.html file will reside.

Configure Shared Storages to be Used by Apache

Once all required information for Apache under Oracle Solaris Cluster build is collected, it's time to start with the configuration of shared disks allocated for Apache shared data store.

Disable Existing Apache Service

If Apache is already installed as a part of default Oracle Solaris 10 installation, then make sure Apache Services are disabled (as the services should be starting through cluster services).

> bash#cd /etc/apache/

> bash#mv httpd.conf.sample httpd.conf

> update ServerName with web-lh

> Disable /etc/rc3.d/S50apache (not to start apache at reboot) – Rename it to bkp.S50apache as

> bash#mv /etc/rc3.d/S50apache /etc/rc3.d/bkp.S50apache

To start with UFS filesystem, create metadevices and set up cluster device. For this purpose, select the required disks under the format command, create required partitions, and then set up metadevices.

Verify Shared Storages Allocated for Apache

Run format command and select the disk to be partitioned and verify disks allocated for Apache.

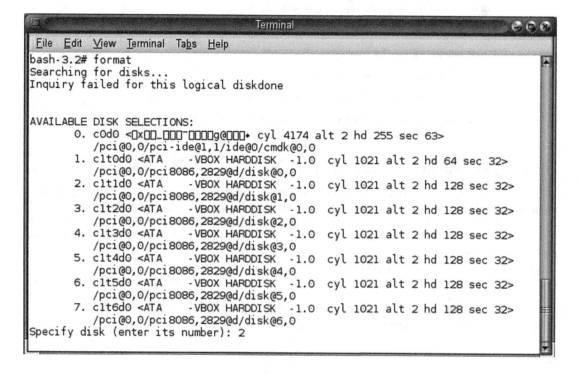

```
bash-3.2# format
Searching for disks...
Inquiry failed for this logical diskdone


AVAILABLE DISK SELECTIONS:
       0. c0d0 <☐x☐☐_☐☐☐¯☐☐☐☐g@☐☐☐• cyl 4174 alt 2 hd 255 sec 63>
          /pci@0,0/pci-ide@1,1/ide@0/cmdk@0,0
       1. c1t0d0 <ATA     -VBOX HARDDISK  -1.0  cyl 1021 alt 2 hd 64 sec 32>
          /pci@0,0/pci8086,2829@d/disk@0,0
       2. c1t1d0 <ATA     -VBOX HARDDISK  -1.0  cyl 1021 alt 2 hd 128 sec 32>
          /pci@0,0/pci8086,2829@d/disk@1,0
       3. c1t2d0 <ATA     -VBOX HARDDISK  -1.0  cyl 1021 alt 2 hd 128 sec 32>
          /pci@0,0/pci8086,2829@d/disk@2,0
       4. c1t3d0 <ATA     -VBOX HARDDISK  -1.0  cyl 1021 alt 2 hd 128 sec 32>
          /pci@0,0/pci8086,2829@d/disk@3,0
       5. c1t4d0 <ATA     -VBOX HARDDISK  -1.0  cyl 1021 alt 2 hd 128 sec 32>
          /pci@0,0/pci8086,2829@d/disk@4,0
       6. c1t5d0 <ATA     -VBOX HARDDISK  -1.0  cyl 1021 alt 2 hd 128 sec 32>
          /pci@0,0/pci8086,2829@d/disk@5,0
       7. c1t6d0 <ATA     -VBOX HARDDISK  -1.0  cyl 1021 alt 2 hd 128 sec 32>
          /pci@0,0/pci8086,2829@d/disk@6,0
Specify disk (enter its number): 2
```

Select disk 2 allocated for Apache Data Service shared disk. Configure them if the disk is not already configured as below.

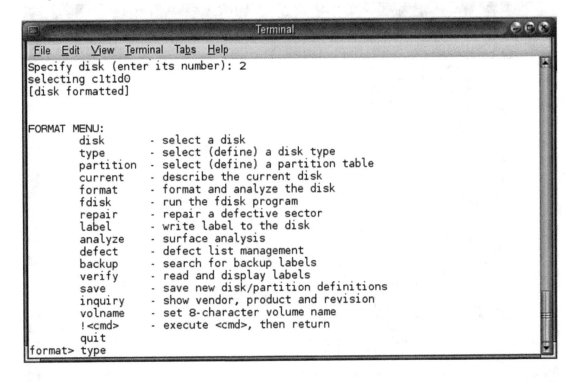

```
Specify disk (enter its number): 2
selecting c1t1d0
[disk formatted]


FORMAT MENU:
        disk       - select a disk
        type       - select (define) a disk type
        partition  - select (define) a partition table
        current    - describe the current disk
        format     - format and analyze the disk
        fdisk      - run the fdisk program
        repair     - repair a defective sector
        label      - write label to the disk
        analyze    - surface analysis
        defect     - defect list management
        backup     - search for backup labels
        verify     - read and display labels
        save       - save new disk/partition definitions
        inquiry    - show vendor, product and revision
        volname    - set 8-character volume name
        !<cmd>     - execute <cmd>, then return
        quit
format> type
```

Select Type as 0 (Autoconfigure).

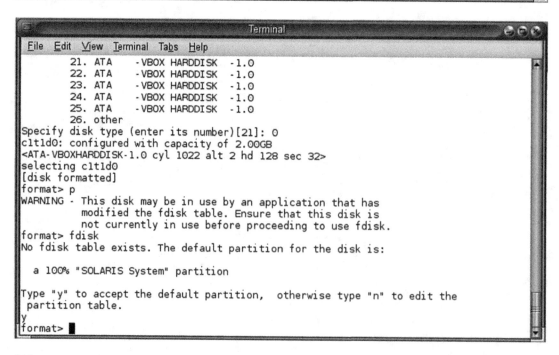

Partition the Disk

And now create the partition and label them as below.

```
                                    Terminal
 File  Edit  View  Terminal  Tabs  Help
 partition table.
y
format> p


PARTITION MENU:
        0      - change `0' partition
        1      - change `1' partition
        2      - change `2' partition
        3      - change `3' partition
        4      - change `4' partition
        5      - change `5' partition
        6      - change `6' partition
        7      - change `7' partition
        select - select a predefined table
        modify - modify a predefined partition table
        name   - name the current table
        print  - display the current table
        label  - write partition map and label to the disk
        !<cmd> - execute <cmd>, then return
        quit
partition> p
Current partition table (default):
Total disk cylinders available: 1020 + 2 (reserved cylinders)

Part      Tag    Flag     Cylinders       Size            Blocks
  0 unassigned    wm       0               0         (0/0/0)          0
  1 unassigned    wm       0               0         (0/0/0)          0
  2     backup    wu       0 - 1019        1.99GB    (1020/0/0) 4177920
  3 unassigned    wm       0               0         (0/0/0)          0
  4 unassigned    wm       0               0         (0/0/0)          0
  5 unassigned    wm       0               0         (0/0/0)          0
  6 unassigned    wm       0               0         (0/0/0)          0
  7 unassigned    wm       0               0         (0/0/0)          0
  8       boot    wu       0 -    0        2.00MB    (1/0/0)       4096
  9 unassigned    wm       0               0         (0/0/0)          0

partition> █
```

147

```
partition> 0
Part      Tag     Flag    Cylinders        Size           Blocks
   0 unassigned    wm          0            0        (0/0/0)            0

Enter partition id tag[unassigned]:
Enter partition permission flags[wm]:
Enter new starting cyl[0]:
Enter partition size[0b, 0c, 0e, 0.00mb, 0.00gb]: 1.7g
partition> p
Current partition table (unnamed):
Total disk cylinders available: 1020 + 2 (reserved cylinders)

Part      Tag     Flag    Cylinders        Size           Blocks
   0 unassigned    wm      0 -   870       1.70GB   (871/0/0)   3567616
   1 unassigned    wm          0            0        (0/0/0)            0
   2     backup    wu      0 -  1019       1.99GB   (1020/0/0)  4177920
   3 unassigned    wm          0            0        (0/0/0)            0
   4 unassigned    wm          0            0        (0/0/0)            0
   5 unassigned    wm          0            0        (0/0/0)            0
   6 unassigned    wm          0            0        (0/0/0)            0
   7 unassigned    wm          0            0        (0/0/0)            0
   8       boot    wu      0 -     0       2.00MB   (1/0/0)         4096
   9 unassigned    wm          0            0        (0/0/0)            0
```

Repeat above steps for disk 2 allocated for Apache and label.

Create Metaset and Mirror Disks for Apache Data Services

Let's now create a metaset and add disks to the metaset to be used by the cluster resource.

```
bash#metaset -s apache-data -a –h demo-clus1 demo-clus2
bash#metaset -s apache-data -t -f              - (Taken ownership of metaset)
```

To add the shared disks to this metaset, first run scdidadm -L and find out the disk set for Apache Data Service as below.

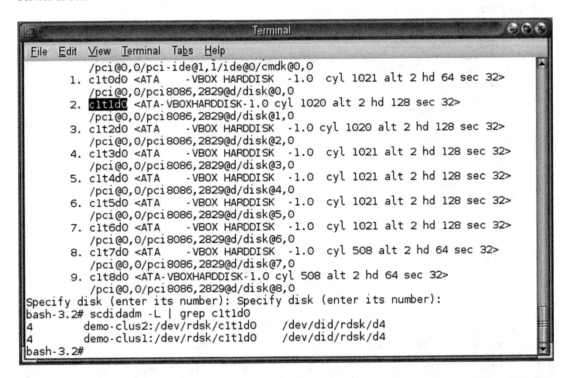

```
                   /pci@0,0/pci-ide@1,1/ide@0/cmdk@0,0
    1. c1t0d0 <ATA    -VBOX HARDDISK  -1.0 cyl 1021 alt 2 hd 64 sec 32>
                   /pci@0,0/pci8086,2829@d/disk@0,0
    2. c1t1d0 <ATA-VBOXHARDDISK-1.0 cyl 1020 alt 2 hd 128 sec 32>
                   /pci@0,0/pci8086,2829@d/disk@1,0
    3. c1t2d0 <ATA    -VBOX HARDDISK  -1.0 cyl 1020 alt 2 hd 128 sec 32>
                   /pci@0,0/pci8086,2829@d/disk@2,0
    4. c1t3d0 <ATA    -VBOX HARDDISK  -1.0 cyl 1021 alt 2 hd 128 sec 32>
                   /pci@0,0/pci8086,2829@d/disk@3,0
    5. c1t4d0 <ATA    -VBOX HARDDISK  -1.0 cyl 1021 alt 2 hd 128 sec 32>
                   /pci@0,0/pci8086,2829@d/disk@4,0
    6. c1t5d0 <ATA    -VBOX HARDDISK  -1.0 cyl 1021 alt 2 hd 128 sec 32>
                   /pci@0,0/pci8086,2829@d/disk@5,0
    7. c1t6d0 <ATA    -VBOX HARDDISK  -1.0 cyl 1021 alt 2 hd 128 sec 32>
                   /pci@0,0/pci8086,2829@d/disk@6,0
    8. c1t7d0 <ATA    -VBOX HARDDISK  -1.0 cyl 508 alt 2 hd 64 sec 32>
                   /pci@0,0/pci8086,2829@d/disk@7,0
    9. c1t8d0 <ATA-VBOXHARDDISK-1.0 cyl 508 alt 2 hd 64 sec 32>
                   /pci@0,0/pci8086,2829@d/disk@8,0
Specify disk (enter its number): Specify disk (enter its number):
bash-3.2# scdidadm -L | grep c1t1d0
4       demo-clus2:/dev/rdsk/c1t1d0    /dev/did/rdsk/d4
4       demo-clus1:/dev/rdsk/c1t1d0    /dev/did/rdsk/d4
bash-3.2#
```

```
bash-3.2# metaset -s apache-data -a /dev/did/rdsk/d4
```

And then create Raid 0 mirroring as below.

```
bash-3.2# metainit -s apache-data d41 1 1 /dev/did/rdsk/d4s0
apache-data/d41: Concat/Stripe is setup
bash-3.2# metainit -s apache-
bash-3.2# metainit -s apache-data d41 1 1 /dev/did/rdsk/d4s0
bash-3.2# scdidadm -L | grep c1t2d0
5       demo-clus2:/dev/rdsk/c1t2d0    /dev/did/rdsk/d5
5       demo-clus1:/dev/rdsk/c1t2d0    /dev/did/rdsk/d5
bash-3.2# metaset -s apache-data -a /dev/did/rdsk/d5
bash-3.2# metainit -s apache-data d42 1 1 /dev/did/rdsk/d5s0
apache-data/d42: Concat/Stripe is setup
bash-3.2# metainit -s apache-data d40 -m d41
apache-data/d40: Mirror is setup
```

Finally

```
bash.3.2#metattach -s apache-data d40 d42
```

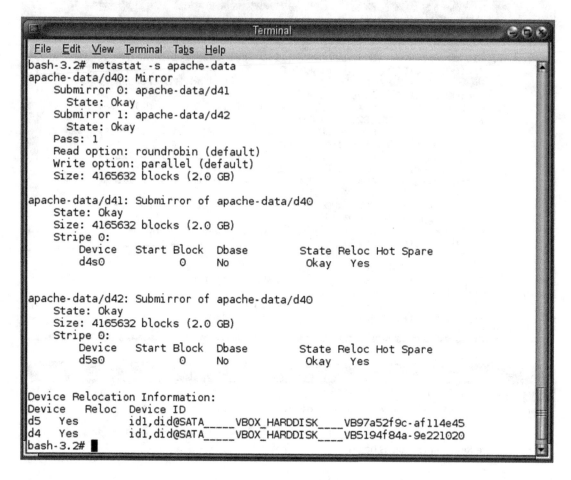

Update md.tab file to ensure metadevices can be recovered in the future.

```
bash# metastat -s apache-data -p >> /etc/lvm/md.tab
```

Setting Shared Data Filesystem

bash# newfs /dev/md/apache-data/rdsk/d40

bash#mkdir /web-data

update /etc/vfstab on both hosts

/dev/md/apache-data/dsk/d40 /dev/md/apache-data/rdsk/d40 /web-data ufs 1 no -

```
Terminal
File  Edit  View  Terminal  Tabs  Help
bash-3.2# newfs /dev/md/apache-data/rdsk/d40
newfs: construct a new file system /dev/md/apache-data/rdsk/d40: (y/n)? y
/dev/md/apache-data/rdsk/d40:   4165632 sectors in 1017 cylinders of 128 tracks,
 32 sectors
        2034.0MB in 45 cyl groups (23 c/g, 46.00MB/g, 11264 i/g)
super-block backups (for fsck -F ufs -o b=#) at:
 32, 94272, 188512, 282752, 376992, 471232, 565472, 659712, 753952, 848192,
 3298432, 3392672, 3486912, 3581152, 3675392, 3769632, 3863872, 3958112,
 4052352, 4146592
bash-3.2#
bash-3.2#
bash-3.2#
```

Repeated above steps on second node demo-clus2

```
Terminal
File  Edit  View  Terminal  Tabs  Help
bash-3.2# metaset -s apache-data -t

bash-3.2#
bash-3.2# metaset -s apache-data

Set name = apache-data, Set number = 1

Host               Owner
  demo-clus1
  demo-clus2        Yes

Driv Dbase

d4   Yes

d5   Yes
bash-3.2# mount /web-data
```

Verify /web data as below:

```
bash.3.2# cd /web-data
```

```
                                              Terminal                              ● ● ●
  File  Edit  View  Terminal  Tabs  Help
 bash-3.2# mount /web-data
 bash-3.2# df -h
 Filesystem               size    used   avail  capacity   Mounted on
 rpool/ROOT/s10_1-13       31G    5.8G    23G     20%      /
 /devices                  OK      OK     OK      0%       /devices
 ctfs                      OK      OK     OK      0%       /system/contract
 proc                      OK      OK     OK      0%       /proc
 mnttab                    OK      OK     OK      0%       /etc/mnttab
 swap                     971M    468K   970M     1%       /etc/svc/volatile
 objfs                     OK      OK     OK      0%       /system/object
 sharefs                   OK      OK     OK      0%       /etc/dfs/sharetab
 /usr/lib/libc/libc_hwcap1.so.1
                           29G    5.8G    23G     20%      /lib/libc.so.1
 fd                        OK      OK     OK      0%       /dev/fd
 swap                     970M     72K   970M     1%       /tmp
 swap                     970M     40K   970M     1%       /var/run
 rpool/export              31G     32K    23G     1%       /export
 rpool/export/home         31G     32K    23G     1%       /export/home
 rpool                     31G     42K    23G     1%       /rpool
 /dev/lofi/127            781M    5.8M   728M     1%       /global/.devices/node@1
 /dev/lofi/126            781M    5.8M   728M     1%       /global/.devices/node@2
 /dev/md/apache-data/dsk/d40
                          1.9G    2.0M   1.9G     1%       /web-data
 bash-3.2# exit
```

Create a dummy index.html file under /webdata/htdocs directory, as this will be the first landing at the start of Apache web service. This page should be accessible if one of the nodes is brought down by failing over its respective cluster resource group to active cluster node.

```
bash.3.2# mkdir /web-data/htdocs
bash.3.2# vi index.html
```

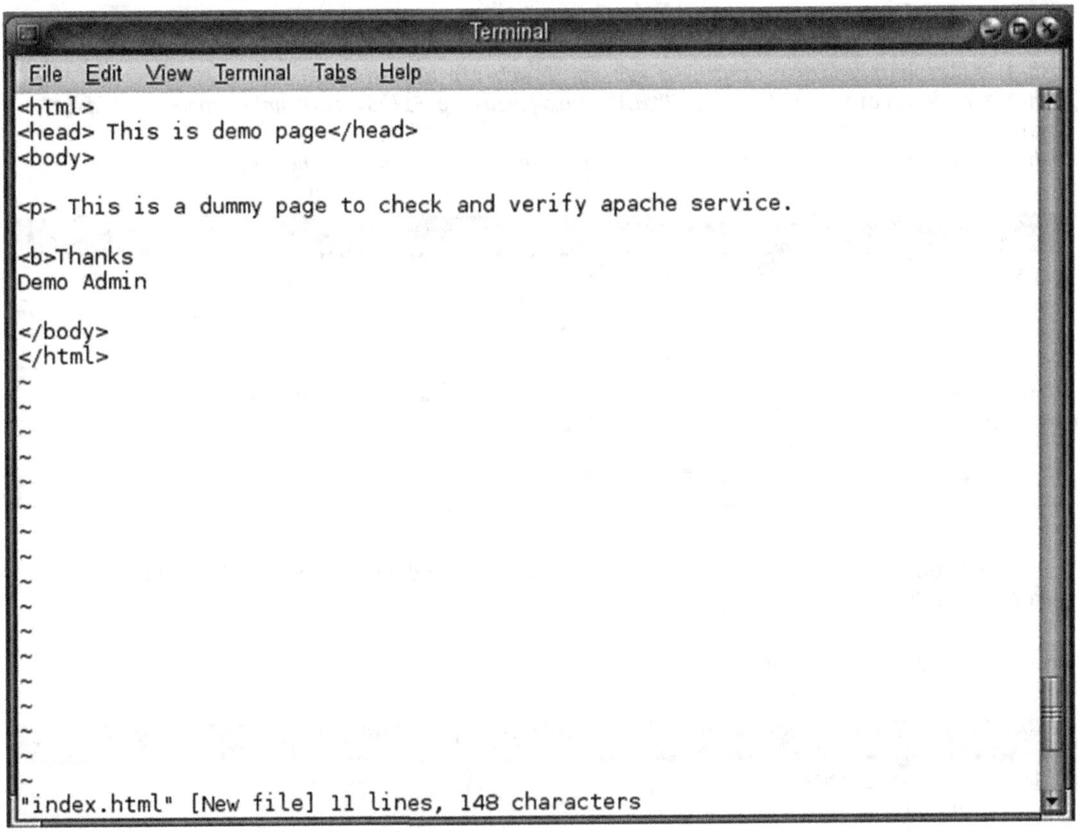

```
Terminal
File  Edit  View  Terminal  Tabs  Help
<html>
<head> This is demo page</head>
<body>

<p> This is a dummy page to check and verify apache service.

<b>Thanks
Demo Admin

</body>
</html>
~
~
~
~
~
~
~
~
~
~
~
~
~
~
~
~
~
"index.html" [New file] 11 lines, 148 characters
```

Create Apache Data Services

Create Apache cluster resource group named web-rg:

bash-3.2#clrg create web-rg

Register SUNW.HAStoragePlus and SUNW.apache resource types:

bash-3.2#clrt register SUNW.HAStoragePlus
bash-3.2#clrt register SUNW.apache

Create Apache cluster resources:

```
bash-3.2#clrssharedaddress create -g web-rg -h web-vip web-lh
bash-3.2#clrs create -g web-rg -t SUNW.HAStoragePlus -p FileSystemMountPoints="/web-data"
webstore-rs
bash-3.2#clrs create -g web-rg -t SUNW.apache -p Bin_dir=/usr/apache/bin web-rs
```

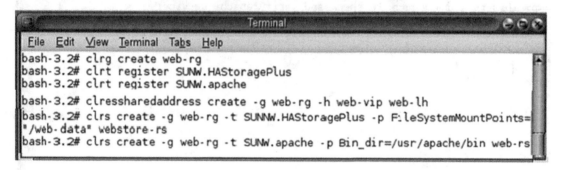

Reboot both hosts to ensure both hosts are up and running under cluster control. Bring the Apache Data Service online.

```
bash-3.2# clrg online -M web-rg
```

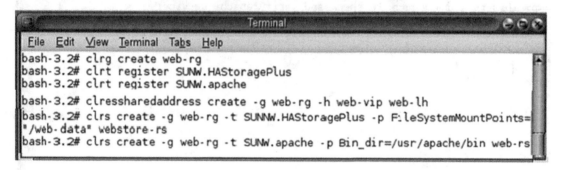

Test and Verify Failover and Failback of Apache Services

To test and verify if the Apache Data Service is successfully implemented it should do the following:
Show online status of Apache resource group and resources status on demo-clus1 node,

```
bash-3.2# clrg status web-rg

=== Cluster Resource Groups ===

Group Name      Node Name       Suspended       Status
----------      ---------       ---------       ------
web-rg          demo-clus2      No              Offline
                demo-clus1      No              Online

bash-3.2# clrs status -g web-rg

=== Cluster Resources ===

Resource Name   Node Name       State           Status Message
-------------   ---------       -----           --------------
apache-rs       demo-clus2      Offline         Offline
                demo-clus1      Online          Online - Service is online.

webstore-rs     demo-clus2      Offline         Offline
                demo-clus1      Online          Online

web-lh          demo-clus2      Offline         Offline
                demo-clus1      Online          Online - SharedAddress online.

bash-3.2#
```

Successfully failover Apache DS from demo-clus1 to demo-clus2 node.

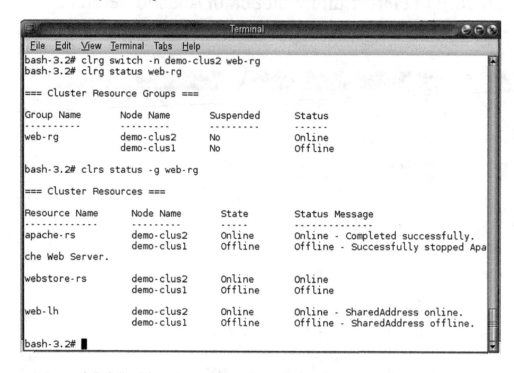

Successfully failback from demo-clus2 to demo-clus1 node.

Keep pinging to the web-vip IP address from the main desktop command line and find out the packet loss due to failover of cluster services.

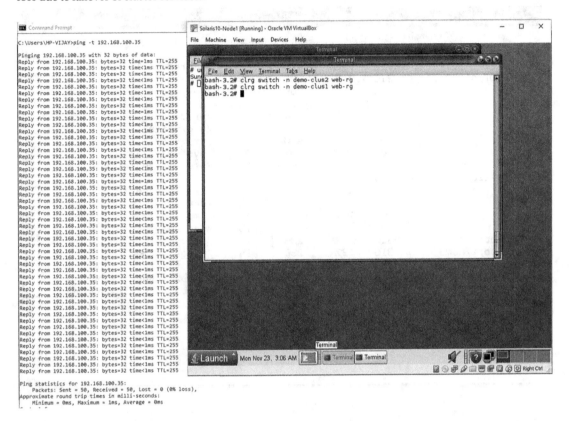

If you observe this carefully, there is hardly any packet loss during the failover, as the setup is in virtual environment under VirtualBox, so the failover of virtual IP is quick.

And the last test is bringing down one node should failover occur from Apache Services to other node.

Phase I – Both NFS and Apache resource groups are running on demo-clus1 node as below.

Demo-clus1 node, neither /web-data nor /nfs-data is mounted as below.

```
bash-3.2# df -h
Filesystem                    size    used   avail  capacity   Mounted on
rpool/ROOT/s10_1-13            31G    5.8G    23G      20%      /
/devices                       OK      OK     OK       0%      /devices
ctfs                           OK      OK     OK       0%      /system/contract
proc                           OK      OK     OK       0%      /proc
mnttab                         OK      OK     OK       0%      /etc/mnttab
swap                          795M    500K   795M      1%      /etc/svc/volatile
objfs                          OK      OK     OK       0%      /system/object
sharefs                        OK      OK     OK       0%      /etc/dfs/sharetab
/usr/lib/libc/libc_hwcap1.so.1
                               29G    5.8G    23G      20%      /lib/libc.so.1
fd                             OK      OK     OK       0%      /dev/fd
swap                          795M    104K   795M      1%      /tmp
swap                          795M     48K   795M      1%      /var/run
rpool/export                   31G     32K    23G       1%      /export
rpool/export/home              31G     32K    23G       1%      /export/home
rpool                          31G     42K    23G       1%      /rpool
/dev/lofi/126                 781M    5.8M   728M       1%      /global/.devices/node@2
/dev/lofi/127                 781M    5.8M   728M       1%      /global/.devices/node@1
bash-3.2# █
```

Because this host is not running any cluster data services, rather all cluster data services are running on demo-clus2 node as below.

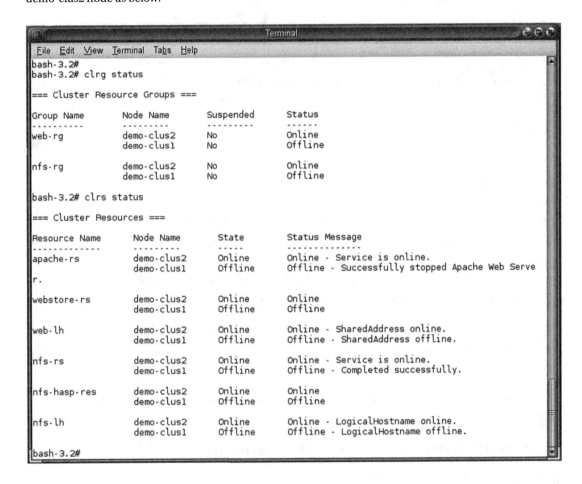

Let's now halt and then power off the cluster node demo-clus2; both NFS and Apache resource groups and resources should move from demo-clus2 to demo-clus1 node as below.

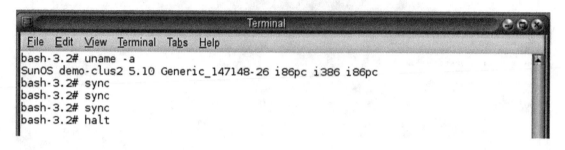

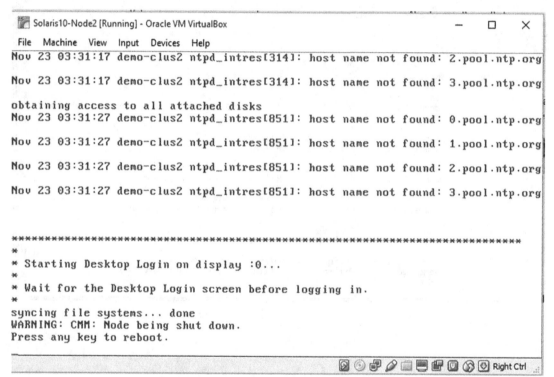

Click on the top left X to power off the host.

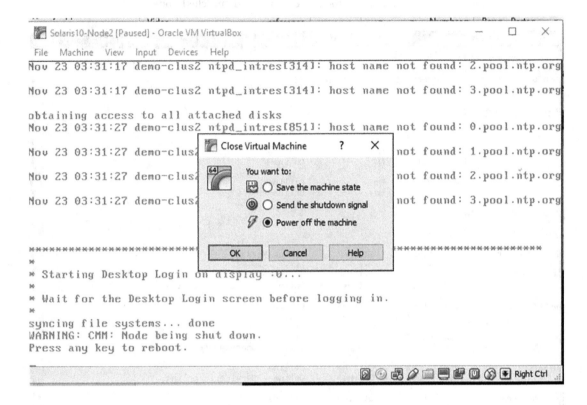

Press ok to Power off the machine.

So let's run the cluster commands to see the cluster status on demo-clus1 node.

```
Terminal
File  Edit  View  Terminal  Tabs  Help
bash-3.2# uname -a
SunOS demo-clus1 5.10 Generic_147148-26 i86pc i386 i86pc
bash-3.2# clrg status

=== Cluster Resource Groups ===

Group Name       Node Name        Suspended     Status
----------       ---------        ---------     ------
web-rg           demo-clus2       No            Offline
                 demo-clus1       No            Online

nfs-rg           demo-clus2       No            Offline
                 demo-clus1       No            Online

bash-3.2# clrs status

=== Cluster Resources ===

Resource Name    Node Name        State         Status Message
-------------    ---------        -----         --------------
apache-rs        demo-clus2       Offline       Offline
                 demo-clus1       Online        Online - Service is online.

webstore-rs      demo-clus2       Offline       Offline
                 demo-clus1       Online        Online

web-lh           demo-clus2       Offline       Offline
                 demo-clus1       Online        Online - SharedAddress online.

nfs-rs           demo-clus2       Offline       Offline
                 demo-clus1       Online        Online - Service is online.

nfs-hasp-res     demo-clus2       Offline       Offline
                 demo-clus1       Online        Online

nfs-lh           demo-clus2       Offline       Offline
                 demo-clus1       Online        Online - LogicalHostname online.

bash-3.2#
```

As you see above, cluster data services have successfully failed over to demo-clus1 node. And the respective directories /web-data and /nfs-data are mounted as below.

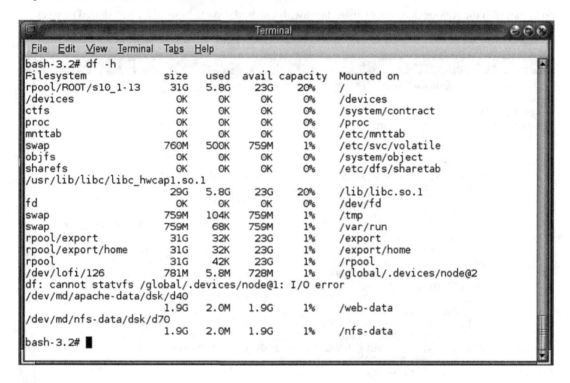

```
bash-3.2# df -h
Filesystem              size    used    avail  capacity  Mounted on
rpool/ROOT/s10_1-13     31G     5.8G    23G    20%       /
/devices                OK      OK      OK     0%        /devices
ctfs                    OK      OK      OK     0%        /system/contract
proc                    OK      OK      OK     0%        /proc
mnttab                  OK      OK      OK     0%        /etc/mnttab
swap                    760M    500K    759M   1%        /etc/svc/volatile
objfs                   OK      OK      OK     0%        /system/object
sharefs                 OK      OK      OK     0%        /etc/dfs/sharetab
/usr/lib/libc/libc_hwcap1.so.1
                        29G     5.8G    23G    20%       /lib/libc.so.1
fd                      OK      OK      OK     0%        /dev/fd
swap                    759M    104K    759M   1%        /tmp
swap                    759M    68K     759M   1%        /var/run
rpool/export            31G     32K     23G    1%        /export
rpool/export/home       31G     32K     23G    1%        /export/home
rpool                   31G     42K     23G    1%        /rpool
/dev/lofi/126           781M    5.8M    728M   1%        /global/.devices/node@2
df: cannot statvfs /global/.devices/node@1: I/O error
/dev/md/apache-data/dsk/d40
                        1.9G    2.0M    1.9G   1%        /web-data
/dev/md/nfs-data/dsk/d70
                        1.9G    2.0M    1.9G   1%        /nfs-data
bash-3.2# █
```

Setting up NFS Cluster Resource Environment

NFS is network file system protocol, used for remotely mounting filesystems using IP addresses of the NFS server. Before starting with the NFS service running as cluster environment, make sure all existing NFS OS services are disabled.

Verify Shared Storages Allocated for NFS

So to start with the NFS service under cluster, first identify shared disks to be used for NFS shared services. Run format command and select the disk to be partitioned and then verify disks allocated.

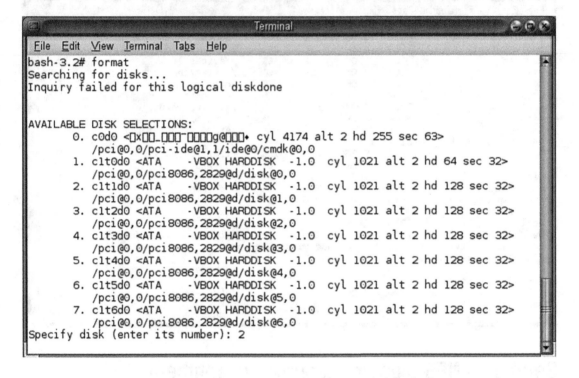

```
bash-3.2# format
Searching for disks...
Inquiry failed for this logical diskdone


AVAILABLE DISK SELECTIONS:
       0. c0d0 <□x□□_□□□¯□□□□g@□□□♦ cyl 4174 alt 2 hd 255 sec 63>
          /pci@0,0/pci-ide@1,1/ide@0/cmdk@0,0
       1. c1t0d0 <ATA    -VBOX HARDDISK  -1.0  cyl 1021 alt 2 hd 64 sec 32>
          /pci@0,0/pci8086,2829@d/disk@0,0
       2. c1t1d0 <ATA    -VBOX HARDDISK  -1.0  cyl 1021 alt 2 hd 128 sec 32>
          /pci@0,0/pci8086,2829@d/disk@1,0
       3. c1t2d0 <ATA    -VBOX HARDDISK  -1.0  cyl 1021 alt 2 hd 128 sec 32>
          /pci@0,0/pci8086,2829@d/disk@2,0
       4. c1t3d0 <ATA    -VBOX HARDDISK  -1.0  cyl 1021 alt 2 hd 128 sec 32>
          /pci@0,0/pci8086,2829@d/disk@3,0
       5. c1t4d0 <ATA    -VBOX HARDDISK  -1.0  cyl 1021 alt 2 hd 128 sec 32>
          /pci@0,0/pci8086,2829@d/disk@4,0
       6. c1t5d0 <ATA    -VBOX HARDDISK  -1.0  cyl 1021 alt 2 hd 128 sec 32>
          /pci@0,0/pci8086,2829@d/disk@5,0
       7. c1t6d0 <ATA    -VBOX HARDDISK  -1.0  cyl 1021 alt 2 hd 128 sec 32>
          /pci@0,0/pci8086,2829@d/disk@6,0
Specify disk (enter its number): 2
```

Select disk 4 allocated for NFS Data Service shared disk. Configure the disk if the disk is not already configured as shown below.

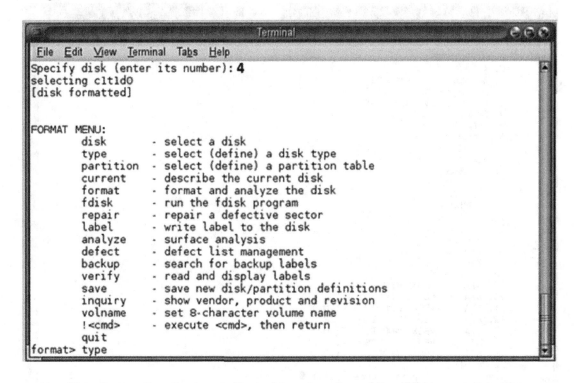

Select Type as 0 (Autoconfigure).

```
AVAILABLE DRIVE TYPES:
        0. Auto configure
        1. Quantum ProDrive 80S
        2. Quantum ProDrive 105S
        3. CDC Wren IV 94171-344
        4. SUN0104
        5. SUN0207
        6. SUN0327
        7. SUN0340
        8. SUN0424
        9. SUN0535
        10. SUN0669
        11. SUN1.0G
        12. SUN1.05
        13. SUN1.3G
        14. SUN2.1G
        15. SUN2.9G
        16. Zip 100
        17. Zip 250
        18. Peerless 10GB
        19. ATA     -VBOX HARDDISK   -1.0
        20. ATA     -VBOX HARDDISK   -1.0
        21. ATA     -VBOX HARDDISK   -1.0
        22. ATA     -VBOX HARDDISK   -1.0
        23. ATA     -VBOX HARDDISK   -1.0
        24. ATA     -VBOX HARDDISK   -1.0
        25. ATA     -VBOX HARDDISK   -1.0
        26. other
Specify disk type (enter its number)[21]: █
```

```
        21. ATA     -VBOX HARDDISK   -1.0
        22. ATA     -VBOX HARDDISK   -1.0
        23. ATA     -VBOX HARDDISK   -1.0
        24. ATA     -VBOX HARDDISK   -1.0
        25. ATA     -VBOX HARDDISK   -1.0
        26. other
Specify disk type (enter its number)[21]: 0
c1t1d0: configured with capacity of 2.00GB
<ATA-VBOXHARDDISK-1.0 cyl 1022 alt 2 hd 128 sec 32>
selecting c1t1d0
[disk formatted]
format> p
WARNING - This disk may be in use by an application that has
          modified the fdisk table. Ensure that this disk is
          not currently in use before proceeding to use fdisk.
format> fdisk
No fdisk table exists. The default partition for the disk is:

  a 100% "SOLARIS System" partition

Type "y" to accept the default partition,  otherwise type "n" to edit the
 partition table.
y
format> █
```

Partition the Disk

And now create the partitions and label them. It depends on the size of the disk. Set partition 0 having the maximum disk size allocated.

```
                                       Terminal
 File  Edit  View  Terminal  Tabs  Help
 partition table.
y
format> p


PARTITION MENU:
        0       - change `0' partition
        1       - change `1' partition
        2       - change `2' partition
        3       - change `3' partition
        4       - change `4' partition
        5       - change `5' partition
        6       - change `6' partition
        7       - change `7' partition
        select  - select a predefined table
        modify  - modify a predefined partition table
        name    - name the current table
        print   - display the current table
        label   - write partition map and label to the disk
        !<cmd>  - execute <cmd>, then return
        quit
partition> p
Current partition table (default):
Total disk cylinders available: 1020 + 2 (reserved cylinders)

Part      Tag    Flag     Cylinders        Size            Blocks
  0 unassigned    wm       0               0          (0/0/0)           0
  1 unassigned    wm       0               0          (0/0/0)           0
  2     backup    wu       0 - 1019        1.99GB     (1020/0/0) 4177920
  3 unassigned    wm       0               0          (0/0/0)           0
  4 unassigned    wm       0               0          (0/0/0)           0
  5 unassigned    wm       0               0          (0/0/0)           0
  6 unassigned    wm       0               0          (0/0/0)           0
  7 unassigned    wm       0               0          (0/0/0)           0
  8       boot    wu       0 -    0        2.00MB     (1/0/0)        4096
  9 unassigned    wm       0               0          (0/0/0)           0

partition> █
```

Repeat above steps for partitioning disk 5 allocated for NFS.

Create Metaset and Mirror Disks for Apache Data Services

Let's now create a metaset and add disks to the metaset to be used by the cluster resource.

```
bash#metaset -s nfs-data -a -h demo-clus1 demo-clus2
bash#metaset -s nfs-data -t -f (Taken ownership of metaset)
```

167

To add the shared disks to this metaset, first run scdidadm -L and find out the disk set for Apache Data Service as below.

```
Specify disk (enter its number): Specify disk (enter its number):
bash-3.2#
bash-3.2#
bash-3.2#
bash-3.2# scdidadm -L
1        demo-clus2:/dev/rdsk/c0d0        /dev/did/rdsk/d1
2        demo-clus2:/dev/rdsk/c1t0d0      /dev/did/rdsk/d2
2        demo-clus1:/dev/rdsk/c1t0d0      /dev/did/rdsk/d2
3        demo-clus2:/dev/rdsk/c1t6d0      /dev/did/rdsk/d3
3        demo-clus1:/dev/rdsk/c1t6d0      /dev/did/rdsk/d3
4        demo-clus2:/dev/rdsk/c1t1d0      /dev/did/rdsk/d4
4        demo-clus1:/dev/rdsk/c1t1d0      /dev/did/rdsk/d4
5        demo-clus2:/dev/rdsk/c1t2d0      /dev/did/rdsk/d5
5        demo-clus1:/dev/rdsk/c1t2d0      /dev/did/rdsk/d5
6        demo-clus2:/dev/rdsk/c1t5d0      /dev/did/rdsk/d6
6        demo-clus1:/dev/rdsk/c1t5d0      /dev/did/rdsk/d6
7        demo-clus2:/dev/rdsk/c1t4d0      /dev/did/rdsk/d7
7        demo-clus1:/dev/rdsk/c1t4d0      /dev/did/rdsk/d7
8        demo-clus2:/dev/rdsk/c1t3d0      /dev/did/rdsk/d8
8        demo-clus1:/dev/rdsk/c1t3d0      /dev/did/rdsk/d8
9        demo-clus1:/dev/rdsk/c0d0        /dev/did/rdsk/d9
10       demo-clus2:/dev/rdsk/c1t7d0      /dev/did/rdsk/d10
11       demo-clus2:/dev/rdsk/c1t8d0      /dev/did/rdsk/d11
12       demo-clus1:/dev/rdsk/c1t7d0      /dev/did/rdsk/d12
13       demo-clus1:/dev/rdsk/c1t8d0      /dev/did/rdsk/d13
bash-3.2# ■                                      Workspace Switcher
```

Once the disks are selected and configured, create metasets and Raid 0 mirroring as below.

```
bash-3.2# metaset -s nfs-data -a /dev/did/rdsk/d7
bash-3.2# metainit -s nfs-data d71 1 1 /dev/did/rdsk/d7s0
nfs-data/d71: Concat/Stripe is setup
bash-3.2# metaset -s nfs-data -a /dev/did/rdsk/d8
bash-3.2# metainit -s nfs-data d72 1 1 /dev/did/rdsk/d8s0
nfs-data/d72: Concat/Stripe is setup
bash-3.2# metainit -s nfs-data d70 -m d71
nfs-data/d70: Mirror is setup
bash-3.2# metattach -s nfs-data d70 d72
nfs-data/d70: submirror nfs-data/d72 is attached
bash-3.2#
```

Verify metaset configuration for NFS shared disks below.

```
bash-3.2# metastat -s nfs-data
nfs-data/d70: Mirror
    Submirror 0: nfs-data/d71
      State: Okay
    Submirror 1: nfs-data/d72
      State: Okay
    Pass: 1
    Read option: roundrobin (default)
    Write option: parallel (default)
    Size: 4165632 blocks (2.0 GB)

nfs-data/d71: Submirror of nfs-data/d70
    State: Okay
    Size: 4165632 blocks (2.0 GB)
    Stripe 0:
        Device    Start Block  Dbase        State Reloc Hot Spare
        d7s0           0       No           Okay  Yes


nfs-data/d72: Submirror of nfs-data/d70
    State: Okay
    Size: 4165632 blocks (2.0 GB)
    Stripe 0:
        Device    Start Block  Dbase        State Reloc Hot Spare
        d8s0           0       No           Okay  Yes


Device Relocation Information:
Device    Reloc   Device ID
d8   Yes         id1,did@SATA_____VBOX_HARDDISK____VB373f5931-20324cd6
d7   Yes         id1,did@SATA_____VBOX_HARDDISK____VB0f029f90-c3a6aa7b
bash-3.2#
```

Update md.tab file to ensure metadevices can be recovered in future.

bash# metastat –s nfs-data –p >> /etc/lvm/md.tab (update this on both cluster nodes)

Setting Shared Data Filesystem

bash# newfs /dev/md/apache-data/rdsk/d70 as below:

bash#mkdir /nfs-data

update /etc/vfstab

/dev/md/apache-data/dsk/d70 /dev/md/apache-data/rdsk/d70 /nfs-data ufs 1 no -

```
┌─────────────────────────────── Terminal ─────────────────────────────┐
│ File  Edit  View  Terminal  Tabs  Help                                │
│ newfs: construct a new file system /dev/md/nfs-data/rdsk/d70: (y/n)? y │
│ /dev/md/nfs-data/rdsk/d70:     4165632 sectors in 1017 cylinders of 128 tracks │
│ , 32 sectors                                                          │
│     2034.0MB in 45 cyl groups (23 c/g, 46.00MB/g, 11264 i/g)          │
│ super-block backups (for fsck -F ufs -o b=#) at:                      │
│  32, 94272, 188512, 282752, 376992, 471232, 565472, 659712, 753952, 848192, │
│  3298432, 3392672, 3486912, 3581152, 3675392, 3769632, 3863872, 3958112, │
│  4052352, 4146592                                                     │
│ bash-3.2#                                                             │
└───────────────────────────────────────────────────────────────────────┘
```

Repeat these steps on second node demo-clus2 and then check the status as below.

```
┌─────────────────────────────── Terminal ─────────────────────────────┐
│ File  Edit  View  Terminal  Tabs  Help                                │
│ bash-3.2# metaset -s nfs-data                                        │
│                                                                       │
│ Set name = nfs-data, Set number = 2                                   │
│                                                                       │
│ Host                Owner                                             │
│   demo-clus1          Yes                                             │
│   demo-clus2                                                          │
│                                                                       │
│ Driv Dbase                                                           │
│                                                                       │
│ d7   Yes                                                             │
│                                                                       │
│ d8   Yes                                                             │
│ bash-3.2#                                                            │
└───────────────────────────────────────────────────────────────────────┘
```

Verify /nfs-data shared file system can be mounted successfully.

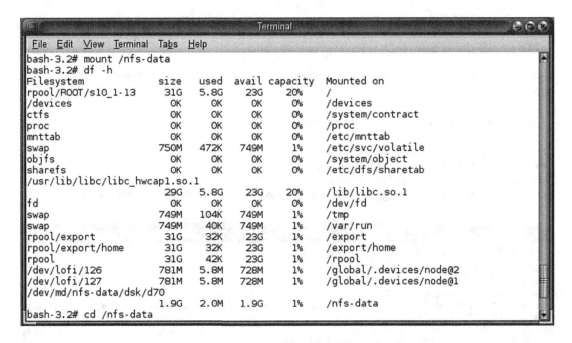

Let's now set up NFS configuration required prior to setting up NFS cluster resource group and resources:

        bash.3.2# cd /nfs-data

For NFS cluster service configuration follow these steps:

        bash.3.2#mkdir -p /nfs-data/SUNW.nfs

        bash.3.2#cd /nfs-data/SUNW.nfs

        bash.3.2#vi dfstab.nfs-rs   (where nfs-rs will be used as cluster resource name)

Insert line to dfstab.nfs-rs and save the file:

share -F nfs -o rw,anon=0 -d "Nfs Home Dir" /nfs-data

Create NFS Data Services

Create NFS Cluster resource group named nfs-rg:

bash.3.2#clrg create nfs-rg

Register SUNW.HAStoragePlus and SUNW.nfs resource types:

bash.3.2#clrt register SUNW.HAStoragePlus
bash-3.2#clrt register SUNW.nfs

Create NFS cluster resources for failover virtual IP:

```
bash.3.2#clreslogicalhostname create -g nfs-rg -h nfs-vip nfs-lh
```

Create NFS cluster resource for failover storage /nfs-data:

```
bash.3.2#clrs create -g nfs-rg -t SUNW.HAStoragePlus -p FileSystemMountPoints="/nfs-data"
nfs-hasp-res
```

Bring the nfs-rg resource group online and do the failover and failback test as below:

```
bash.3.2#clrg switch -n demo-clus1 nfs-rg
bash.3.2#clrg switch -n demo-clus2 nfs-rg
bash.3.2#clrg set -p PathPrefix=/nfs-data
bash.3.2#clrs create -g nfs-rg -t SUNW.nfs -p Resource_dependencies=nfs-hasp-res nfs-rs
```

```
Terminal
File  Edit  View  Terminal  Tabs  Help
bash-3.2# clrg create nfs-rg
bash-3.2# clrt register SUNW.nfs
bash-3.2# clreslogicalhostname create -g nfs-rg -h nfs-vip nfs-lh
bash-3.2# clrs create -g nfs-rg -t SUNW.HAStoragePlus -p FilesystemMountPoints="
/mfs-data" nfs-hasp-res
bash-3.2# clrg online -M nfs-rg
bash-3.2# clrg switch -n clus-demo2 nfs-rg
bash-3.2# clrg switch -n clus-demo1 nfs-rg
bash-3.2# clrg set -p PathPrefix=/nfs-data
bash-3.2# clrs create -g nfs-rg -t SUNW.nfs -p Resource_dependencies=nfs-hasp-re
s nfs-rs
bash-3.2# ▮
```

Bring the NFS Data Service online:

```
bash-3.2# clrg online -M nfs-rg
```

```
bash-3.2# clrg status nfs-rg

=== Cluster Resource Groups ===

Group Name        Node Name        Suspended        Status
----------        ----------       ----------       ------
nfs-rg            demo-clus2       No               Online
                  demo-clus1       No               Offline

bash-3.2# clrs status -g nfs-rg

=== Cluster Resources ===

Resource Name     Node Name        State        Status Message
-------------     ----------       -----        --------------
nfs-rs            demo-clus2       Online       Online - Service is online.
                  demo-clus1       Offline      Offline - Completed successfully
.

nfs-hasp-res      demo-clus2       Online       Online
                  demo-clus1       Offline      Offline

nfs-lh            demo-clus2       Online       Online - LogicalHostname online.
                  demo-clus1       Offline      Offline - LogicalHostname offlin
e.

bash-3.2#
```

Test and Verify Failover and Failback of NFS Cluster Services

As of now the NFS cluster Data Service is started successfully on demo-clus2 node. Let's now failover and failback the cluster resource group and verify that it's up and running.

Failover to demo-clus1 node:

```
bash-3.2# clrg switch -n demo-clus1 nfs-rg
bash-3.2# clrg status nfs-rg

=== Cluster Resource Groups ===

Group Name          Node Name         Suspended         Status
----------          ---------         ---------         ------
nfs-rg              demo-clus2        No                Offline
                    demo-clus1        No                Online

bash-3.2# clrs status -g nfs-rg

=== Cluster Resources ===

Resource Name       Node Name         State             Status Message
-------------       ---------         -----             --------------
nfs-rs              demo-clus2        Offline           Offline - Completed successfully.
                    demo-clus1        Online            Online - Successfully started NFS
service.

nfs-hasp-res        demo-clus2        Offline           Offline
                    demo-clus1        Online            Online

nfs-lh              demo-clus2        Offline           Offline - LogicalHostname offline.
                    demo-clus1        Online            Online - LogicalHostname online.

bash-3.2#
```

Check /nfs-data filesystem mounted on demo-clus1 node:

```
bash-3.2# uname -a
SunOS demo-clus1 5.10 Generic_147148-26 i86pc i386 i86pc
bash-3.2# df -h
Filesystem              size   used  avail capacity  Mounted on
rpool/ROOT/s10_1-13      31G   5.8G    23G    20%     /
/devices                 OK     OK     OK     0%      /devices
ctfs                     OK     OK     OK     0%      /system/contract
proc                     OK     OK     OK     0%      /proc
mnttab                   OK     OK     OK     0%      /etc/mnttab
swap                    710M   504K   710M    1%      /etc/svc/volatile
objfs                    OK     OK     OK     0%      /system/object
sharefs                  OK     OK     OK     0%      /etc/dfs/sharetab
/usr/lib/libc/libc_hwcap1.so.1
                         29G   5.8G    23G    20%     /lib/libc.so.1
fd                       OK     OK     OK     0%      /dev/fd
swap                    710M   104K   710M    1%      /tmp
swap                    710M    68K   710M    1%      /var/run
rpool/export             31G    32K    23G    1%      /export
rpool/export/home        31G    32K    23G    1%      /export/home
rpool                    31G    42K    23G    1%      /rpool
/dev/lofi/126           781M   5.8M   728M    1%      /global/.devices/node@2
/dev/md/apache-data/dsk/d40
                        1.9G   2.0M   1.9G    1%      /web-data
/dev/lofi/127           781M   5.8M   728M    1%      /global/.devices/node@1
/dev/md/nfs-data/dsk/d70
                        1.9G   2.0M   1.9G    1%      /nfs-data
bash-3.2#
```

Also test if /nfs-data can be mounted on demo-clus2 at /mnt directory:

```
bash-3.2# uname -a
SunOS demo-clus2 5.10 Generic_147148-26 i86pc i386 i86pc
bash-3.2# mount nfs-vip:/nfs-data /mnt
bash-3.2# df -h
Filesystem              size   used  avail capacity  Mounted on
rpool/ROOT/s10_1-13      31G   6.0G    23G    21%     /
/devices                 OK     OK     OK     0%      /devices
ctfs                     OK     OK     OK     0%      /system/contract
proc                     OK     OK     OK     0%      /proc
mnttab                   OK     OK     OK     0%      /etc/mnttab
swap                    795M   496K   795M    1%      /etc/svc/volatile
objfs                    OK     OK     OK     0%      /system/object
sharefs                  OK     OK     OK     0%      /etc/dfs/sharetab
/usr/lib/libc/libc_hwcap1.so.1
                         29G   6.0G    23G    21%     /lib/libc.so.1
fd                       OK     OK     OK     0%      /dev/fd
swap                    795M   104K   795M    1%      /tmp
swap                    795M    48K   795M    1%      /var/run
rpool/export             31G    32K    23G    1%      /export
rpool/export/home        31G    32K    23G    1%      /export/home
rpool                    31G    42K    23G    1%      /rpool
/dev/lofi/126           781M   5.8M   728M    1%      /global/.devices/node@2
/dev/lofi/127           781M   5.8M   728M    1%      /global/.devices/node@1
nfs-vip:/nfs-data       1.9G   2.0M   1.9G    1%      /mnt
bash-3.2#
```

Now let's failback nfs-rg to demo-clus2 node and verify these tests. First unmount /mnt from demo-clus2 node. Check NFS cluster resource groups and resources status and mount NFS to demo-clus1.

```
bash-3.2# uname -a
SunOS demo-clus2 5.10 Generic_147148-26 i86pc i386 i86pc
bash-3.2# umount /mnt
bash-3.2# clrg switch -n demo-clus2 nfs-rg
bash-3.2# clrg status nfs-rg

=== Cluster Resource Groups ===

Group Name          Node Name          Suspended          Status
----------          ----------         ----------         ------
nfs-rg              demo-clus2         No                 Online
                    demo-clus1         No                 Offline

bash-3.2# clrs status -g nfs-rg

=== Cluster Resources ===

Resource Name       Node Name          State              Status Message
-------------       ----------         -----              --------------
nfs-rs              demo-clus2         Online             Online - Successfully started NFS serv
ice.
                    demo-clus1         Offline            Offline - Completed successfully.

nfs-hasp-res        demo-clus2         Online             Online
                    demo-clus1         Offline            Offline

nfs-lh              demo-clus2         Online             Online - LogicalHostname online.
                    demo-clus1         Offline            Offline - LogicalHostname offline.

bash-3.2#
```

```
Terminal
File  Edit  View  Terminal  Tabs  Help
bash-3.2# uname -a
SunOS demo-clus1 5.10 Generic_147148-26 i86pc i386 i86pc
bash-3.2# mount nfs-vip:/nfs-data /mnt
bash-3.2# df -h
Filesystem              size   used  avail capacity  Mounted on
rpool/ROOT/s10_1-13      31G   5.8G    23G    20%     /
/devices                  OK     OK     OK     0%     /devices
ctfs                      OK     OK     OK     0%     /system/contract
proc                      OK     OK     OK     0%     /proc
mnttab                    OK     OK     OK     0%     /etc/mnttab
swap                    718M   504K   717M     1%     /etc/svc/volatile
objfs                     OK     OK     OK     0%     /system/object
sharefs                   OK     OK     OK     0%     /etc/dfs/sharetab
/usr/lib/libc/libc_hwcap1.so.1
                         29G   5.8G    23G    20%     /lib/libc.so.1
fd                        OK     OK     OK     0%     /dev/fd
swap                    717M   104K   717M     1%     /tmp
swap                    717M    52K   717M     1%     /var/run
rpool/export             31G    32K    23G     1%     /export
rpool/export/home        31G    32K    23G     1%     /export/home
rpool                    31G    42K    23G     1%     /rpool
/dev/lofi/126           781M   5.8M   728M     1%     /global/.devices/node@2
/dev/md/apache-data/dsk/d40
                        1.9G   2.0M   1.9G     1%     /web-data
/dev/lofi/127           781M   5.8M   728M     1%     /global/.devices/node@1
nfs-vip:/nfs-data       1.9G   2.0M   1.9G     1%     /mnt
bash-3.2#
```

As you can see above, the filesystem is successfully mounted on the cluster node demo-clus1 from demo-clus2 node as NFS share.

And this completes the Apache and NFS Data Services build process.

CHAPTER 6

■ ■ ■

Veritas Clustering – (Solaris)

The focus of this chapter is to help build Veritas Cluster environments on personal laptops or desktops. As was the case in the previous chapter with Oracle Solaris Cluster, steps will be for a simulated cluster environment, although we will cover all steps required for the cluster build with some limitations and restrictions. To begin with the cluster build, keep the build plan ready with all required information.

Veritas Cluster Planning

Veritas cluster planning involves similar phases of activities starting from design phase to hardware procurement to network configuration to storage configuration; installing and configuring cluster components; configuring Cluster resource groups and resources; and, finally, testing and verification of failover services.

The following list of activities reduces the efforts of cluster build activities. Keep all the below information handy before proceeding further with the Cluster installation and configuration process.

Veritas Cluster Planning	
High-Level Cluster Design	High-Level Cluster design, Decision on Cluster Topology, Cost Estimation
Hardware Planning	Servers, PCI Cards, CPU, Memory, Storage, Network, Power
	Rack Mount
	Cabling, Patching.
Cluster software planning	Prerequisite for cluster build (Licensing)
	Cluster Name
	Software versions compatibility
	OS and software patches
Network Planning	Port configuration for Channel Port and Trunking Firewall port access,
	List of FQDN hostnames for each subnet
	Network Subnet for public, core, and private network
	Floating IP DNS names required by applications/Databases
Storage planning	Dedicated and multihome disks (Storage LUNs), NAS drive, etc.
	Disk Layouts, Filesystem Layout

(continued)

Veritas Cluster Planning	
Cluster Data Services planning	Number of Cluster nodes
	Cluster Resource Name/s
	Cluster Resource Dependencies
	Cluster resource VIP (Virtual floating IP), with FQDN name
	Cluster resource group names
	Cluster group dependencies
Switchover testing	Testing cases resource group for failover and verifying application availability
	Failover cluster resource group

This list of planning information will help in small, large, or enterprise-scale cluster builds, as a part of installation and configuration tasks. For the purpose of simulated cluster build environments, we may not follow all the steps, but we will walk through each step as part of the process in general.

High-Level Cluster Design

As a first step toward cluster build prepare a high architecture diagram. A high-level design should be constructed based on the respective application/business requirements and solution design. The high-level cluster design should cover the server's layout, network connections diagram, and storage design. High-level design should be approved by both the application owners and infrastructure architect before signing off to the next level of low-level design.

For the cluster build, using virtual hosts as illustrated below is high-level design:

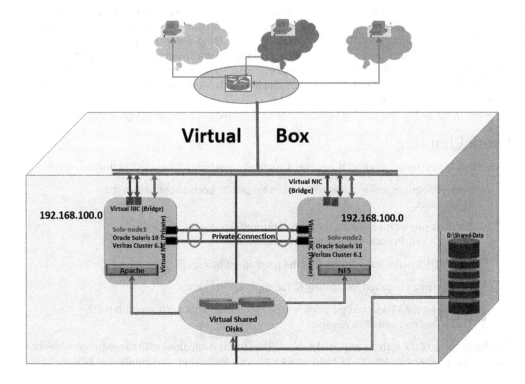

Figure 6-1.

The topology adopted here is for the two-node cluster along with shared virtual disks. As per the design, there will be four interfaces configured, out of which one interface as a bridge interface used for connecting to the virtual host from Laptop/Desktop command line, the second interface is a Host-Only-Adapter to be used for application communication, and the remaining two interfaces will be configured for the private interconnect (Heartbeat).

Hardware Planning

Once the design is reviewed by respective architects, it's time to procure hardware. Hardware planning involves planning for the right kind of server in terms of capacity (CPU and memory) and other configuration components such as HBA and PCI cards. The choice of right kind of hardware should be based on the workload, performance, and redundancy requirements. Additionally, procurement of network devices such as switches, routers, or firewalls or using existing hardware capacity, cabling, and patching are other important parts of hardware planning.

For the purpose of writing this book, two virtual hosts under the VirtualBox environment were required to have Desktop/Laptop with necessary configuration (Min Quad Core CPU and 6 GB RAM) as stated in Table 3–1 in the chapter "Preparation for the Cluster Build."

Cluster Software Planning

Keep all the required software for cluster build ready. The software requirement is already listed in Table 6-1 in the chapter "Preparation for the Cluster Build" along with compatible versions and patches. In addition to this software, also have required application software with start/stop and probe methods ready.

For purpose-stated VirtualBox setup, we will be working on Apache and NFS as two cluster services. Make sure software is downloaded with the necessary license. (Solaris 10 and VirtualBox do not require licenses). Steps to download and install VirtualBox and Solaris 10 virtual host environments are already explained in the previous chapter.

Network Planning

As per the High-Level Design, keep all the network requirements ready. These will include:

> Firewall requirement to allow connection to specific ports to connect to the application.

> Network subnet information for each communication network layer (Public, Core, Private, and Management/console).

> FQDN DNS name setup for each of the participant hosts.

> FQDN names required for floating IP for application failover.

> Decide on the VLAN configuration for the specific network ports and submit the Trunk Port configuration request.

For the purpose of the stated setup, make sure VirtualBox is configured with the required network interfaces and keep the hostname and IP addresses list handy for further configuration as below.

Cluster Hosts	IP Address	Name
Hostnames	192.168.100.61	solv-node1
(Host Management)	192.168.100.62	solv-node2
Cluster Node 1	192.168.20.10	app-node1
Cluster Node 2	192.168.20.20	app-node2
Sun Cluster HA for Apache logical hostname	192.168.100.30	app02-vip
Sun Cluster HA for NFS logical hostname	192.168.100.40	app01-vip
Cluster Name		sol-vcs

Storage Planning

Storage planning is the most critical part of the cluster configuration. As a part of planning, keep the requirements ready:

> To decide on local host storage capacity as well as storage from SAN or NAS device.

> Mark the list of storage LUNs pointing to multiple hosts and which storage LUN should point to which cluster node.

> To decide on storage LUN, based on IOPS and nature of read and write.

To decide on storage replication if required.

Mapping of NAS device (if used), pointing to specific host and specified permissions.

Decide on the number of quorum devices based on the number of hosts.

To decide on layout of filesystem of storage LUN.

Decide the disks used for creating mirrored disks and metasets.

For the purpose of Virtual Host cluster builds, only the shared disks used by applications and one quorum device will be required. Below is the list of disk configurations that will be used for each Data Service visible through both cluster hosts.

Apache:	D:\Shared-Disks\VCLUDSH_01
	D:\Shared-Disks\ VCLUDSH_02
NFS:	D:\Shared-Disks\ VCLUDSH_03
	D:\Shared-Disks\ VCLUDSH_04

Cluster Data Service/Resource Group and Resource

Before setting up cluster environments, be ready with the following information:

List of cluster resource groups.

List of cluster resources.

Dependencies of cluster resource groups and resources.

Timeout, failover, failback, etc., configuration parameters.

Cluster start/stop and probe scripts required to start, stop or probing required cluster services.

For the purpose of VirtualHost cluster build, Apache and NFS applications will be used. They will be set up with the following names, types, and dependencies:

Apache Data Service

Resource Group APPGP02

Resource   *web-lh – Logical Host resource for Apache (VIP for apache failover).*

                 apache-rs – Apache resource for running apache binaries.

                 webstore-rs – Apache datastore for keeping DocumentRoot (Index.html)

Resource Type SUNW.apache

Dependencies *For Apache web service (apache-rs) to run,*

                 First floating IP should be configured (web-lh)

                 And webstore-rs should be in place to invoke apache service. So the dependencies are

                 apache-rs depends on web-lh and webstore-rs

NFS Data Service

Resource Group *APPGP01*

Resource   *nfs-lh – Logical Host resource for NFS*

                   nfs-res – NFS resource to start NFS services.

Resource Type *SUNW.nfs*

Dependencies *nfs-res will be dependent on nfs-lh*

Failover Test Plans

Keep the test plans ready to ensure the application starts up and shuts down cleanly. Also ensure successful failovers of resource groups within participated cluster nodes. Verify that cluster resource groups failover if one of the nodes shuts down or powers down.

Veritas Cluster Implementation
VirtualBox Network Configuration for Veritas Cluster Hosts

VirtualBox network configuration for Veritas Cluster hosts is similar to the way it has been set in previous chapters for Oracle Cluster configuration except that for this lab setup, we will not be using IPMP configuration. So we will dedicate the first interface for Host Management as a bridge interface and the second interface as Host-Only-Adapter. The remaining two interfaces will be configured the same as before for private interconnects.

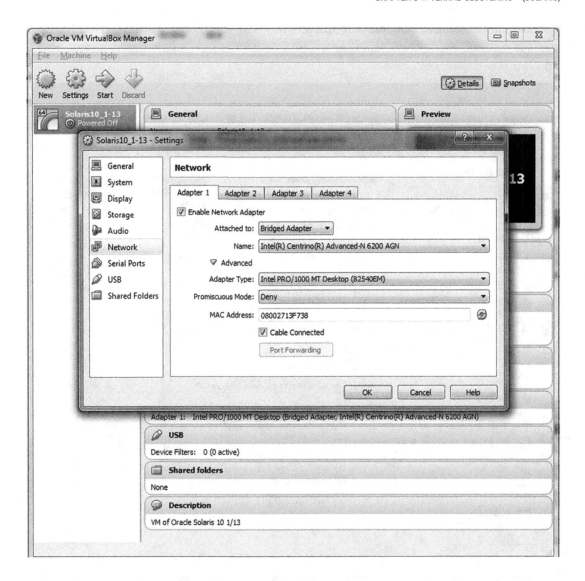

Configure the Adapter 2 with Host-Only-Adapter:

The third and fourth adapters are to be set up as Internal Networks and to be used for Private Connections. Configure private interfaces as shown here:

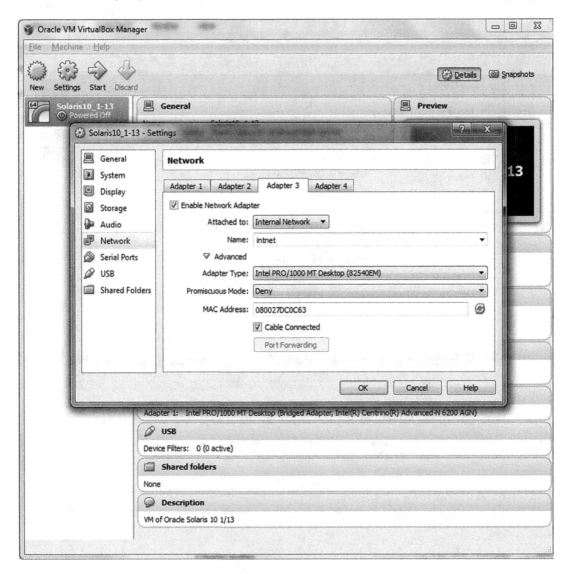

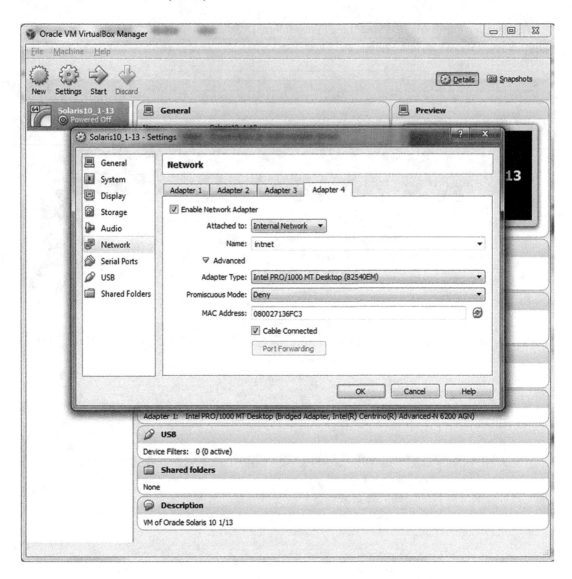

Installation of Veritas Cluster Software
Prerequisite Configuration for Cluster Setup
Extract the software

To install Veritas Cluster Software, go to the directory where the Veritas Cluster Server Software is downloaded. Unzip and tar extract the software and choose the directory location for the installation.

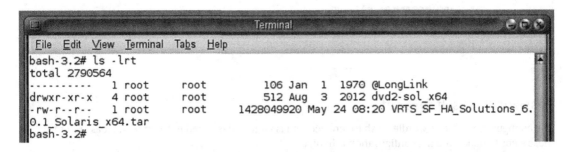

```
Terminal
File  Edit  View  Terminal  Tabs  Help
bash-3.2# gunzip VRTS_SF_HA_Solutions_6.0.1_Solaris_x64.tar.gz
bash-3.2# tar xf VRTS_SF_HA_Solutions_6.0.1_Solaris_x64.tar
bash-3.2#
bash-3.2#
bash-3.2#
```

```
Terminal
File  Edit  View  Terminal  Tabs  Help
bash-3.2# ls -lrt
total 2790564
----------   1 root      root             106 Jan  1  1970 @LongLink
drwxr-xr-x   4 root      root             512 Aug  3  2012 dvd2-sol_x64
-rw-r--r--   1 root      root      1428049920 May 24 08:20 VRTS_SF_HA_Solutions_6.
0.1_Solaris_x64.tar
bash-3.2#
```

```
Terminal
File  Edit  View  Terminal  Tabs  Help
total 4
drwxr-xr-x  17 root      root             512 Aug  3  2012 sol10_x64
drwxr-xr-x  17 root      root             512 Aug  3  2012 sol11_x64
bash-3.2# cd sol10_x64/
bash-3.2# ls
cluster_server
copyright
docs
dynamic_multipathing
file_system
installer
perl
pkgs
scripts
storage_foundation
storage_foundation_cluster_file_system_ha
storage_foundation_for_oracle_rac
storage_foundation_high_availability
virtualstore
volume_manager
webinstaller
windows
xprtl
bash-3.2#
```

189

Update /etc/hosts File

Update /etc/hosts for the cluster hostnames and application node names.

```
bash-3.2# cat /etc/hosts
#
# Internet host table
#
::1        localhost
127.0.0.1          localhost
192.168.100.61  solv-node1        loghost
192.168.100.62  solv-node2

# Application nodes
192.168.20.10    app-node1
192.168.20.20    app-node2
bash-3.2# █

bash-3.2# cat /etc/hostname.e1000g1
app-node1
bash-3.2# █
```

Passwordless ssh for root

The configuration for passwordless ssh to root account is already described in Chapter 4. Please refer to these steps to make sure the configuration is in place.

Installing Veritas Cluster Software

Go to the directory where Veritas Cluster software is extracted.

```
192.168.100.61 - PuTTY                                        —    □    ×
bash-3.2# ls -lrt
total 82
drwxrwxr-x   4 root     root          512 May  7  2012 perl
-rwxr-xr-x   1 root     root        18325 Jul 24  2012 webinstaller
drwxrwxr-x   4 root     root          512 Jul 24  2012 xprtl
-rwxr-xr-x   1 root     root         6316 Jul 24  2012 installer
-rw-r--r--   1 root     root          860 Aug  3  2012 copyright
drwxrwxr-x   4 root     root          512 Aug  3  2012 storage_foundation
drwxrwxr-x   3 root     root          512 Aug  3  2012 file_system
drwxrwxr-x   3 root     root          512 Aug  3  2012 dynamic_multipathing
drwxrwxr-x   3 root     root          512 Aug  3  2012 virtualstore
drwxrwxr-x   4 root     root          512 Aug  3  2012 storage_foundation_high_av
ailability
drwxrwxr-x   4 root     root          512 Aug  3  2012 storage_foundation_for_ora
cle_rac
drwxrwxr-x   4 root     root          512 Aug  3  2012 storage_foundation_cluster
_file_system_ha
drwxrwxr-x  10 root     root          512 Aug  3  2012 docs
drwxrwxr-x   2 root     root         1024 Aug  3  2012 pkgs
drwxrwxr-x   2 root     root          512 Aug  3  2012 windows
drwxrwxr-x   3 root     root          512 Aug  3  2012 volume_manager
drwxrwxr-x   7 root     root          512 Aug  3  2012 scripts
drwxrwxr-x   4 root     root          512 Aug  3  2012 cluster_server
bash-3.2#
```

Run **installer** program to start with the Veritas Cluster Software installation process as shown here.

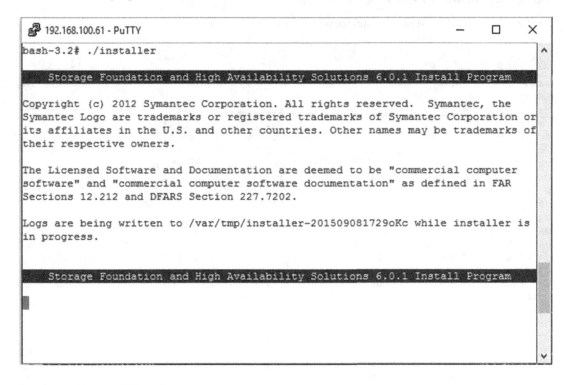

Preinstallation Checks

Select the Preinstallation checks to ensure the required preconfiguration information is in place.

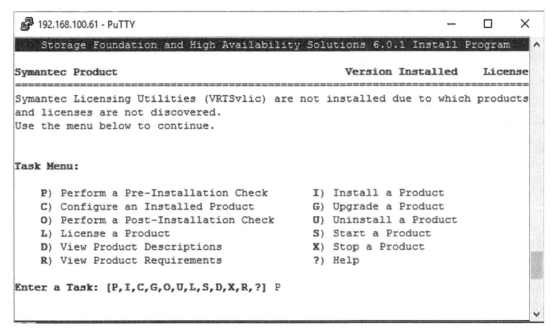

Select option 4 for performing preinstallation check for Veritas Storage Foundation and High Availability (SFHA) as shown below and press Enter to continue.

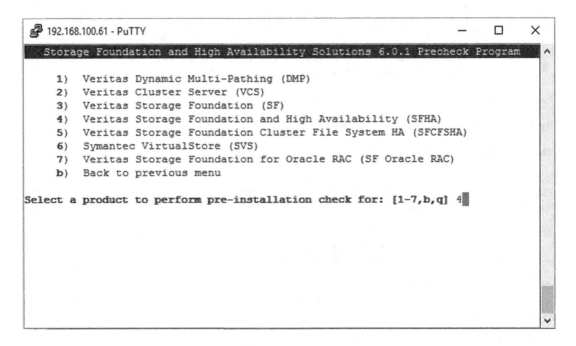

The following will show the cluster preinstallation check status. In case any of the configuration checks are at the failed state, verify and check and fix them prior to installation.

```
192.168.100.61 - PuTTY                                              —    □    ✕

      Checking installed product ........................................ Done
      Checking prerequisite patches and packages ....................... Done
      Checking platform version ........................................ Done
      Checking file system free space .................................. Done
      Checking product licensing ....................................... Done
      Performing product prechecks ..................................... Done

Precheck report completed

System verification checks completed

The following warnings were discovered on the systems:

CPI WARNING V-9-40-4970 To avoid a potential reboot after installation, you
should modify the /etc/system file on solv-node1 with the appropriate values,
and reboot prior to package installation.

Appropriate /etc/system file entries are shown below:
      set lwp_default_stksize=0x6000
      set rpcmod:svc_default_stksize=0x6000

CPI WARNING V-9-40-4970 To avoid a potential reboot after installation, you
should modify the /etc/system file on solv-node2 with the appropriate values,
and reboot prior to package installation.
```

```
Appropriate /etc/system file entries are shown below:
      set lwp_default_stksize=0x6000
      set rpcmod:svc_default_stksize=0x6000

installer log files, summary file, and response file are saved at:

      /opt/VRTS/install/logs/installer-201509081729oKc

Would you like to view the summary file? [y,n,q] (n)
```

Update /etc/system file with below two entries and reboot the hosts and try installer command again and select the preinstallation to verify if this is fixed.

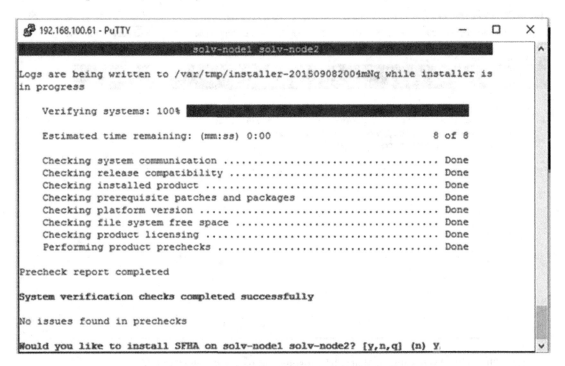

Post pre-checks verification, continue with the installation of SFHA software on both cluster nodes. Select option 2 to install recommended packages.

Install Veritas Cluster Software (SFHA)

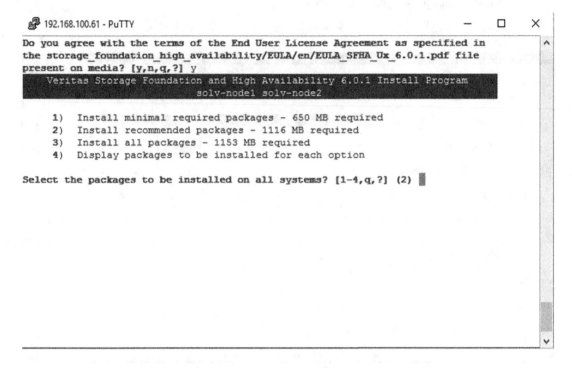

This will give the list of software that will be installed as part of the cluster build.

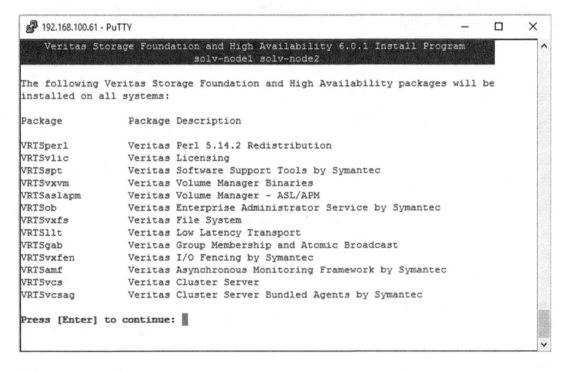

The list will go on by pressing Enter.

```
Press [Enter] to continue:
VRTSvcsea          Veritas Cluster Server Enterprise Agents by Symantec
VRTSdbed           Veritas Storage Foundation Databases
VRTSodm            Veritas Oracle Disk Manager
VRTSsfmh           Veritas Storage Foundation Managed Host by Symantec
VRTSvbs            Veritas Virtual Business Service
VRTSsfcpi601       Veritas Storage Foundation Installer

Press [Enter] to continue: █
```

And finally the packages will be installed as below:

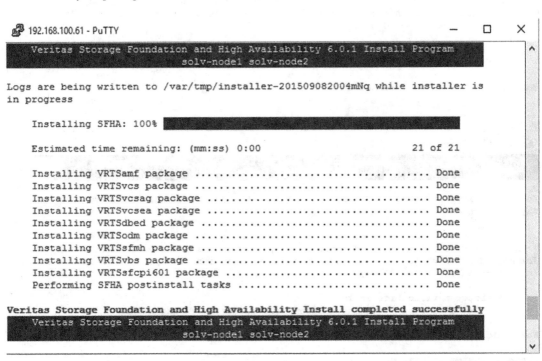

```
192.168.100.61 - PuTTY                                              —    □    ×
      Veritas Storage Foundation and High Availability 6.0.1 Install Program
                          solv-node1 solv-node2

Logs are being written to /var/tmp/installer-201509082004mNq while installer is
in progress

    Installing SFHA: 100%

    Estimated time remaining: (mm:ss) 0:00                         21 of 21

    Installing VRTSamf package ..................................... Done
    Installing VRTSvcs package ..................................... Done
    Installing VRTSvcsag package .................................. Done
    Installing VRTSvcsea package .................................. Done
    Installing VRTSdbed package ................................... Done
    Installing VRTSodm package .................................... Done
    Installing VRTSsfmh package ................................... Done
    Installing VRTSvbs package .................................... Done
    Installing VRTSsfcpi601 package .............................. Done
    Performing SFHA postinstall tasks ............................ Done

Veritas Storage Foundation and High Availability Install completed successfully
      Veritas Storage Foundation and High Availability 6.0.1 Install Program
                          solv-node1 solv-node2
```

License Veritas Cluster Installation

Once all packages are installed, the software will be required to be licensed. If you don't have a license (and setting up cluster build for learning), choose option 2 to enable keyless licensing.

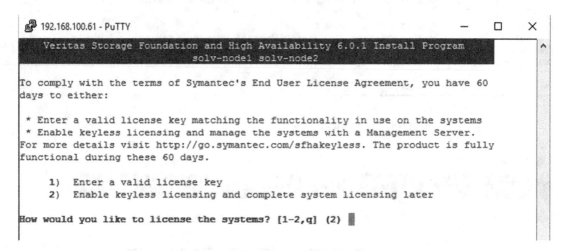

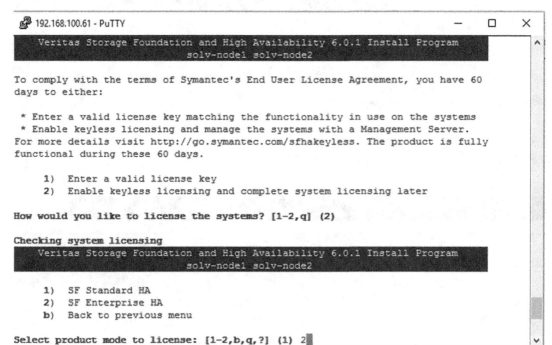

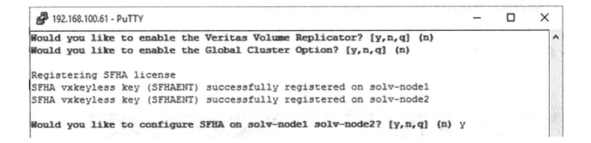

Setting up Veritas Cluster framework

Once the installation process is completed, the next steps are for setting up of Veritas Cluster. For this exercise do not select Veritas Volume Replicator and Global Cluster Options, but apply the license as accepted in the previous step.

Enable I/O Fencing

To start with the setup, first configure I/O fencing. As discussed before, I/O fencing prevents shared disks from data corruption.

```
I/O Fencing

It needs to be determined at this time if you plan to configure I/O Fencing in
enabled or disabled mode, as well as help in determining the number of network
interconnects (NICS) required on your systems. If you configure I/O Fencing in
enabled mode, only a single NIC is required, though at least two are
recommended.

A split brain can occur if servers within the cluster become unable to
communicate for any number of reasons. If I/O Fencing is not enabled, you run
the risk of data corruption should a split brain occur. Therefore, to avoid
data corruption due to split brain in CFS environments, I/O Fencing has to be
enabled.

If you do not enable I/O Fencing, you do so at your own risk
```

So enable I/O fencing by selecting y and continue as below.

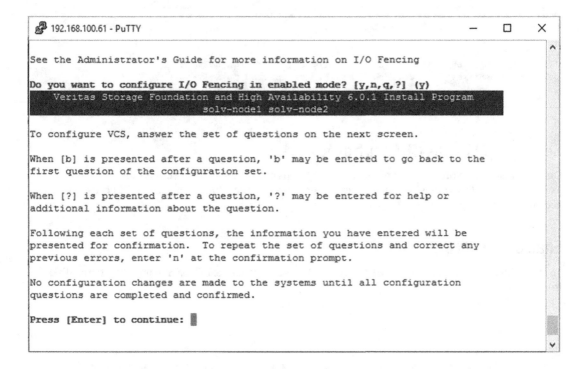

Set Cluster Name

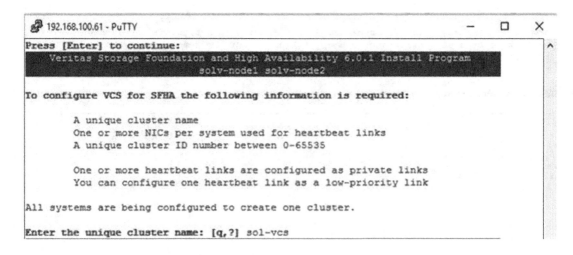

Configure Heartbeat

Once the cluster name is set, the next step is to set up LLT, private interconnect, or heartbeat connections.

```
Veritas Storage Foundation and High Availability 6.0.1 Install Program
                     solv-node1 solv-node2

    1)   Configure heartbeat links using LLT over Ethernet
    2)   Configure heartbeat links using LLT over UDP
    3)   Automatically detect configuration for LLT over Ethernet
    b)   Back to previous menu

How would you like to configure heartbeat links? [1-3,b,q,?] (1)
```

Choose interfaces to be used for private interconnects (heartbeat):

```
    Discovering NICs on solv-node1  Discovered e1000g0 e1000g1 e1000g2 e1000g3

Enter the NIC for the first private heartbeat link on solv-node1: [b,q,?]
(e1000g0) e1000g2
Would you like to configure a second private heartbeat link? [y,n,q,b,?] (n) y
Enter the NIC for the second private heartbeat link on solv-node1: [b,q,?]
(e1000g0) e1000g3
Would you like to configure a third private heartbeat link? [y,n,q,b,?] (n)
Do you want to configure an additional low-priority heartbeat link? [y,n,q,b,?]
(n)
Are you using the same NICs for private heartbeat links on all systems?
[y,n,q,b,?] (y)
    Checking media speed for e1000g2 on solv-node1 .............. 1000 Mbps
    Checking media speed for e1000g3 on solv-node1 .............. 1000 Mbps
    Checking media speed for e1000g2 on solv-node2 .............. 1000 Mbps
    Checking media speed for e1000g3 on solv-node2 .............. 1000 Mbps

Enter a unique cluster ID number between 0-65535: [b,q,?] (7)
```

Give a unique ID for the cluster to isolate this from any other cluster.
Verify heartbeat interfaces and choose y to continue.

```
192.168.100.61 - PuTTY                                          —    □    ✕

Enter a unique cluster ID number between 0-65535: [b,q,?] (7) 500

The cluster cannot be configured if the cluster ID 500 is in use by another
cluster. Installer can perform a check to determine if the cluster ID is
duplicate. The check will take less than a minute to complete.

Would you like to check if the cluster ID is in use by another cluster? [y,n,q]
(y) y

    Checking cluster ID ............................................ Done

Duplicated cluster ID detection passed. The cluster ID 500 can be used for the
cluster.

Press [Enter] to continue:
        Veritas Storage Foundation and High Availability 6.0.1 Install Program
                          solv-node1 solv-node2

Cluster information verification:

        Cluster Name:       sol-vcs
        Cluster ID Number: 500
        Private Heartbeat NICs for solv-node1:
                link1=e1000g2
                link2=e1000g3
        Private Heartbeat NICs for solv-node2:
                link1=e1000g2
                link2=e1000g3

Is this information correct? [y,n,q,?] (y) ▊
```

```
        Veritas Storage Foundation and High Availability 6.0.1 Install Program
                          solv-node1 solv-node2

The following data is required to configure the Virtual IP of the Cluster:

        A public NIC used by each system in the cluster
        A Virtual IP address and netmask

Do you want to configure the Virtual IP? [y,n,q,?] (n) y

Active NIC devices discovered on solv-node1: e1000g0

Enter the NIC for Virtual IP of the Cluster to use on solv-node1: [b,q,?]
(e1000g0) e1000g1
e1000g1 does not appear to be an active NIC
Are you sure you want to use NIC e1000g1 ? [y,n,q,b,?] (n) y
Is e1000g1 to be the public NIC used by all systems? [y,n,q,b,?] (y)
Enter the Virtual IP address for the Cluster: [b,q,?] 192.168.20.30
Enter the NetMask for IP 192.168.20.30: [b,q,?] (255.255.255.0)
        Veritas Storage Foundation and High Availability 6.0.1 Install Program
                          solv-node1 solv-node2

Cluster Virtual IP verification:

        NIC: e1000g1
        IP: 192.168.20.30
        NetMask: 255.255.255.0

Is this information correct? [y,n,q] (y) ▊
```

Cluster Security Configuration

At this stage of cluster configuration, select n for not configuring cluster in secure mode and n to add additional user.

```
    Veritas Storage Foundation and High Availability 6.0.1 Install Program
                         solv-node1 solv-node2

Veritas Cluster Server can be configured in secure mode

Running VCS in Secure Mode guarantees that all inter-system communication is
encrypted, and users are verified with security credentials.

When running VCS in Secure Mode, NIS and system usernames and passwords are
used to verify identity. VCS usernames and passwords are no longer utilized
when a cluster is running in Secure Mode.

Would you like to configure the VCS cluster in secure mode? [y,n,q,?] (n)
    Veritas Storage Foundation and High Availability 6.0.1 Install Program
                         solv-node1 solv-node2

The following information is required to add VCS users:

        A user name
        A password for the user
        User privileges (Administrator, Operator, or Guest)

Do you wish to accept the default cluster credentials of 'admin/password'?
[y,n,q] (y)

Do you want to add another user to the cluster? [y,n,q] (n)
```

Default users will be configured for administering and managing clusters. Next is setting the MTP configuration. Again, the VCS cluster under VirtualBox needs not be configured for SMTP, so we will skip it.

```
    Veritas Storage Foundation and High Availability 6.0.1 Install Program
                         solv-node1 solv-node2

VCS User verification:

        User: admin     Privilege: Administrators

        Passwords are not displayed

Is this information correct? [y,n,q] (y)
    Veritas Storage Foundation and High Availability 6.0.1 Install Program
                         solv-node1 solv-node2

The following information is required to configure SMTP notification:

        The domain-based hostname of the SMTP server
        The email address of each SMTP recipient
        A minimum severity level of messages to send to each recipient

Do you want to configure SMTP notification? [y,n,q,?] (n)
    Veritas Storage Foundation and High Availability 6.0.1 Install Program
                         solv-node1 solv-node2

The following information is required to configure SNMP notification:

        System names of SNMP consoles to receive VCS trap messages
```

Stop and Start Cluster Processes

As a part of cluster configuration, it will automatically stop and start all cluster services with the configuration chosen before.

```
          SNMP trap daemon port numbers for each console
          A minimum severity level of messages to send to each console

Do you want to configure SNMP notification? [y,n,q,?] (n)

All SFHA processes that are currently running must be stopped

Do you want to stop SFHA processes now? [y,n,q,?] (y)
       Veritas Storage Foundation and High Availability 6.0.1 Install Program
                            solv-node1 solv-node2

Logs are being written to /var/tmp/installer-201509082004mNq while installer is
in progress

    Stopping SFHA: 100%

    Estimated time remaining: (mm:ss) 0:00                         9 of 9

    Performing SFHA prestop tasks ................................... Done
    Stopping sfmh-discovery ......................................... Done
    Stopping vxdclid ................................................ Done
    Stopping had .................................................... Done
    Stopping CmdServer .............................................. Done
    Stopping amf .................................................... Done
    Stopping vxfen .................................................. Done
    Stopping gab .................................................... Done
```

```
    Stopping llt .................................................... Done

Veritas Storage Foundation and High Availability Shutdown completed
successfully
       Veritas Storage Foundation and High Availability 6.0.1 Install Program
                            solv-node1 solv-node2

Logs are being written to /var/tmp/installer-201509082004mNq while installer is
in progress

    Starting SFHA: 100%

    Estimated time remaining: (mm:ss) 0:00                        20 of 20

    Starting vxportal ............................................... Done
    Starting fdd .................................................... Done
    Starting llt .................................................... Done
    Starting gab .................................................... Done
    Starting amf .................................................... Done
    Starting had .................................................... Done
    Starting CmdServer .............................................. Done
    Starting vxdbd .................................................. Done
    Starting odm .................................................... Done
    Performing SFHA poststart tasks ................................. Done

Veritas Storage Foundation and High Availability Startup completed successfully
```

For choosing disk fencing for SATA (not SCSI disks), select n for not having disk base fencing.

```
 Veritas Storage Foundation and High Availability 6.0.1 Install Program
                      solv-node1 solv-node2

Fencing configuration
    1)   Configure Coordination Point client based fencing
    2)   Configure disk based fencing

Select the fencing mechanism to be configured in this Application Cluster:
[1-2,q] 2

This fencing configuration option requires a restart of VCS. Installer will
stop VCS at a later stage in this run. Do you want to continue? [y,n,q,b,?] y

Do you have SCSI3 PR enabled disks? [y,n,q,b] (y) n

Since you don't have SCSI3 PR enabled disks, you cannot configure disk based
fencing but you can use Coordination Point client based fencing

Do you want to retry fencing configuration? [y,n,q,b] (n)

The updates to VRTSaslapm package are released via the Symantec SORT web page:
https://sort.symantec.com/asl. To make sure you have the latest version of
VRTSaslapm (for up to date ASLs and APMs), download and install the latest
package from the SORT web page.
```

And this will complete the installation and configuration of a base Veritas Cluster framework.

```
installer log files, summary file, and response file are saved at:

        /opt/VRTS/install/logs/installer-201509082004mNq

Would you like to view the summary file? [y,n,q] (n)

bash-3.2#
```

Verify and Test Cluster Configuration

Check the cluster status as below.

```
bash-3.2# ifconfig -a
lo0: flags=2001000849<UP,LOOPBACK,RUNNING,MULTICAST,IPv4,VIRTUAL> mtu 8232 index
 1
        inet 127.0.0.1 netmask ff000000
e1000g0: flags=1000843<UP,BROADCAST,RUNNING,MULTICAST,IPv4> mtu 1500 index 2
        inet 192.168.100.61 netmask ffffff00 broadcast 192.168.100.255
        ether 8:0:27:ac:21:57
e1000g1: flags=1000843<UP,BROADCAST,RUNNING,MULTICAST,IPv4> mtu 1500 index 3
        inet 192.168.20.10 netmask ffffff00 broadcast 192.168.20.255
        ether 8:0:27:d8:22:36
bash-3.2# /opt/VRTS/bin/hastatus -sum

-- SYSTEM STATE
-- System              State              Frozen

A  solv-node1          RUNNING            0
A  solv-node2          RUNNING            0

-- GROUP STATE
-- Group         System          Probed     AutoDisabled     State


B  ClusterService  solv-node1     Y          N                OFFLINE

B  ClusterService  solv-node2     Y          N                ONLINE

bash-3.2#
```

Verify resource group failover to different nodes and check the status.

```
bash-3.2# /opt/VRTS/bin/hagrp -switch ClusterService -to solv-node1
bash-3.2# /opt/VRTS/bin/hastatus -sum

-- SYSTEM STATE
-- System              State              Frozen

A  solv-node1          RUNNING            0
A  solv-node2          RUNNING            0

-- GROUP STATE
-- Group         System          Probed     AutoDisabled     State

B  ClusterService  solv-node1     Y          N                ONLINE
B  ClusterService  solv-node2     Y          N                OFFLINE
bash-3.2#
```

Check the cluster network status (Virtual IP plumbed to solv-node1).

```
bash-3.2# ifconfig -a
lo0: flags=2001000849<UP,LOOPBACK,RUNNING,MULTICAST,IPv4,VIRTUAL> mtu 8232 index 1
        inet 127.0.0.1 netmask ff000000
e1000g0: flags=1000843<UP,BROADCAST,RUNNING,MULTICAST,IPv4> mtu 1500 index 2
        inet 192.168.100.61 netmask ffffff00 broadcast 192.168.100.255
        ether 8:0:27:ac:21:57
e1000g1: flags=1000843<UP,BROADCAST,RUNNING,MULTICAST,IPv4> mtu 1500 index 3
        inet 192.168.20.10 netmask ffffff00 broadcast 192.168.20.255
        ether 8:0:27:d8:22:36
e1000g1:1: flags=1000843<UP,BROADCAST,RUNNING,MULTICAST,IPv4> mtu 1500 index 3
        inet 192.168.20.30 netmask ffffff00 broadcast 192.168.20.255
bash-3.2# 
```

■ ■ ■

## CHAPTER 7

Setting Up Apache and NFS Services in Veritas Cluster

The very first step for setting up the applications under a cluster environment is to set the PATH to the Veritas Cluster binaries, thereby allowing commands to run without giving a full path every time.

```
#vi /.profile
Shift+G (To go to the end of the file)
      i (to start typing into the .profile file)
      PATH=$PATH:/usr/sbin:/usr/openwin/bin:/opt/VRTSvcs/bin
      export PATH
```

Adding Shared Disks and Setting Up Volumes
Add Shared Disks

Before proceeding to create cluster resource groups, have shared disks allocated and then configured as Veritas Volume managed disks. To add disks, as a good practice, shut down both nodes and add the disks as shared disks to be used by the cluster nodes. Add them using the GUI or command line. Steps for creating shared disks are already mentioned in Chapter 4, while setting up shared disks for Oracle Solaris Cluster. Below is a list of commands that will help in creating disks of 2Gb each.

```
C:\Program Files\Oracle\VirtualBox\VBoxManage.exe createhd -filename
d:\Shared-Disks\VCLUSDSH_01.vdi -size 2049 -format VDI -variant Fixed

C:\Program Files\Oracle\VirtualBox\VBoxManage.exe createhd -filename
d:\Shared-Disks\VCLUSDSH_01.vdi -size 2049 -format VDI -variant Fixed

C:\Program Files\Oracle\VirtualBox\VBoxManage.exe createhd -filename
d:\Shared-Disks\VCLUSDSH_01.vdi -size 2049 -format VDI -variant Fixed

C:\Program Files\Oracle\VirtualBox\VBoxManage.exe createhd -filename
d:\Shared-Disks\VCLUSDSH_01.vdi -size 2049 -format VDI -variant Fixed
```

```
Command Prompt                                            —    □    ×

C:\Program Files\Oracle\VirtualBox>VBoxManage.exe createhd --filename d:\Shared-Disks\
VCLUDSH_01.vdi --size 2048 --format VDI --variant Fixed
0%...10%...20%...30%...40%...50%...60%...70%...80%...90%...100%
Medium created. UUID: 60721308-103f-4679-9752-7853b4051739

C:\Program Files\Oracle\VirtualBox>VBoxManage.exe createhd --filename d:\Shared-Disks\
VCLUDSH_02.vdi --size 2048 --format VDI --variant Fixed
0%...10%...20%...30%...40%...50%...60%...70%...80%...90%...100%
Medium created. UUID: 42754b40-bf97-46d3-be7c-9aacee92faa2

C:\Program Files\Oracle\VirtualBox>VBoxManage.exe createhd --filename d:\Shared-Disks\
VCLUDSH_03.vdi --size 2048 --format VDI --variant Fixed
0%...10%...20%...30%...40%...50%...60%...70%...80%...90%...100%
Medium created. UUID: db6e4fe9-cfa5-4366-8f4d-0770a3b418ec

C:\Program Files\Oracle\VirtualBox>VBoxManage.exe createhd --filename d:\Shared-Disks\
VCLUDSH_04.vdi --size 2048 --format VDI --variant Fixed
0%...10%...20%...30%...40%...50%...60%...70%...80%...90%...100%
Medium created. UUID: f13395fa-37d9-404a-a4d0-b9ce66cd2d44

C:\Program Files\Oracle\VirtualBox>
```

Attach these disks to both cluster nodes and mark them as shareable using these commands:

```
C:\Program Files\Oracle\VirtualBox\VBoxManage.exe storageattach
Solv-Node1—storagectl "SATA Controller" -port 0 -device 0 -type hdd -medium
d:\Shared-Disks\VCLUSDSH_01.vdi -mtype shareable

C:\Program Files\Oracle\VirtualBox\VBoxManage.exe storageattach
Solv-Node1—storagectl "SATA Controller" -port 1 -device 0 -type hdd -medium
d:\Shared-Disks\VCLUSDSH_02.vdi -mtype shareable

C:\Program Files\Oracle\VirtualBox\VBoxManage.exe storageattach
Solv-Node1—storagectl "SATA Controller" -port 2 -device 0 -type hdd -medium
d:\Shared-Disks\VCLUSDSH_03.vdi -mtype shareable

C:\Program Files\Oracle\VirtualBox\VBoxManage.exe storageattach
Solv-Node1—storagectl "SATA Controller" -port 3 -device 0 -type hdd -medium
d:\Shared-Disks\VCLUSDSH_04.vdi -mtype shareable
```

```
Command Prompt                                          —    □    ×

C:\Program Files\Oracle\VirtualBox>VBoxManage.exe storageattach Solv-Node1 --storagect
l "SATA Controller" --port 0 --device 0 --type hdd --medium D:\Shared-Disks\VCQDSK.vdi
 --mtype shareable

C:\Program Files\Oracle\VirtualBox>VBoxManage.exe storageattach Solv-Node1 --storagect
l "SATA Controller" --port 1 --device 0 --type hdd --medium D:\Shared-Disks\VCLUDSH_01
.vdi --mtype shareable

C:\Program Files\Oracle\VirtualBox>VBoxManage.exe storageattach Solv-Node1 --storagect
l "SATA Controller" --port 2 --device 0 --type hdd --medium D:\Shared-Disks\VCLUDSH_02
.vdi --mtype shareable

C:\Program Files\Oracle\VirtualBox>VBoxManage.exe storageattach Solv-Node1 --storagect
l "SATA Controller" --port 3 --device 0 --type hdd --medium D:\Shared-Disks\VCLUDSH_03
.vdi --mtype shareable

C:\Program Files\Oracle\VirtualBox>VBoxManage.exe storageattach Solv-Node1 --storagect
l "SATA Controller" --port 4 --device 0 --type hdd --medium D:\Shared-Disks\VCLUDSH_04
.vdi --mtype shareable

C:\Program Files\Oracle\VirtualBox>
```

And repeat the previous commands based on second cluster node (solv-node2) as below:

```
C:\Program Files\Oracle\VirtualBox\VBoxManage.exe storageattach
Solv-Node2–storagectl "SATA Controller" -port 0 -device 0 -type hdd -medium
d:\Shared-Disks\VCLUSDSH_01.vdi -mtype shareable

C:\Program Files\Oracle\VirtualBox\VBoxManage.exe storageattach
Solv-Node2–storagectl "SATA Controller" -port 1 -device 0 -type hdd -medium
d:\Shared-Disks\VCLUSDSH_02.vdi -mtype shareable

C:\Program Files\Oracle\VirtualBox\VBoxManage.exe storageattach
Solv-Node2–storagectl "SATA Controller" -port 2 -device 0 -type hdd -medium
d:\Shared-Disks\VCLUSDSH_03.vdi -mtype shareable

C:\Program Files\Oracle\VirtualBox\VBoxManage.exe storageattach
Solv-Node2–storagectl "SATA Controller" -port 3 -device 0 -type hdd -medium
d:\Shared-Disks\VCLUSDSH_04.vdi -mtype shareable
```

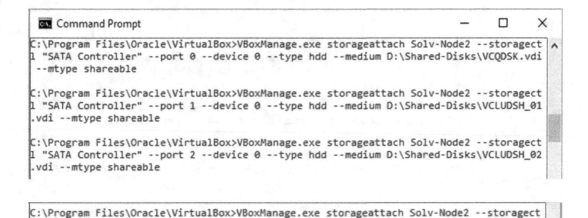

```
Command Prompt                                            —      □      ×

C:\Program Files\Oracle\VirtualBox>VBoxManage.exe storageattach Solv-Node2 --storagect
l "SATA Controller" --port 0 --device 0 --type hdd --medium D:\Shared-Disks\VCQDSK.vdi
--mtype shareable

C:\Program Files\Oracle\VirtualBox>VBoxManage.exe storageattach Solv-Node2 --storagect
l "SATA Controller" --port 1 --device 0 --type hdd --medium D:\Shared-Disks\VCLUDSH_01
.vdi --mtype shareable

C:\Program Files\Oracle\VirtualBox>VBoxManage.exe storageattach Solv-Node2 --storagect
l "SATA Controller" --port 2 --device 0 --type hdd --medium D:\Shared-Disks\VCLUDSH_02
.vdi --mtype shareable


C:\Program Files\Oracle\VirtualBox>VBoxManage.exe storageattach Solv-Node2 --storagect
l "SATA Controller" --port 3 --device 0 --type hdd --medium D:\Shared-Disks\VCLUDSH_03
.vdi --mtype shareable


C:\Program Files\Oracle\VirtualBox>
```

Either reboot both cluster nodes and/or run devfsadm –Cv command on both cluster nodes to refresh/ re-create device trees.

```
bash-3.2# devfsadm –Cv
devfsadm[4122]: verbose: symlink /dev/cfg/sata0/0 -> ../../../devices/pci@0,0/pc
i8086,2829@d:0
devfsadm[4122]: verbose: symlink /dev/cfg/sata0/1 -> ../../../devices/pci@0,0/pc
i8086,2829@d:1
devfsadm[4122]: verbose: symlink /dev/cfg/sata0/2 -> ../../../devices/pci@0,0/pc
i8086,2829@d:2
devfsadm[4122]: verbose: symlink /dev/cfg/sata0/3 -> ../../../devices/pci@0,0/pc
i8086,2829@d:3
devfsadm[4122]: verbose: symlink /dev/cfg/sata0/4 -> ../../../devices/pci@0,0/pc
i8086,2829@d:4
```

Run dclisetup.sh on both to run vxdclid daemon for running vxlist commands.

```
192.168.100.61 - PuTTY                                     —      □      ×

bash-3.2# /opt/VRTSsfmh/adm/dclisetup.sh
bash-3.2#
```

```
192.168.100.62 - PuTTY                                     —      □      ×

bash-3.2#  /opt/VRTSsfmh/adm/dclisetup.sh
bash-3.2#
```

Run vxlist command to check the status of the disks added and their device names as below; all the disks will be in an uninitialized state.

```
bash-3.2# /usr/lib/vxvm/bin/vxlist
TY    DEVICE    DISK    DISKGROUP      SIZE    FREE  STATUS
disk  c0d0s2    -       -                -       -  uninitialized
disk  disk_0    -       -                -       -  uninitialized
disk  disk_1    -       -                -       -  uninitialized
disk  disk_2    -       -                -       -  uninitialized
disk  disk_3    -       -                -       -  uninitialized
disk  disk_4    -       -                -       -  uninitialized

TY    FS      FSTYPE      SIZE      FREE    %USED  DEVICE_PATH          MOUNT_POINT
fs    /       ufs        8.10g     3.05g      62%  /dev/dsk/c0d0s0      /
fs    home    ufs        7.09g     4.34g      39%  /dev/dsk/c0d0s7      /export/home

TY    NAME    TYPE    STATE     WWN    PNAME
hba   c0      FC      offline   -      /pci@0,0/pci-ide@1,1/ide@0
hba   c2      SCSI    online    -      /pci@0,0/pci8086,2829@d

TY    ENCLR_NAME      ENCLR_MODEL    ARRAY_TYPE    STATUS        ENCLR_SNO
encl  disk            ATA            Disk          connected     DISKS
encl  other_disks     VERITAS        OTHER_DISKS   connected     OTHER_DISKS
bash-3.2#
```

And to this, run vxdisk list to check if all stated disks are online and that extended disks have native disk names. The type shown here has none.

```
bash-3.2# vxdisk list
DEVICE       TYPE          DISK        GROUP        STATUS
c0d0s2       auto:none     -           -            online invalid
disk_0       auto:none     -           -            online invalid
disk_1       auto:none     -           -            online invalid
disk_2       auto:none     -           -            online invalid
disk_3       auto:none     -           -            online invalid
disk_4       auto:none     -           -            online invalid
bash-3.2# vxdisk -e list
DEVICE       TYPE          DISK      GROUP       STATUS         OS_NATIVE_NAME    ATTR
c0d0s2       auto:none     -         -           online invalid  c0d0s2           -
disk_0       auto:none     -         -           online invalid  c2t0d0s2         -
disk_1       auto:none     -         -           online invalid  c2t2d0s2         -
disk_2       auto:none     -         -           online invalid  c2t1d0s2         -
disk_3       auto:none     -         -           online invalid  c2t3d0s2         -
disk_4       auto:none     -         -           online invalid  c2t4d0s2         -
bash-3.2#
```

213

Bring Shared Disks Under Veritas Control

Change to directory /etc/vx/bin and run the command vxdisksetup to set up disks as a Veritas-controlled volume manager as below.

```
192.168.100.61 - PuTTY
bash-3.2# pwd
/etc/vx/bin
bash-3.2# ./vxdisksetup -i disk_0
bash-3.2# ./vxdisksetup -i disk_1
bash-3.2# ./vxdisksetup -i disk_2
bash-3.2# ./vxdisksetup -i disk_3
bash-3.2# ./vxdisksetup -i disk_4
bash-3.2# vxdisk list
DEVICE        TYPE          DISK      GROUP        STATUS
c0d0s2        auto:none     -         -            online invalid
disk_0        auto:cdsdisk  -         -            online
disk_1        auto:cdsdisk  -         -            online
disk_2        auto:cdsdisk  -         -            online
disk_3        auto:cdsdisk  -         -            online
disk_4        auto:cdsdisk  -         -            online
```

Check the disks status again, and now the Type appears as cdsdisk.

```
bash-3.2# vxdisk -e list
DEVICE        TYPE          DISK    GROUP     STATUS            OS_NATIVE_NAME   ATTR
c0d0s2        auto:none     -       -         online invalid    c0d0s2           -
disk_0        auto:cdsdisk  -       -         online            c2t0d0s2         -
disk_1        auto:cdsdisk  -       -         online            c2t2d0s2         -
disk_2        auto:cdsdisk  -       -         online            c2t1d0s2         -
disk_3        auto:cdsdisk  -       -         online            c2t3d0s2         -
disk_4        auto:cdsdisk  -       -         online            c2t4d0s2         -
bash-3.2#
```

Configure Disks Using Format Command

Check the disks added using format as below, and select each disk for setting them as Solaris partition disks.

```
bash-3.2# format
Searching for disks...
Inquiry failed for this logical diskdone


AVAILABLE DISK SELECTIONS:
       0. c0d0 <███x██████████@███ cyl 2085 alt 2 hd 255 sec 63>
          /pci@0,0/pci-ide@1,1/ide@0/cmdk@0,0
       1. c2t0d0 <ATA-VBOXHARDDISK-1.0 cyl 21843 alt 2 hd 16 sec 3>
          /pci@0,0/pci8086,2829@d/disk@0,0
       2. c2t1d0 <ATA-VBOXHARDDISK-1.0 cyl 52426 alt 2 hd 16 sec 5>
          /pci@0,0/pci8086,2829@d/disk@1,0
       3. c2t2d0 <ATA-VBOXHARDDISK-1.0 cyl 52426 alt 2 hd 16 sec 5>
          /pci@0,0/pci8086,2829@d/disk@2,0
       4. c2t3d0 <ATA-VBOXHARDDISK-1.0 cyl 52426 alt 2 hd 16 sec 5>
          /pci@0,0/pci8086,2829@d/disk@3,0
       5. c2t4d0 <ATA-VBOXHARDDISK-1.0 cyl 52426 alt 2 hd 16 sec 5>
          /pci@0,0/pci8086,2829@d/disk@4,0
Specify disk (enter its number): 1
selecting c2t0d0
[disk formatted]
```

```
FORMAT MENU:
        disk       - select a disk
        type       - select (define) a disk type
        partition  - select (define) a partition table
        current    - describe the current disk
        format     - format and analyze the disk
        fdisk      - run the fdisk program
        repair     - repair a defective sector
        label      - write label to the disk
        analyze    - surface analysis
        defect     - defect list management
        backup     - search for backup labels
        verify     - read and display labels
        save       - save new disk/partition definitions
        inquiry    - show vendor, product and revision
        volname    - set 8-character volume name
        !<cmd>     - execute <cmd>, then return
        quit
```

```
format> fdisk
No fdisk table exists. The default partition for the disk is:

  a 100% "SOLARIS System" partition

Type "y" to accept the default partition,  otherwise type "n" to edit the
 partition table.
y
```

Repeat for all the other remaining four disks. Check the disks using the format command as shown below.

```
bash-3.2# echo | format
Searching for disks...
Inquiry failed for this logical diskdone


AVAILABLE DISK SELECTIONS:
       0. c0d0 <▒x▒▒▒▒▒▒▒▒|@▒▒▒ cyl 2085 alt 2 hd 255 sec 63>
          /pci@0,0/pci-ide@1,1/ide@0/cmdk@0,0
       1. c2t0d0 <ATA     -VBOX HARDDISK  -1.0  cyl 509 alt 2 hd 64 sec 32>
          /pci@0,0/pci8086,2829@d/disk@0,0
       2. c2t1d0 <ATA     -VBOX HARDDISK  -1.0  cyl 1021 alt 2 hd 128 sec 32>
          /pci@0,0/pci8086,2829@d/disk@1,0
       3. c2t2d0 <ATA     -VBOX HARDDISK  -1.0  cyl 1021 alt 2 hd 128 sec 32>
          /pci@0,0/pci8086,2829@d/disk@2,0
       4. c2t3d0 <ATA     -VBOX HARDDISK  -1.0  cyl 1021 alt 2 hd 128 sec 32>
          /pci@0,0/pci8086,2829@d/disk@3,0
       5. c2t4d0 <ATA     -VBOX HARDDISK  -1.0  cyl 1021 alt 2 hd 128 sec 32>
          /pci@0,0/pci8086,2829@d/disk@4,0
Specify disk (enter its number): Specify disk (enter its number):
bash-3.2# vxdisk -e list
DEVICE       TYPE         DISK       GROUP       STATUS          OS_NATIVE_NAME   ATTR

c0d0s2       auto:none    -          -           online invalid  c0d0s2           -

disk_0       auto:cdsdisk -          -           online          c2t0d0s2         -

disk_1       auto:cdsdisk -          -           online          c2t2d0s2         -

disk_2       auto:cdsdisk -          -           online          c2t1d0s2         -

disk_3       auto:cdsdisk -          -           online          c2t3d0s2         -

disk_4       auto:cdsdisk -          -           online          c2t4d0s2         -

bash-3.2# █
```

Create Disk Group

Now run the vxdg command to create disk groups DGRP01 out of disk_1 and disk_2 (output of Device Name from vxdisk –e list command).

```
bash-3.2# vxdg init DGRP01 DGRP01_1=disk_1 DGRP01_2=disk_2
bash-3.2# vxdisk -e list
DEVICE       TYPE           DISK         GROUP        STATUS          OS_NAT
IVE_NAME     ATTR
c0d0s2       auto:none      -            -            online invalid  c0d0s2
             -
disk_0       auto:cdsdisk   -            -            online          c2t0d0
s2           -
disk_1       auto:cdsdisk   DGRP01_1     DGRP01       online          c2t2d0
s2           -
disk_2       auto:cdsdisk   DGRP01_2     DGRP01       online          c2t1d0
s2           -
disk_3       auto:cdsdisk   -            -            online          c2t3d0
s2           -
disk_4       auto:cdsdisk   -            -            online          c2t4d0
s2           -
bash-3.2# vxdg init DGRP02 DGRP02_1=disk_3 DGRP02_2=disk_4
bash-3.2# vxdisk -e list
DEVICE       TYPE           DISK         GROUP        STATUS          OS_NAT
IVE_NAME     ATTR
c0d0s2       auto:none      -            -            online invalid  c0d0s2
             -
disk_0       auto:cdsdisk   -            -            online          c2t0d0
s2           -
disk_1       auto:cdsdisk   DGRP01_1     DGRP01       online          c2t2d0
s2           -
disk_2       auto:cdsdisk   DGRP01_2     DGRP01       online          c2t1d0
s2           -
disk_3       auto:cdsdisk   DGRP02_1     DGRP02       online          c2t3d0
s2           -
disk_4       auto:cdsdisk   DGRP02_2     DGRP02       online          c2t4d0
s2           -
bash-3.2#
```

Verify Disk Groups

Assign full-disk sizes to the disk groups DGRP01 and DGRP02.

Verify disk groups can be deported and imported back with no errors observed as below. This test will help in making sure that disks can failover successfully by using deport and import commands.

```
bash-3.2# vxassist -g DGRP01 maxsize
Maximum volume size: 8255488 (4031Mb)
bash-3.2# vxassist -g DGRP02 maxsize
Maximum volume size: 8255488 (4031Mb)
bash-3.2# vxdg deport DGRP01
bash-3.2# vxdg list
NAME          STATE          ID
DGRP02        enabled,cds          1442312370.13.solv-node1
bash-3.2# vxdg import DGRP01
bash-3.2# vxdg list
NAME          STATE          ID
DGRP02        enabled,cds          1442312370.13.solv-node1
DGRP01        enabled,cds          1442312321.11.solv-node1
bash-3.2# vxdg deport DGRP02
bash-3.2# vxdg list
NAME          STATE          ID
DGRP01        enabled,cds          1442312321.11.solv-node1
bash-3.2# vxdg import DGRP02
bash-3.2# vxdg list
NAME          STATE          ID
DGRP01        enabled,cds          1442312321.11.solv-node1
DGRP02        enabled,cds          1442312370.13.solv-node1
bash-3.2# 
```

Create Volume

Now Create Disk Volumes.

```
bash-3.2# vxassist -g DGRP01 make VOL_APP01 4031M
bash-3.2# vxassist -g DGRP02 make VOL_APP02 4031M
bash-3.2# vxprint -v
Disk group: DGRP01

TY NAME          ASSOC          KSTATE    LENGTH    PLOFFS    STATE     TUTIL0    PUTIL0
v  VOL_APP01     fsgen          ENABLED   8255488   -         ACTIVE    -         -

Disk group: DGRP02

TY NAME          ASSOC          KSTATE    LENGTH    PLOFFS    STATE     TUTIL0    PUTIL0
v  VOL_APP02     fsgen          ENABLED   8255488   -         ACTIVE    -         -
```

And print the disks volumes created.

```
bash-3.2# vxprint -vth
Disk group: DGRP01

V  NAME          RVG/VSET/CO  KSTATE    STATE     LENGTH   READPOL    PREFPLEX UTYPE
PL NAME          VOLUME       KSTATE    STATE     LENGTH   LAYOUT     NCOL/WID MODE
SD NAME          PLEX         DISK      DISKOFFS  LENGTH   [COL/]OFF  DEVICE   MODE
SV NAME          PLEX         VOLNAME   NVOLLAYR  LENGTH   [COL/]OFF  AM/NM    MODE
SC NAME          PLEX         CACHE     DISKOFFS  LENGTH   [COL/]OFF  DEVICE   MODE
DC NAME          PARENTVOL    LOGVOL
SP NAME          SNAPVOL      DCO
EX NAME          ASSOC        VC                           PERMS     MODE      STATE

v  VOL_APP01     -            ENABLED   ACTIVE    8255488  SELECT     -        fsgen
pl VOL_APP01-01 VOL_APP01    ENABLED   ACTIVE    8255488  CONCAT     -        RW
sd DGRP01_1-01  VOL_APP01-01 DGRP01_1  0         4128288  0          disk_1   ENA
sd DGRP01_2-01  VOL_APP01-01 DGRP01_2  0         4127200  4128288    disk_2   ENA

Disk group: DGRP02

V  NAME          RVG/VSET/CO  KSTATE    STATE     LENGTH   READPOL    PREFPLEX UTYPE
PL NAME          VOLUME       KSTATE    STATE     LENGTH   LAYOUT     NCOL/WID MODE
SD NAME          PLEX         DISK      DISKOFFS  LENGTH   [COL/]OFF  DEVICE   MODE
SV NAME          PLEX         VOLNAME   NVOLLAYR  LENGTH   [COL/]OFF  AM/NM    MODE
SC NAME          PLEX         CACHE     DISKOFFS  LENGTH   [COL/]OFF  DEVICE   MODE
DC NAME          PARENTVOL    LOGVOL
SP NAME          SNAPVOL      DCO
EX NAME          ASSOC        VC                           PERMS     MODE      STATE

v  VOL_APP02     -            ENABLED   ACTIVE    8255488  SELECT     -        fsgen
pl VOL_APP02-01 VOL_APP02    ENABLED   ACTIVE    8255488  CONCAT     -        RW
sd DGRP02_1-01  VOL_APP02-01 DGRP02_1  0         4128288  0          disk_3   ENA
sd DGRP02_2-01  VOL_APP02-01 DGRP02_2  0         4127200  4128288    disk_4   ENA
bash-3.2#
```

Create Veritas File Systems

Last, create Veritas file systems on VOL_APP01 and VOL_APP02 volumes.

```
bash-3.2# mkfs -F vxfs /dev/vx/rdsk/DGRP01/VOL_APP01
    version 9 layout
    8255488 sectors, 4127744 blocks of size 1024, log size 16384 blocks
    rcq size 1024 blocks
    largefiles supported
bash-3.2# mkfs -F vxfs /dev/vx/rdsk/DGRP02/VOL_APP02
    version 9 layout
    8255488 sectors, 4127744 blocks of size 1024, log size 16384 blocks
    rcq size 1024 blocks
    largefiles supported
bash-3.2#
```

Mount File Systems

Create two app directories and check if they can be mounted using about volumes.

```
bash-3.2# mkdir /app02
bash-3.2# mount -f vxfs /dev/vx/
clust       dmp/        dsk/        info        netiod      rdsk/       taskmon     vcevent
config      dmpconfig   esd         iod         rdmp/       task        trace
bash-3.2# mount -f vxfs /dev/vx/dsk/DGRP01/VOL_APP01 /app01
```

```
bash-3.2# mount -f vxfs /dev/vx/dsk/DGRP02/VOL_APP02 /app02
bash-3.2# df -h
Filesystem             size   used  avail capacity  Mounted on
/dev/dsk/c0d0s0        8.1G   5.0G   3.1G    62%     /
/devices                0K     0K     0K     0%     /devices
ctfs                    0K     0K     0K     0%     /system/contract
proc                    0K     0K     0K     0%     /proc
mnttab                  0K     0K     0K     0%     /etc/mnttab
swap                   1.1G   1.1M   1.1G     1%     /etc/svc/volatile
objfs                   0K     0K     0K     0%     /system/object
sharefs                 0K     0K     0K     0%     /etc/dfs/sharetab
swap                   1.1G     0K   1.1G     0%     /dev/vx/dmp
swap                   1.1G     0K   1.1G     0%     /dev/vx/rdmp
/usr/lib/libc/libc_hwcap1.so.1
                       8.1G   5.0G   3.1G    62%     /lib/libc.so.1
fd                      0K     0K     0K     0%     /dev/fd
swap                   1.1G    36K   1.1G     1%     /tmp
swap                   1.1G    32K   1.1G     1%     /var/run
/dev/dsk/c0d0s7        7.1G   2.7G   4.3G    39%     /export/home
/dev/odm                0K     0K     0K     0%     /dev/odm
/dev/vx/dsk/DGRP01/VOL_APP01
                       3.9G    19M   3.7G     1%     /app01
/dev/vx/dsk/DGRP02/VOL_APP02
                       3.9G    19M   3.7G     1%     /app02
```

Create directories /app01 and /app02 on the second host as well: to get them mounted via cluster-controlled commands.

```
192.168.100.62 - PuTTY                                    —    □    ×

bash-3.2# mkdir /app01
bash-3.2# mkdir /app02
bash-3.2#
```

Set Up Resource Groups and Cluster Resources

Now it's time to create cluster resources and resource groups. But before this, to configure veritas cluster resource groups and resources, let's first make man.cf file as read-write.

```
bash-3.2# /opt/VRTSvcs/bin/haconf -makerw
bash-3.2# cd /etc/VRTS
VRTS/        VRTSagents/ VRTSvbs/      VRTSvcs/
bash-3.2# cd /etc/VRTSvcs/conf/config/
```

To create cluster resource groups for app01 and app02, follow the steps below:

1.   Create cluster resource groups.

2.   Add Veritas disk group cluster resources to respective groups.

3.   Add cluster volume cluster resources to the respective group.

4.   Add mount cluster resource to this group.

5.   Add NIC cluster resource to this group.

6.   Add virtual IP cluster resource to this group (NIC resource to failover resource).

7.   Finally, add cluster resource for application service (here it's NFS and Apache).

Creating Cluster Resource Group for NFS

Before starting with the cluster resource group creation, let's first bring the cluster configuration file /etc/ VRTSvcs/conf/config/main.cf into read-write mode as:

>   *haconf -makerw*

Create Cluster Resource Group

Create cluster resource group APPGP01 to be used by the NFS service and point them to cluster nodes solv-node1 and solv-node2. At the beginning, cluster resources will not be set to Critical to stop disabled automated failover. This is needed to test and verify cluster resources. Once they are tested and verified, these cluster resource properties should be set to 0 for automated failover of cluster resources.

```
bash-3.2# /opt/VRTSvcs/bin/hagrp -add APPGP01
bash-3.2#  /opt/VRTSvcs/bin/hagrp -modify APPGP01 SystemList  solv-node1 0 solv-node2 1
bash-3.2# /opt/VRTSvcs/bin/hagrp -modify APPGP01 AutoStartList  solv-node1  solv-node2
```

Add Disk Group DGRP01 Cluster Resource

Add Disk group cluster resource APPGP01_DG01 to the NFS cluster resource group APPGP01.

```
bash-3.2# /opt/VRTSvcs/bin/hares -add APPGP01_DG01 DiskGroup APPGP01
VCS NOTICE V-16-1-10242 Resource added. Enabled attribute must be set before agent monitors
bash-3.2# /opt/VRTSvcs/bin/hares -modify APPGP01_DG01 DiskGroup DGRP01
bash-3.2# /opt/VRTSvcs/bin/hares -modify APPGP01_DG01 Enabled 1
bash-3.2# /opt/VRTSvcs/bin/hares -list
APPGP01_DG01            solv-node1
APPGP01_DG01            solv-node2
csgnic                 solv-node1
csgnic                 solv-node2
webip                  solv-node1
webip                  solv-node2
```

Add Volume Cluster Resource

Add volume APPGP01_VOL01 cluster resource to the resource group APPGP01.

```
bash-3.2# /opt/VRTSvcs/bin/hares -add APPGP01_VOL01 Volume APPGP01
VCS NOTICE V-16-1-10242 Resource added. Enabled attribute must be set before agent monitors
bash-3.2# /opt/VRTSvcs/bin/hares -modify APPGP01_VOL01 Diskgroup DGRP01
bash-3.2# /opt/VRTSvcs/bin/hares -modify APPGP01_VOL01 Volume VOL_APP01
bash-3.2# /opt/VRTSvcs/bin/hares -modify APPGP01_VOL01 Enabled 1
```

Create Mountpoint Cluster Resource

Create mountpoint cluster resource APPGP01_MNT01 pointing to block device. /dev/vx/dsk/DGRP01/VOL_APP01 as vxfs filesystem

```
bash-3.2# /opt/VRTSvcs/bin/hares -add APPGP01_MNT01 Mount APPGP01
VCS NOTICE V-16-1-10242 Resource added. Enabled attribute must be set before agent monitors
bash-3.2# /opt/VRTSvcs/bin/hares -modify APPGP01_MNT01 BlockDevice /dev/vx/dsk/DGRP01/VOL_APP01
bash-3.2# /opt/VRTSvcs/bin/hares -modify APPGP01_MNT01 MountPoint /app01
bash-3.2# /opt/VRTSvcs/bin/hares -modify APPGP01_MNT01 Enabled 1
bash-3.2# /opt/VRTSvcs/bin/hares -modify APPGP01_MNT01 FSType vxfs
```

And set cluster dependencies of mountpoint MNT01 on the VOL01.

```
bash-3.2# haconf -makerw
bash-3.2# hares -link APPGP01_VOL01 APPGP01_DG01
bash-3.2# hares -link APPGP01_MNT01 APPGP01_VOL01
```

Add NIC Device Resource

Add NIC device cluster resource to the APPGP01 as shown below.

```
bash-3.2# /opt/VRTSvcs/bin/hares -add APPGP01_NIC1 NIC APPGP01
VCS NOTICE V-16-1-10242 Resource added. Enabled attribute must be set before age
nt monitors
bash-3.2# /opt/VRTSvcs/bin/hares -modify APPGP01_NIC1 Enabled 1
bash-3.2# /opt/VRTSvcs/bin/hares -modify APPGP01_NIC1 Device e1000g1
```

Create IP Cluster Resource

Create floating IP cluster resource APPGP01_IP01.

```
bash-3.2# /opt/VRTSvcs/bin/hares -add APPGP01_IP01 IP APPGP01
VCS NOTICE V-16-1-10242 Resource added. Enabled attribute must be set before agent monitors
bash-3.2# /opt/VRTSvcs/bin/hares -modify APPGP01_IP01 Device e1000g1
bash-3.2# /opt/VRTSvcs/bin/hares -modify APPGP01_IP01 Address "192.168.20.40"
bash-3.2# /opt/VRTSvcs/bin/hares -modify APPGP01_IP01 NetMask "255.255.255.0"
bash-3.2# /opt/VRTSvcs/bin/hares -modify APPGP01_IP01 Enabled 1
```

Setting up NFS Cluster Resources

To set up the NFS application under Veritas Cluster, first disable and unconfigure all NFS services running as a part of the default Solaris 10 installation.

```
svccfg export svc:/network/nfs/server:default > nfs-server.cfg
svccfg export svc:/network/nfs/server > nfs-server.cfg
svccfg export svc:/network/nfs/status > nfs-status.cfg
svccfg export svc:/network/nfs/nlockmgr > nfs-nlockmgr.cfg
 svccfg export /network/nfs/mapid > nfs-mapid.cfg
svccfg delete -f svc:/network/nfs/server
 svccfg delete -f svc:/network/nfs/status
 svccfg delete -f  svc:/network/nfs/nlockmgr
svccfg delete -f svc:/network/nfs/mapid:default
svcs -a | grep -i nfs
```

Next create cluster resource NFS_Server of type NFS, with property as NServers (Number of Servers). As an example, we are setting this to 10. Further, check the resource properties.

```
bash-3.2# hares -add NFS_Server NFS APPGP01
VCS NOTICE V-16-1-10242 Resource added. Enabled attribute must be set before age
nt monitors
bash-3.2# hares -modify NFS_Server Enabled 1
bash-3.2# hares -modify NFS_Server Nservers 10
bash-3.2# hares -display NFS_Server
#Resource    Attribute        System       Value
NFS_Server   Group            global       APPGP01
NFS_Server   Type             global       NFS
NFS_Server   AutoStart        global       1
NFS_Server   Critical         global       1
NFS_Server   Enabled          global       1
NFS_Server   LastOnline       global       solv-node1
NFS_Server   MonitorOnly      global       0
NFS_Server   ResourceOwner    global
NFS_Server   TriggerEvent     global       0
NFS_Server   ArgListValues    solv-node1 UseSMF   1       0       Nservers
        1        10       LockFileTimeout 1       180     CleanRmtab    1
0
NFS_Server   ArgListValues    solv-node2 UseSMF   1       0       Nservers
        1        10       LockFileTimeout 1       180     CleanRmtab    1
0
```

NFS_Server	ConfidenceLevel	solv-node1 0				
NFS_Server	ConfidenceLevel	solv-node2 0				
NFS_Server	ConfidenceMsg	solv-node1				
NFS_Server	ConfidenceMsg	solv-node2				
NFS_Server	Flags	solv-node1				
NFS_Server	Flags	solv-node2				
NFS_Server	IState	solv-node1 not waiting				
NFS_Server	IState	solv-node2 not waiting				
NFS_Server	MonitorMethod	solv-node1 Traditional				
NFS_Server	MonitorMethod	solv-node2 Traditional				
NFS_Server	Probed	solv-node1 1				
NFS_Server	Probed	solv-node2 1				
NFS_Server	Start	solv-node1 1				
NFS_Server	Start	solv-node2 0				
NFS_Server	State	solv-node1 ONLINE				
NFS_Server	State	solv-node2 OFFLINE				
NFS_Server	CleanRmtab	global	0			
NFS_Server	ComputeStats	global	0			
NFS_Server	ContainerInfo	global	Type		Name	
Enabled						
NFS_Server	LockFileTimeout	global	180			
NFS_Server	Nservers	global	10			
NFS_Server	ResContainerInfo	global	Type		Name	
Enabled						
NFS_Server	ResourceInfo	global	State	Valid	Msg	
TS						
NFS_Server	ResourceRecipients	global				
NFS_Server	TriggerPath	global				
NFS_Server	TriggerResRestart	global	0			
NFS_Server	TriggerResStateChange	global	0			
NFS_Server	TriggersEnabled	global				
NFS_Server	UseSMF	global	0			
NFS_Server	MonitorTimeStats	solv-node1 Avg		0	TS	
NFS_Server	MonitorTimeStats	solv-node2 Avg		0	TS	

Next is to add NFS_Restart NFS cluster resources to ensure that the NFS cluster service can successfully be started/restarted. Also check that the properties post these updates to see if the parameters are added correctly.

```
bash-3.2# hares -add NFS_Restart NFSRestart APPGP01
VCS NOTICE V-16-1-10242 Resource added. Enabled attribute must be set before agent monitors
bash-3.2#  hares -modify NFS_Restart Enabled 1
bash-3.2# hares -modify NFS_Restart NFSRes NFS_Server
bash-3.2# hares -modify NFS_Restart LocksPathName "/opt/VRTSvcs/lock"
bash-3.2# hares -modify NFS_Restart NFSLockFailover  1
bash-3.2#
```

```
bash-3.2# hares -display NFS_Restart
#Resource       Attribute             System      Value
NFS_Restart     Group                 global      APPGP01
NFS_Restart     Type                  global      NFSRestart
NFS_Restart     AutoStart             global      1
NFS_Restart     Critical              global      1
NFS_Restart     Enabled               global      1
NFS_Restart     LastOnline            global
NFS_Restart     MonitorOnly           global      0
NFS_Restart     ResourceOwner         global
NFS_Restart     TriggerEvent          global      0
NFS_Restart     ArgListValues         solv-node1 LocksPathName     1        =
NFSLockFailover 1        1            LockServers    1        20       NFSRes   1
=        NFSRes:Nservers 1            ""         NFSRes:LockFileTimeout 1         ""
NFSRes:UseSMF   1        ""           Lower   1        0        State    1        0
```

```
NFS_Restart     Flags                 solv-node2 |STATE UNKNOWN|
NFS_Restart     IState                solv-node1 not waiting
NFS_Restart     IState                solv-node2 not waiting
NFS_Restart     MonitorMethod         solv-node1 Traditional
NFS_Restart     MonitorMethod         solv-node2 Traditional
NFS_Restart     Probed                solv-node1 0
NFS_Restart     Probed                solv-node2 0
NFS_Restart     Start                 solv-node1 0
NFS_Restart     Start                 solv-node2 0
NFS_Restart     State                 solv-node1 OFFLINE|STATE UNKNOWN
NFS_Restart     State                 solv-node2 OFFLINE|STATE UNKNOWN
NFS_Restart     ComputeStats          global     0
NFS_Restart     ContainerInfo         global     Type              Name
NFS_Restart     LockServers           global     20
NFS_Restart     LocksPathName         global     =
NFS_Restart     Lower                 global     0
NFS_Restart     NFSLockFailover       global     1
NFS_Restart     NFSRes                global     =
NFS_Restart     ResContainerInfo      global     Type              Name
NFS_Restart     ResourceInfo          global     State    Valid    Msg
NFS_Restart     ResourceRecipients    global
NFS_Restart     TriggerPath           global
NFS_Restart     TriggerResRestart     global     0
NFS_Restart     TriggerResStateChange global     0
NFS_Restart     TriggersEnabled       global
NFS_Restart     MonitorTimeStats      solv-node1 Avg      0        TS
```

```
NFS_Restart  ConfidenceLevel       solv-node1 0
NFS_Restart  ConfidenceLevel       solv-node2 0
NFS_Restart  ConfidenceMsg         solv-node1
NFS_Restart  ConfidenceMsg         solv-node2
NFS_Restart  Flags                 solv-node1 |STATE UNKNOWN|
NFS_Restart  Flags                 solv-node2 |STATE UNKNOWN|
NFS_Restart  IState                solv-node1 not waiting
NFS_Restart  IState                solv-node2 not waiting
NFS_Restart  MonitorMethod         solv-node1 Traditional
NFS_Restart  MonitorMethod         solv-node2 Traditional
NFS_Restart  Probed                solv-node1 0
NFS_Restart  Probed                solv-node2 0
NFS_Restart  Start                 solv-node1 0
NFS_Restart  Start                 solv-node2 0
NFS_Restart  State                 solv-node1 OFFLINE|STATE UNKNOWN
NFS_Restart  State                 solv-node2 OFFLINE|STATE UNKNOWN
NFS_Restart  ComputeStats          global     0
NFS_Restart  ContainerInfo         global     Type              Name
Enabled
NFS_Restart  LockServers           global     20
NFS_Restart  LocksPathName         global     =
NFS_Restart  Lower                 global     0
NFS_Restart  NFSLockFailover       global     1
NFS_Restart  NFSRes                global     =
NFS_Restart  ResContainerInfo      global     Type              Name
Enabled
```

```
NFS_Restart  ResourceInfo          global     State    Valid   Msg
TS
NFS_Restart  ResourceRecipients    global
NFS_Restart  TriggerPath           global
NFS_Restart  TriggerResRestart     global     0
NFS_Restart  TriggerResStateChange global     0
NFS_Restart  TriggersEnabled       global
NFS_Restart  MonitorTimeStats      solv-node1 Avg      0       TS
NFS_Restart  MonitorTimeStats      solv-node2 Avg      0       TS
bash-3.2#
```

Next is adding NFS_Share cluster resource to enable share functionality on the NFS server, as the filesystem to be used by the NFS service is /app01. Create NFS directory inside /app01 and set this directory to be used as NFS share path.

```
bash-3.2# hares -add NFS_Share Share APPGP01
VCS NOTICE V-16-1-10242 Resource added. Enabled attribute must be set before agent monitors
bash-3.2# hares -modify NFS_Share Enabled 1
bash-3.2# hares -modify NFS_Share PathName  "/app01/nfs"
bash-3.2# hares -modify NFS_Share Options "rw,anon=0"
bash-3.2#
```

Check the cluster resource NFS_Share properties and verify.

```
bash-3.2# hares -display NFS_Share
#Resource      Attribute                 System       Value
NFS_Share      Group                     global       APPGP01
NFS_Share      Type                      global       Share
NFS_Share      AutoStart                 global       1
NFS_Share      Critical                  global       1
NFS_Share      Enabled                   global       1
NFS_Share      LastOnline                global
NFS_Share      MonitorOnly               global       0
NFS_Share      ResourceOwner             global
NFS_Share      TriggerEvent              global       0
NFS_Share      ArgListValues             solv-node1 PathName   1         =         Options
1       =         NFSRes:State     1       ""
NFS_Share      ArgListValues             solv-node2 PathName   1         =         Options
1       =         NFSRes:State     1       ""
NFS_Share      ConfidenceLevel           solv-node1 0
NFS_Share      ConfidenceLevel           solv-node2 0
NFS_Share      ConfidenceMsg             solv-node1
NFS_Share      ConfidenceMsg             solv-node2
```

```
NFS_Share      Flags                     solv-node1 |STATE UNKNOWN|
NFS_Share      Flags                     solv-node2 |STATE UNKNOWN|
NFS_Share      IState                    solv-node1 not waiting
NFS_Share      IState                    solv-node2 not waiting
NFS_Share      MonitorMethod             solv-node1 Traditional
NFS_Share      MonitorMethod             solv-node2 Traditional
NFS_Share      Probed                    solv-node1 0
NFS_Share      Probed                    solv-node2 0
NFS_Share      Start                     solv-node1 0
NFS_Share      Start                     solv-node2 0
NFS_Share      State                     solv-node1 OFFLINE|STATE UNKNOWN
NFS_Share      State                     solv-node2 OFFLINE|STATE UNKNOWN
NFS_Share      ComputeStats              global       0
NFS_Share      ContainerInfo             global       Type                Name
Enabled
NFS_Share      NFSRes                    global
NFS_Share      Options                   global       =
NFS_Share      PathName                  global       =
NFS_Share      ResContainerInfo          global       Type                Name
Enabled
NFS_Share      ResourceInfo              global       State      Valid    Msg
TS
NFS_Share      ResourceRecipients        global
NFS_Share      TriggerPath               global
NFS_Share      TriggerResRestart         global       0
NFS_Share      TriggerResStateChange global   0
```

```
NFS_Share      TriggersEnabled      global
NFS_Share      MonitorTimeStats     solv-node1 Avg        0        TS
NFS_Share      MonitorTimeStats     solv-node2 Avg        0        TS
bash-3.2#
```

Finally, set cluster dependencies to ensure cluster resources start in sequence.

```
bash-3.2# haconf -makerw
bash-3.2# hares -link APPGP01_VOL01 APPGP01_DG01
bash-3.2# hares -link APPGP01_MNT01 APPGP01_VOL01
bash-3.2# hares -link APPGP02_VOL01 APPGP02_DG01
bash-3.2# hares -link APPGP02_MNT01 APPGP02_VOL01
bash-3.2#
```

```
bash-3.2# /opt/VRTSvcs/bin/haconf -makerw
bash-3.2# hares -link NFS_Restart APPGP01_IP01
bash-3.2# hares -link NFS_Share APPGP01_MNT01
bash-3.2# hares -link NFS_Share NFS_Server
bash-3.2#
bash-3.2#
```

Now as the cluster resource groups and resources are created, bring the main.cf back to read-only mode by using the command below.

```
bash-3.2# /opt/VRTSvcs/bin/haconf -dump -makero
bash-3.2# hares -list | grep -i nfs
NFS_Restart            solv-node1
NFS_Restart            solv-node2
NFS_Server             solv-node1
NFS_Server             solv-node2
NFS_Share              solv-node1
NFS_Share              solv-node2
bash-3.2#
```

```
bash-3.2# more /etc/VRTSvcs/conf/config/main.cf
include "OracleASMTypes.cf"
include "types.cf"
include "Db2udbTypes.cf"
include "OracleTypes.cf"
include "SybaseTypes.cf"

cluster sol-vcs (
        UserNames = { admin = anoGniNkoJooMwoInl }
        ClusterAddress = "192.168.20.30"
        Administrators = { admin }
        )

system solv-node1 (
        )

system solv-node2 (
        )

group APPGP01 (
        SystemList = { solv-node1 = 0, solv-node2 = 1 }
        AutoStartList = { solv-node1 }
        )

        DiskGroup APPGP01_DG01 (
                Critical = 0
                DiskGroup = DGRP01
                StartVolumes = 0
                )

        IP APPGP01_IP01 (
                Critical = 0
                Device = e1000g1
                Address = "192.168.20.40"
                NetMask = "255.255.255.0"
                )

        Mount APPGP01_MNT01 (
                Critical = 0
                MountPoint = "/app01"
                BlockDevice = "/dev/vx/dsk/DGRP01/VOL_APP01"
                FSType = vxfs
                FsckOpt = "-y"
                )

        NFS NFS_Server (
                Nservers = 10
                )

        NFSRestart NFS_Restart (
                NFSRes = "="
                LocksPathName = "="
```

```
                            NFSLockFailover = 1
                            )

                NIC APPGP01_NIC1 (
                            Device = e1000g1
                            )

                Share NFS_Share (
                            PathName = "="
                            Options = "="
                            )

                Volume APPGP01_VOL01 (
                            Critical = 0
                            Volume = VOL_APP01
                            DiskGroup = DGRP01
                            )

                APPGP01_IP01 requires APPGP01_NIC1
                APPGP01_MNT01 requires APPGP01_VOL01
                APPGP01_VOL01 requires APPGP01_DG01


                // resource dependency tree
                //
                //        group APPGP01
                //        {
                //        IP APPGP01_IP01
                //            {
                //            NIC APPGP01_NIC1
                //            }
                //        Mount APPGP01_MNT01
                //            {
                //            Volume APPGP01_VOL01
                //                {
                //                DiskGroup APPGP01_DG01
                //                }
                //            }
                //        NFSRestart NFS_Restart
                //        NFS NFS_Server
                //        Share NFS_Share
                //        }


group APPGP02 (
        SystemList = { solv-node1 = 0, solv-node2 = 1 }
        AutoStartList = { solv-node1, solv-node2 }
        )

        DiskGroup APPGP02_DG01 (
                Critical = 0
                DiskGroup = DGRP02
```

```
                StartVolumes = 0
                )

IP APPGP02_IP01 (
        Critical = 0
        Device = e1000g1
        Address = "192.168.20.50"
        NetMask = "255.255.255.0"
        )

Mount APPGP02_MNT01 (
        Critical = 0
        MountPoint = "/app02"
        BlockDevice = "/dev/vx/dsk/DGRP02/VOL_APP02"
        FSType = vxfs
        FsckOpt = "-y"
        )

NIC APPGP02_NIC1 (
        Device = e1000g1
        )

Volume APPGP02_VOL01 (
        Critical = 0
        Volume = VOL_APP02
        DiskGroup = DGRP02
        )

APPGP02_IP01 requires APPGP02_NIC1
APPGP02_MNT01 requires APPGP02_VOL01
APPGP02_VOL01 requires APPGP02_DG01


// resource dependency tree
//
//      group APPGP02
//      {
//      IP APPGP02_IP01
//          {
//          NIC APPGP02_NIC1
//          }
//      Mount APPGP02_MNT01
//          {
//          Volume APPGP02_VOL01
//              {
//              DiskGroup APPGP02_DG01
//              }
//          }
//      }
```

```
group ClusterService (
        SystemList = { solv-node1 = 0, solv-node2 = 1 }
        AutoStartList = { solv-node1, solv-node2 }
        OnlineRetryLimit = 3
        OnlineRetryInterval = 120
        )

        IP webip (
                Device = e1000g1
                Address = "192.168.20.30"
                NetMask = "255.255.255.0"
                )

        NIC csgnic (
                Device = e1000g1
                )

        webip requires csgnic


        // resource dependency tree
        //
        //        group ClusterService
        //        {
        //        IP webip
        //            {
        //            NIC csgnic
        //            }
        //        }
```

Verify and Test NFS Cluster Service

Offline and Online of NFS Resource Group APPGP01

First bring APPGP01 (NFS cluster resource group) offline, if not already offline and check the status.

```
bash-3.2# hagrp -offline APPGP01 -any
VCS NOTICE V-16-1-50733 Attempting to offline group on system solv-node1
bash-3.2# _
```

```
bash-3.2# hagrp -state
#Group          Attribute              System        Value
APPGP01         State                  solv-node1    |OFFLINE|
APPGP01         State                  solv-node2    |OFFLINE|
ClusterService  State                  solv-node1    |ONLINE|
ClusterService  State                  solv-node2    |OFFLINE|
bash-3.2# █
```

Next is to bring the cluster resource group APPGP01 online on the node solv-node1.

```
bash-3.2# hagrp -online APPGP01 -sys solv-node1
bash-3.2#
```

And check the status as below.

```
bash-3.2# hagrp -state
#Group           Attribute           System        Value
APPGP01          State               solv-node1   |ONLINE|
APPGP01          State               solv-node2   |OFFLINE|
ClusterService   State               solv-node1   |ONLINE|
ClusterService   State               solv-node2   |OFFLINE|
```

Verify NFS mount on other host in the same subnet (for testing purposes) as below.

```
bash-3.2# mount -F nfs solv-node1:/app01/nfs /mnt
bash-3.2# df -h
Filesystem              size   used  avail capacity  Mounted on
/dev/dsk/c0d0s0         8.1G   5.0G   3.0G    63%     /
/devices                 0K     0K     0K     0%     /devices
ctfs                     0K     0K     0K     0%     /system/contract
proc                     0K     0K     0K     0%     /proc
mnttab                   0K     0K     0K     0%     /etc/mnttab
swap                    1.1G   1.1M   1.1G     1%     /etc/svc/volatile
objfs                    0K     0K     0K     0%     /system/object
sharefs                  0K     0K     0K     0%     /etc/dfs/sharetab
swap                    1.1G     0K   1.1G     0%     /dev/vx/dmp
swap                    1.1G     0K   1.1G     0%     /dev/vx/rdmp
/usr/lib/libc/libc_hwcap1.so.1
                        8.1G   5.0G   3.0G    63%     /lib/libc.so.1
fd                       0K     0K     0K     0%     /dev/fd
swap                    1.1G    40K   1.1G     1%     /tmp
swap                    1.1G    32K   1.1G     1%     /var/run
/dev/dsk/c0d0s7         7.1G   448M   6.6G     7%     /export/home
/dev/odm                 0K     0K     0K     0%     /dev/odm
solv-node1:/app01/nfs
                        3.9G    19M   3.7G     1%     /mnt
bash-3.2#
```

Failover and Failback Check for APPGP01

Failover the APPGP01 (nfs resource group) to solv-node2 node and check the status.

```
bash-3.2# hagrp -switch APPGP01 -to solv-node2
```

233

```
bash-3.2# hares -state | grep APPGP01
APPGP01_DG01   State                    solv-node1 OFFLINE
APPGP01_DG01   State                    solv-node2 ONLINE
APPGP01_IP01   State                    solv-node1 OFFLINE
APPGP01_IP01   State                    solv-node2 ONLINE
APPGP01_MNT01 State                     solv-node1 OFFLINE
APPGP01_MNT01 State                     solv-node2 ONLINE
APPGP01_NIC1   State                    solv-node1 ONLINE
APPGP01_NIC1   State                    solv-node2 ONLINE
APPGP01_VOL01 State                     solv-node1 OFFLINE
APPGP01_VOL01 State                     solv-node2 ONLINE
NFS_Restart    State                    solv-node1 OFFLINE
NFS_Restart    State                    solv-node2 ONLINE
NFS_Server     State                    solv-node1 ONLINE
NFS_Server     State                    solv-node2 ONLINE
NFS_Share      State                    solv-node1 OFFLINE
NFS_Share      State                    solv-node2 ONLINE
bash-3.2#
```

And switch back to solv-node1 and check the status.

```
bash-3.2# hagrp -switch APPGP01 -to solv-node1
bash-3.2#
```

```
bash-3.2# hares -state
APPGP01_DG01   State                    solv-node1 ONLINE
APPGP01_DG01   State                    solv-node2 OFFLINE
APPGP01_IP01   State                    solv-node1 ONLINE
APPGP01_IP01   State                    solv-node2 OFFLINE
APPGP01_MNT01 State                     solv-node1 ONLINE
APPGP01_MNT01 State                     solv-node2 OFFLINE
APPGP01_NIC1   State                    solv-node1 ONLINE
APPGP01_NIC1   State                    solv-node2 ONLINE
APPGP01_VOL01 State                     solv-node1 ONLINE
APPGP01_VOL01 State                     solv-node2 OFFLINE
NFS_Restart    State                    solv-node1 ONLINE
NFS_Restart    State                    solv-node2 OFFLINE
NFS_Server     State                    solv-node1 ONLINE
NFS_Server     State                    solv-node2 OFFLINE
NFS_Share      State                    solv-node1 ONLINE
NFS_Share      State                    solv-node2 OFFLINE
bash-3.2#
```

First, offline APPGP01 cluster resource group:

```
bash-3.2# hagrp -offline APPGP01 -any
VCS NOTICE V-16-1-50733 Attempting to offline group on system solv-node1
bash-3.2# ▊
```

Run ifconfig –a on each host:
Solv-node1.

```
bash-3.2# ifconfig -a
lo0: flags=2001000849<UP,LOOPBACK,RUNNING,MULTICAST,IPv4,VIRTUAL> mtu 8232 index 1
        inet 127.0.0.1 netmask ff000000
e1000g0: flags=1000843<UP,BROADCAST,RUNNING,MULTICAST,IPv4> mtu 1500 index 2
        inet 192.168.100.61 netmask ffffff00 broadcast 192.168.100.255
        ether 8:0:27:ac:21:57
e1000g1: flags=1000843<UP,BROADCAST,RUNNING,MULTICAST,IPv4> mtu 1500 index 3
        inet 192.168.20.10 netmask ffffff00 broadcast 192.168.20.255
        ether 8:0:27:d8:22:36
bash-3.2# ▊
```

Solv-node2.

```
bash-3.2# ifconfig -a
lo0: flags=2001000849<UP,LOOPBACK,RUNNING,MULTICAST,IPv4,VIRTUAL> mtu 8232 index 1
        inet 127.0.0.1 netmask ff000000
e1000g0: flags=1000843<UP,BROADCAST,RUNNING,MULTICAST,IPv4> mtu 1500 index 2
        inet 192.168.100.62 netmask ffffff00 broadcast 192.168.100.255
        ether 8:0:27:5b:5e:ca
e1000g1: flags=1000843<UP,BROADCAST,RUNNING,MULTICAST,IPv4> mtu 1500 index 3
        inet 192.168.20.20 netmask ffffff00 broadcast 192.168.20.255
        ether 8:0:27:be:fa:e3
e1000g1:2: flags=1000843<UP,BROADCAST,RUNNING,MULTICAST,IPv4> mtu 1500 index 3
        inet 192.168.20.30 netmask ffffff00 broadcast 192.168.20.255
bash-3.2# ▊
```

Online APPGP01 on solv-node1.

```
bash-3.2# hagrp -switch APPGP01 -to solv-node1
bash-3.2#
```

Run ifconfig –a and see if the NFS floating IP is plumbed in.

```
bash-3.2# ifconfig -a
lo0: flags=2001000849<UP,LOOPBACK,RUNNING,MULTICAST,IPv4,VIRTUAL> mtu 8232 index 1
        inet 127.0.0.1 netmask ff000000
e1000g0: flags=1000843<UP,BROADCAST,RUNNING,MULTICAST,IPv4> mtu 1500 index 2
        inet 192.168.100.61 netmask ffffff00 broadcast 192.168.100.255
        ether 8:0:27:ac:21:57
e1000g1: flags=1000843<UP,BROADCAST,RUNNING,MULTICAST,IPv4> mtu 1500 index 3
        inet 192.168.20.10 netmask ffffff00 broadcast 192.168.20.255
        ether 8:0:27:d8:22:36
e1000g1:1: flags=1000843<UP,BROADCAST,RUNNING,MULTICAST,IPv4> mtu 1500 index 3
        inet 192.168.20.40 netmask ffffff00 broadcast 192.168.20.255
bash-3.2# ▊
```

Run df –h /app01 to see if /app01 is mounted.

```
bash-3.2# df -h /app01
Filesystem                 size   used  avail capacity  Mounted on
/dev/vx/dsk/DGRP01/VOL_APP01
                           3.9G    19M   3.7G      1%   /app01
bash-3.2# 
```

Online APPGP01 on solv-node2.

```
bash-3.2# hagrp -switch APPGP01 -to solv-node2
bash-3.2# 
```

Run df –h /app01 on solv-node2.

```
bash-3.2# df -h /app01
Filesystem                 size   used  avail capacity  Mounted on
/dev/vx/dsk/DGRP01/VOL_APP01
                           3.9G    19M   3.7G      1%   /app01
bash-3.2# 
```

Creating Cluster Resource Group for Apache

Device configurations for both NFS and Apache cluster configurations are already completed. So here we will create Apache cluster resources.

Create/Update ApacheTypes.cf

Create ApacheTypes.cf file in the directory /etc/VRTSvcs/conf for the configuration of ApacheCluster under Veritas.

```
bash-3.2# pwd
/
bash-3.2# cd /etc/VRTSvcs/conf/
bash-3.2# vi vcsApacheTypes.cf 
```

```
192.168.100.61 - PuTTY                                        —    □    ×
type Apache (
  static int RestartLimit = 1
  str ServerRoot
  str PidFile
  ste IPAddr
  int Port
  str TestFile
  static str ArgList[] = { ServerRoot, PidFile, IPAddr, Port, TestFile }
  )
~
~
~
~
~
~
~
~
~
~
~
~
~
~
~
~
~
"vcsApacheTypes.cf" 9 lines, 199 characters
```

Create Cluster Resource Group APPGP02

```
bash-3.2# /opt/VRTSvcs/bin/hagrp -add APPGP02
bash-3.2#  /opt/VRTSvcs/bin/hagrp -modify APPGP02 SystemList  solv-node1 0 solv-node2 1
bash-3.2# /opt/VRTSvcs/bin/hagrp -modify APPGP02 AutoStartList  solv-node1  solv-node2
```

Add Disk Group DGRP02 Cluster Resource

Add Disk group cluster resource APPGP02_DG02 to the NFS cluster resource group APPGP02.

```
bash-3.2# /opt/VRTSvcs/bin/hares -add APPGP02_DG01 DiskGroup APPGP02
VCS NOTICE V-16-1-10242 Resource added. Enabled attribute must be set before agent monitors
bash-3.2# /opt/VRTSvcs/bin/hares -modify APPGP02_DG01 DiskGroup DGRP02
bash-3.2# /opt/VRTSvcs/bin/hares -modify APPGP02_DG01 Enabled 1
```

Add Volume Cluster Resource

Add volume APPGP01_VOL01 cluster resource to the resource group APPGP01.

```
bash-3.2# /opt/VRTSvcs/bin/hares -add APPGP02_VOL01 Volume APPGP02
VCS NOTICE V-16-1-10242 Resource added. Enabled attribute must be set before agent monitors
bash-3.2# /opt/VRTSvcs/bin/hares -modify APPGP02_VOL01 DiskGroup DGRP02
bash-3.2# /opt/VRTSvcs/bin/hares -modify APPGP02_VOL01 Volume VOL_APP02
bash-3.2# /opt/VRTSvcs/bin/hares -modify APPGP02_VOL01 Enabled 1
bash-3.2# /opt/VRTSvcs/bin/hares -list
APPGP01_DG01          solv-node1
APPGP01_DG01          solv-node2
APPGP01_VOL01         solv-node1
APPGP01_VOL01         solv-node2
APPGP02_DG01          solv-node1
APPGP02_DG01          solv-node2
APPGP02_VOL01         solv-node1
APPGP02_VOL01         solv-node2
csgnic                solv-node1
csgnic                solv-node2
webip                 solv-node1
webip          _      solv-node2
webip                 solv-node1
webip          _      solv-node2
```

Create Mountpoint Cluster Resource

Create mountpoint cluster resource APPGP02_MNT01 pointing to block device: /dev/vx/dsk/DGRP02/VOL_APP02 as vxfs filesystem.

```
bash-3.2# /opt/VRTSvcs/bin/hares -add APPGP02_MNT01 Mount APPGP02
VCS NOTICE V-16-1-10242 Resource added. Enabled attribute must be set before agent monitors
bash-3.2# /opt/VRTSvcs/bin/hares -modify APPGP02_MNT01 BlockDevice /dev/vx/dsk/DGRP02/VOL_APP02
bash-3.2# /opt/VRTSvcs/bin/hares -modify APPGP02_MNT01 MountPoint /app02
bash-3.2# /opt/VRTSvcs/bin/hares -modify APPGP02_MNT01 FSType vxfs
bash-3.2# /opt/VRTSvcs/bin/hares -modify APPGP02_MNT01 FsckOpt %-y
bash-3.2# /opt/VRTSvcs/bin/hares -modify APPGP02_MNT01 Enabled 1
```

Add NIC Device Resource

Add NIC device cluster resource to the APPGP02 as below:

```
bash-3.2# /opt/VRTSvcs/bin/hares -add APPGP02_NIC1 NIC APPGP02
VCS NOTICE V-16-1-10242 Resource added. Enabled attribute must be set before age
nt monitors
bash-3.2# /opt/VRTSvcs/bin/hares -modify APPGP02_NIC1 Enabled 1
bash-3.2# /opt/VRTSvcs/bin/hares -modify APPGP02_NIC1 Device e1000g1
bash-3.2#
```

Create IP Cluster Resource

Create floating IP cluster resource APPGP02_IP01:

```
bash-3.2# /opt/VRTSvcs/bin/hares -add APPGP02_IP01 IP APPGP02
VCS NOTICE V-16-1-10242 Resource added. Enabled attribute must be set before agent monitors
bash-3.2# /opt/VRTSvcs/bin/hares -modify APPGP02_IP01 Device e1000g1
bash-3.2# /opt/VRTSvcs/bin/hares -modify APPGP02_IP01 Address "192.168.20.50"
bash-3.2# /opt/VRTSvcs/bin/hares -modify APPGP02_IP01 NetMask "255.255.255.0"
bash-3.2# /opt/VRTSvcs/bin/hares -modify APPGP02_IP01 Enabled 1
bash-3.2#
```

Create Apache Cluster Resource

To set up an Apache cluster resource, please keep the following information handy prior to the setup:

> The default installed apache is in /usr/apache2 directory and configuration is in /etc/apache2.

> Make changes below to the httpd.conf file:

>> ServerRoot /usr/apache2

>> PidFile /var/apache2/logs/httpd.pid

>> Listen 192.168.20.50:80 (This is floating IP address)

>> User webservd, Group webservd

>> ServerName solv-node1 (or solv-node2 for each node)

>> DocumentRoot "/app02"

>> Update <Directory "/app02"> - After the comment # This should be changed to whatever you set DocumentRoot to

Post above configuration changes to httpd.conf file; now create cluster resource for Apache-type Veritas Cluster service as below:
hconf –makerw (to make the main.cf file read+write)
Next add cluster resource and configuration parameters as below:

```
bash-3.2# hares -.add Apache_Host APPGP02
bash-3.2# hares -add Apache_Host Apache APPGP02
bash-3.2# hares -modify Apache_Host httpdDir "/usr/apache2/bin"
bash-3.2# hares -modify Apache_Host ConfigFile "/etc/apache2/httpd.conf"
bash-3.2# hares -online Apache_Host Enabled 1
bash-3.2#
```

And next is to create cluster resource dependencies for the Apache_Host cluster resource as below:

```
bash-3.2# hares -link Apache_Host APPGPO2_MNTO1
bash-3.2# hares -link Apache_Host APPGPO2_IPO1
bash-3.2# █
```

And finally run command to save the main.cf file read-only as below:
#haconf –dump –makero
And check the status of the cluster resource group and resources:

```
bash-3.2# hagrp -state
#Group          Attribute         System       Value
APPGPO1         State             solv-node1  |ONLINE|
APPGPO1         State             solv-node2  |OFFLINE|
APPGPO2         State             solv-node1  |ONLINE|
APPGPO2         State             solv-node2  |OFFLINE|
ClusterService  State             solv-node1  |ONLINE|
ClusterService  State             solv-node2  |OFFLINE|
bash-3.2# █
```

```
bash-3.2# hares -state
#Resource        Attribute      System      Value
APPGPO1_DG01     State          solv-node1  ONLINE
APPGPO1_DG01     State          solv-node2  OFFLINE
APPGPO1_IP01     State          solv-node1  ONLINE
APPGPO1_IP01     State          solv-node2  OFFLINE
APPGPO1_MNTO1    State          solv-node1  ONLINE
APPGPO1_MNTO1    State          solv-node2  OFFLINE
APPGPO1_NIC1     State          solv-node1  ONLINE
APPGPO1_NIC1     State          solv-node2  ONLINE
APPGPO1_VOL01    State          solv-node1  ONLINE
APPGPO1_VOL01    State          solv-node2  OFFLINE
APPGPO2_DG01     State          solv-node1  ONLINE
APPGPO2_DG01     State          solv-node2  OFFLINE
APPGPO2_IP01     State          solv-node1  ONLINE
APPGPO2_IP01     State          solv-node2  OFFLINE
APPGPO2_MNTO1    State          solv-node1  ONLINE
APPGPO2_MNTO1    State          solv-node2  OFFLINE
APPGPO2_NIC1     State          solv-node1  ONLINE
APPGPO2_NIC1     State          solv-node2  ONLINE
APPGPO2_VOL01    State          solv-node1  ONLINE
APPGPO2_VOL01    State          solv-node2  OFFLINE
Apache_Host      State          solv-node1  ONLINE
Apache_Host      State          solv-node2  OFFLINE
NFS_Restart      State          solv-node1  ONLINE
NFS_Restart      State          solv-node2  OFFLINE
NFS_Server       State          solv-node1  ONLINE
NFS_Server       State          solv-node2  OFFLINE
NFS_Share        State          solv-node1  ONLINE
NFS_Share        State          solv-node2  OFFLINE
csgnic           State          solv-node1  ONLINE
csgnic           State          solv-node2  ONLINE
webip            State          solv-node1  ONLINE
webip            State          solv-node2  OFFLINE
bash-3.2#
```

```
bash-3.2# hastatus -sum

-- SYSTEM STATE
-- System              State            Frozen

A  solv-node1          RUNNING            0
A  solv-node2          RUNNING            0

-- GROUP STATE
-- Group          System          Probed    AutoDisabled    State

B  APPGP01        solv-node1        Y          N            ONLINE
B  APPGP01        solv-node2        Y          N            OFFLINE
B  APPGP02        solv-node1        Y          N            ONLINE
B  APPGP02        solv-node2        Y          N            OFFLINE
B  ClusterService solv-node1        Y          N            ONLINE
B  ClusterService solv-node2        Y          N            OFFLINE
bash-3.2#
```

Test and Verify Apache Cluster Resource
Resource Failover and Failback Tests

```
bash-3.2# hagrp -state
#Group          Attribute         System      Value
APPGP01         State             solv-node1  |ONLINE|
APPGP01         State             solv-node2  |OFFLINE|
APPGP02         State             solv-node1  |ONLINE|
APPGP02         State             solv-node2  |OFFLINE|
ClusterService  State             solv-node1  |ONLINE|
ClusterService  State             solv-node2  |OFFLINE|
bash-3.2# hagrp -switch APPGP02 -to solv-node2
bash-3.2# hagrp -state
#Group          Attribute         System      Value
APPGP01         State             solv-node1  |ONLINE|
APPGP01         State             solv-node2  |OFFLINE|
APPGP02         State             solv-node1  |OFFLINE|
APPGP02         State             solv-node2  |ONLINE|
ClusterService  State             solv-node1  |ONLINE|
ClusterService  State             solv-node2  |OFFLINE|
bash-3.2# hagrp -switch APPGP02 -to solv-node1
bash-3.2# hagrp -state
#Group          Attribute         System      Value
APPGP01         State             solv-node1  |ONLINE|
APPGP01         State             solv-node2  |OFFLINE|
APPGP02         State             solv-node1  |ONLINE|
APPGP02         State             solv-node2  |OFFLINE|
ClusterService  State             solv-node1  |ONLINE|
ClusterService  State             solv-node2  |OFFLINE|
bash-3.2#
```

Also parallel check the web page and accept IP address http://192.168.20.50
And run the ping from the desktop/laptop command line on 192.168.20.50 and look for the packet loss.

Shut Down Cluster Node

Shut down one of the cluster nodes (solv-node1); Apache service should move to other cluster nodes as below:

```
bash-3.2# hagrp -state
#Group          Attribute          System      Value
APPGP01         State              solv-node1  |OFFLINE|
APPGP01         State              solv-node2  |ONLINE|
APPGP02         State              solv-node1  |OFFLINE|
APPGP02         State              solv-node2  |ONLINE|
ClusterService State              solv-node1  |OFFLINE|
ClusterService State              solv-node2  |ONLINE|
bash-3.2# df -h
Filesystem           size   used  avail capacity  Mounted on
/dev/dsk/c0d0s0      8.1G   5.1G   2.9G    64%     /
/devices               OK     OK     OK     0%     /devices
ctfs                   OK     OK     OK     0%     /system/contract
proc                   OK     OK     OK     0%     /proc
mnttab                 OK     OK     OK     0%     /etc/mnttab
swap                 934M   1.1M   933M     1%     /etc/svc/volatile
objfs                  OK     OK     OK     0%     /system/object
sharefs                OK     OK     OK     0%     /etc/dfs/sharetab
swap                 933M     OK   933M     0%     /dev/vx/dmp
swap                 933M     OK   933M     0%     /dev/vx/rdmp
/usr/lib/libc/libc_hwcap1.so.1
                     8.1G   5.1G   2.9G    64%     /lib/libc.so.1
fd                     OK     OK     OK     0%     /dev/fd
swap                 933M    76K   933M     1%     /tmp
swap                 933M    32K   933M     1%     /var/run
/dev/dsk/c0d0s7      7.1G   448M   6.6G     7%     /export/home
/dev/odm               OK     OK     OK     0%     /dev/odm
/dev/vx/dsk/DGRP01/VOL_APP01
                     3.9G    19M   3.7G     1%     /app01
/dev/vx/dsk/DGRP02/VOL_APP02
                     3.9G    19M   3.7G     1%     /app02
bash-3.2#
```

```
bash-3.2# ifconfig -a
lo0: flags=2001000849<UP,LOOPBACK,RUNNING,MULTICAST,IPv4,VIRTUAL> mtu 8232 index 1
        inet 127.0.0.1 netmask ff000000
e1000g0: flags=1000843<UP,BROADCAST,RUNNING,MULTICAST,IPv4> mtu 1500 index 2
        inet 192.168.100.62 netmask ffffff00 broadcast 192.168.100.255
        ether 8:0:27:5b:5e:ca
e1000g1: flags=1000843<UP,BROADCAST,RUNNING,MULTICAST,IPv4> mtu 1500 index 3
        inet 192.168.20.20 netmask ffffff00 broadcast 192.168.20.255
        ether 8:0:27:be:fa:e3
e1000g1:1: flags=1000843<UP,BROADCAST,RUNNING,MULTICAST,IPv4> mtu 1500 index 3
        inet 192.168.20.40 netmask ffffff00 broadcast 192.168.20.255
e1000g1:2: flags=1000843<UP,BROADCAST,RUNNING,MULTICAST,IPv4> mtu 1500 index 3
        inet 192.168.20.30 netmask ffffff00 broadcast 192.168.20.255
e1000g1:3: flags=1000843<UP,BROADCAST,RUNNING,MULTICAST,IPv4> mtu 1500 index 3
        inet 192.168.20.50 netmask ffffff00 broadcast 192.168.20.255
bash-3.2#
```

As you see above, 192.168.20.50 is the floating IP address used for Apache cluster service.

■ ■ ■

## CHAPTER 8

Graphical User Interface for Cluster Management

Both Oracle Solaris Cluster and Veritas Cluster provide cluster management tools/webgui for management and administration of cluster environments. These include the following: adding/Removing Data Services; adding/removing cluster nodes; adding/removing cluster resources; enable/disable cluster resource; offline/online Data Services; Device group management for adding/removing/online and offline activities; adding/removing quorum device.

Oracle Solaris Web GUI

To access Oracle Solaris Cluster web GUI, log in to any of the cluster nodes, as in the stated examples in the previous chapters for NFS and Apache.

```
https://192.168.100.20:6789
```

This should open the following login screen and allow us to log in to the cluster management screen. Log in with the access provided while configuring the cluster or with the root account (if you are managing it as a part of your personal lab setup).

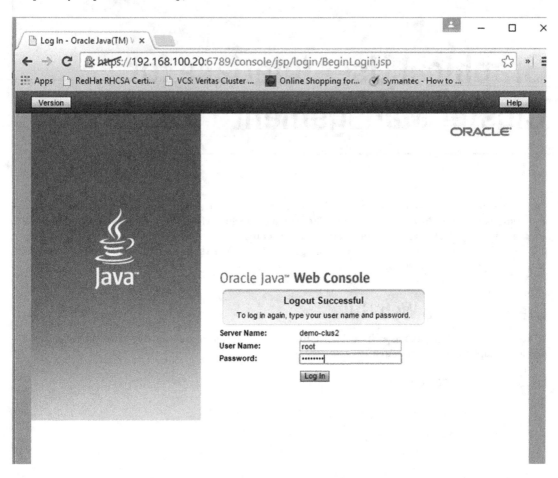

Once clicked in, the "Log In" button, the following screen will appear for managing Oracle Solaris cluster. Click on Oracle Solaris Cluster Manager to manage the existing cluster setup.

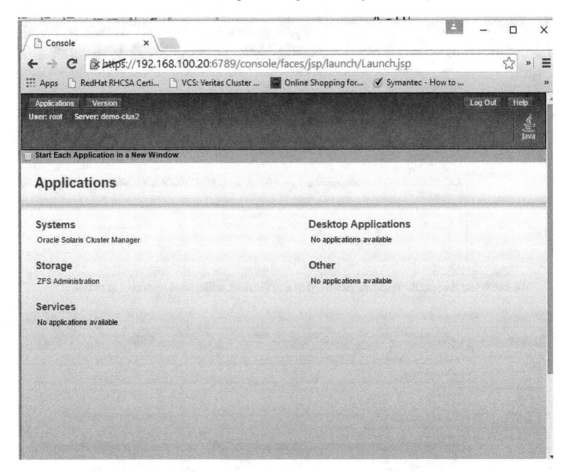

Once selected, the screen will show the name of the cluster, cluster nodes, and cluster resource groups (Service Groups) status.

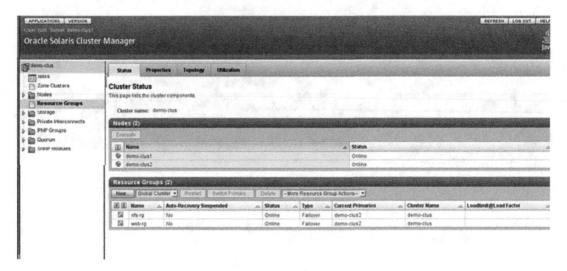

You can select the specific resource group (NFS) and see their underlined resources as below.

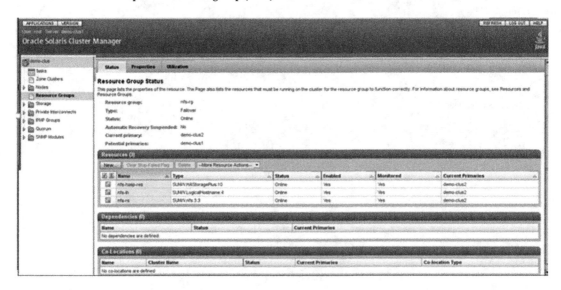

And here it shows the list of resources as part of the Apache resource group. You can further see the properties of the resource group and resource utilization by the group.

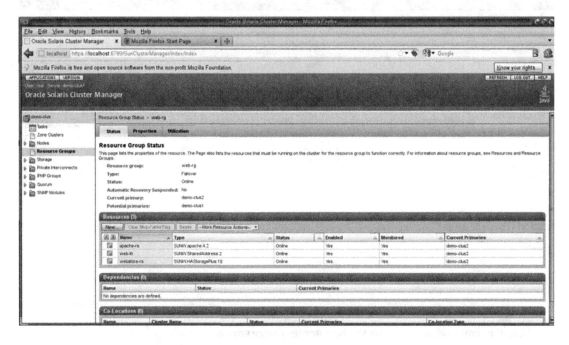

By clicking on the Nodes, you can see the list of cluster nodes connected to the cluster and their status online/offline.

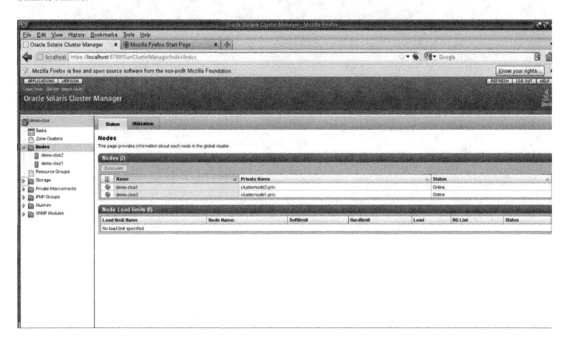

Next to this is the storage option, which is used for managing storage, device groups, disks, etc.

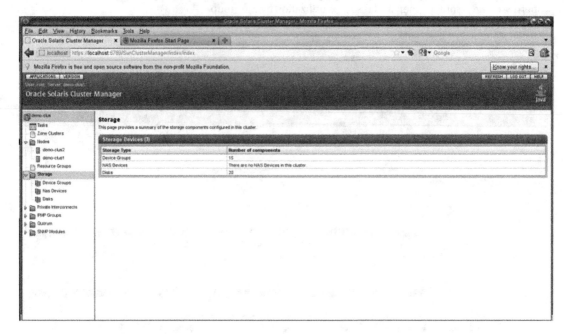

Next, the screen below shows the status of storage device groups.

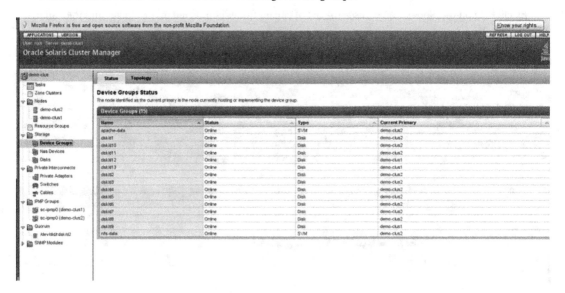

By selecting the Disks inside Storage, it shows all the disks configured as a part of cluster build and their statuses as online/offline.

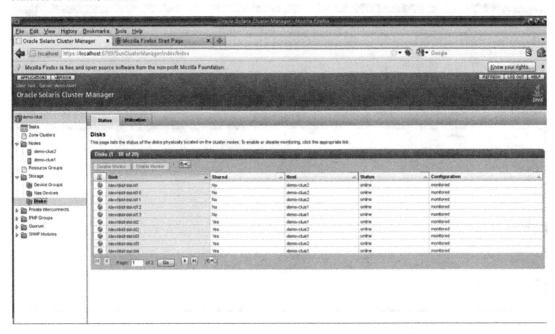

Next is to view and manage Private Interfaces. By selecting the private adapters, it will show all adaptors configured as a part of cluster build for private connections across the node.

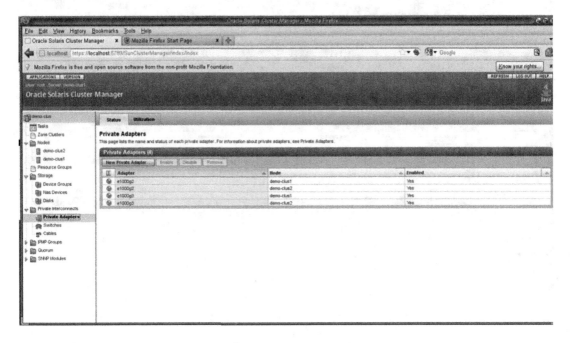

The next screen shows the IPMP group configured as a part of the build.

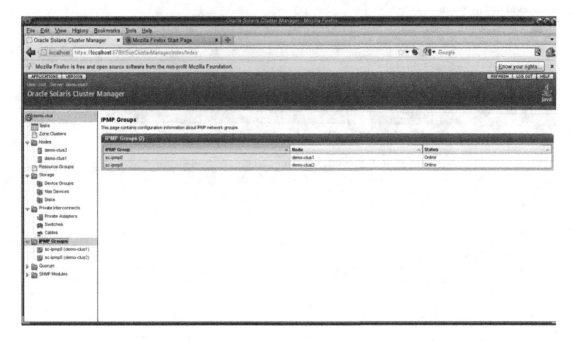

The last option here is to view add/remove the quorum device.

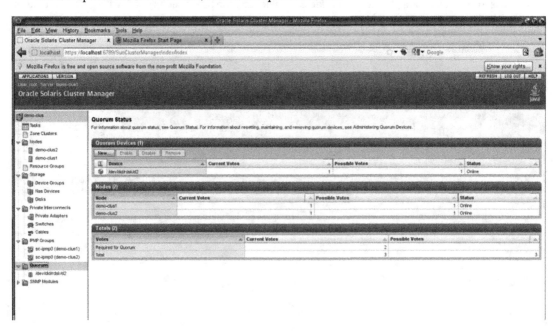

The examples below show how to switchover/failover cluster resource groups from one node to other. For this purpose, first select the respective cluster resource group as below and select option Switchover to switch to a different cluster node.

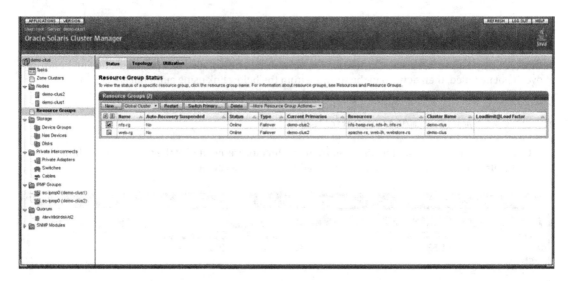

Select a different cluster node as below:

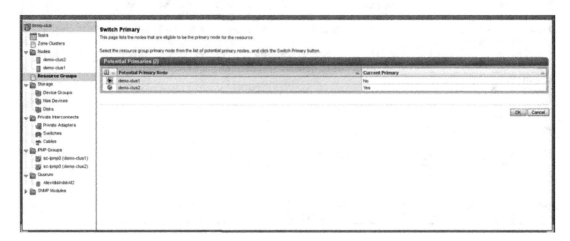

After clicking Ok above, cluster should start the switchover of cluster resources from one node to another. Initially it will show the status as pending online for the online process to finish. Once switchover is completed, it should show the Resource Group being online on the other cluster node.

Veritas Cluster GUI

Veritas GUI, also known as Veritas Cluster Java Console, should be installed as a part of the default build above. If not installed, then download the software from the below link using authenticated login and password access to the Symantec site:

https://www4.symantec.com/Vrt/vrtcontroller#

Once downloaded, transfer the file to /opt/cluster directory as created at the time of cluster build. Extract the file and add the package using the pkgadd command as below:

```
                                        Terminal
 File  Edit  View  Terminal  Tabs  Help
drwxr-xr-x   2 65530      119            512 Aug 17  2012 install
drwxr-xr-x   4 65530      119            512 Aug 17  2012 reloc
bash-3.2# cd ..
bash-3.2# ls -lrt
total 3104486
----------   1 root       root           106 Jan  1  1970 @LongLink
drwxr-xr-x   4 root       root           512 Aug  3  2012 dvd2-sol_x64
drwxr-xr-x   4 65530      119            512 Aug 17  2012 VRTScscm
-rw-r--r--   1 root       root      1428049920 May 24  2015 VRTS_SF_HA_Solutions_6.
0.1_Solaris_x64.tar
-rw-r--r--   1 root       root       160636928 Nov 27 11:55 VCS_Cluster_Manager_Java
_Console_6.0.1_for_Solaris_x86.tar
bash-3.2#
bash-3.2#
bash-3.2#
bash-3.2#
bash-3.2# pkgadd -d .

The following packages are available:
  1  VRTScscm      Veritas Cluster Server Cluster Manager by Symantec
                   (i386) 6.0

Select package(s) you wish to process (or 'all' to process
all packages). (default: all) [?,??,q]: █
```

Set the environment variable PKGPARAM to avoid jre error.

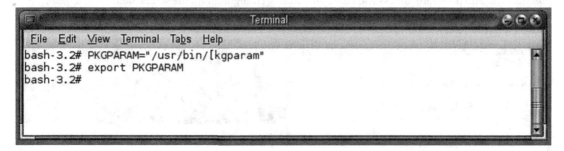

Run /opt/VRTS/bin/hagui command to initiate the GUI console for managing the Veritas Cluster below.

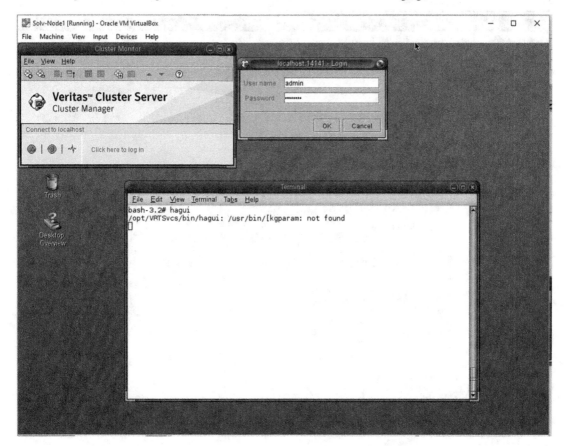

Click on the place where it says "Click here to log in" and at the login prompt use admin/password (default login and password, unless you changed it during configuration); the screen below will appear, which will show the high-level cluster status.

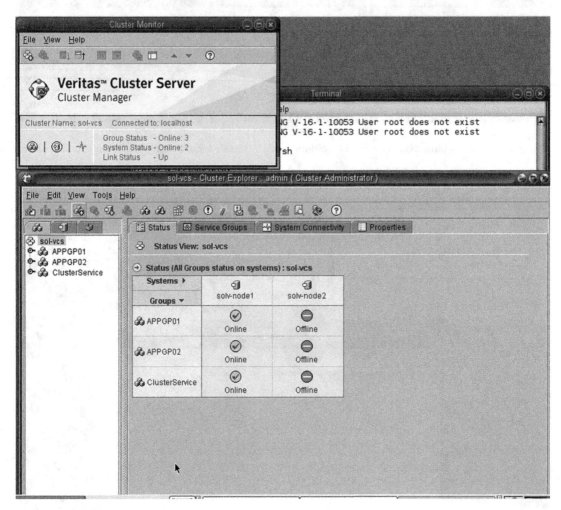

The next screen shows the cluster name and the host this is connected to (here it is local host, unless you provide the name/IP of the cluster host). It also shows Group Status and System Status.

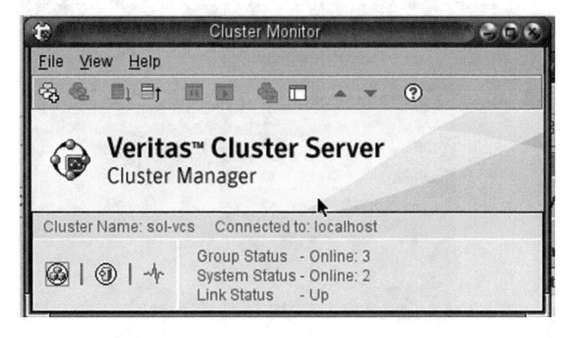

A quick note on the options you will see on the main cluster management GUI as below:

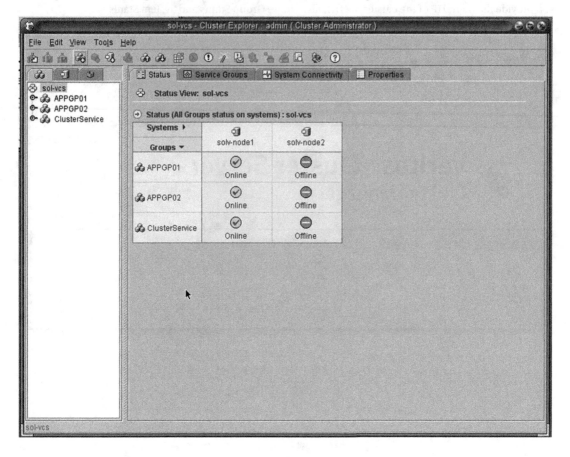

These are extracted as below:

The above options will help in managing cluster nodes, resource groups, resources, devices, and command-line options. Following the order of the picture above, these options are:

Open configuration, Save configuration, save and close configuration, Add Service Group, Add Resource, Add System, Manage Systems for service group, Online Service Group, Offline Service Group, Show Command Center, Show Shell Command Windows, Show the Logs, Launch Configuration Wizard, Launch Notifier Resource Configuration Wizard, Launch Remote Group Resource Wizard, Add/Delete Remote Clusters, Configure Global Groups, Query, and Virtual Fire Drill

And options in the second line are:

Service Groups, Systems, and Types

Let's now see some other options as a part of cluster management:

First you will see Service groups (Resource groups) created (APPGP01 and APPGP02). Further clicking on the APPGP01 (on the left side), you will see options of managing DiskGroup, IP, Mount, NFS, NFSRestart, NIC, Share, and Volume. These resources are set up as a part of the group. On the right-hand side of the screen, you will see the status of the service group, which node is online, and the resource status.

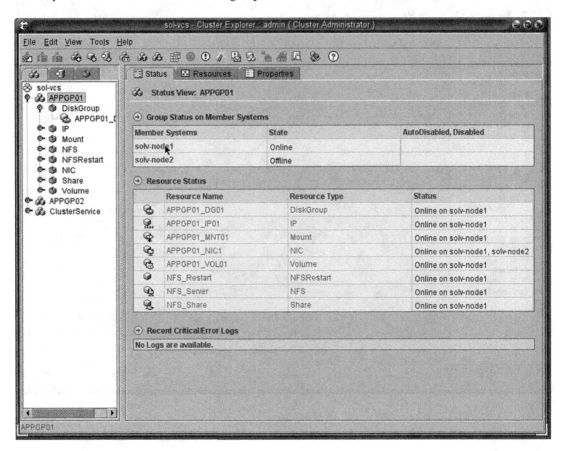

A high-level view of the NFS cluster resources along with their dependency matrix is shown by clicking Resources option as below.

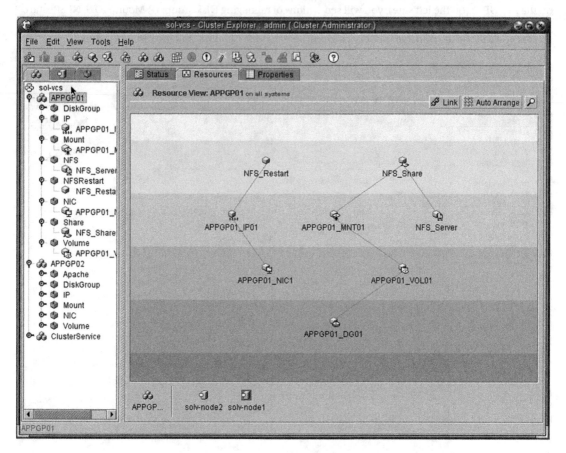

And here is another example of showing Apache cluster resources and their dependencies chart:

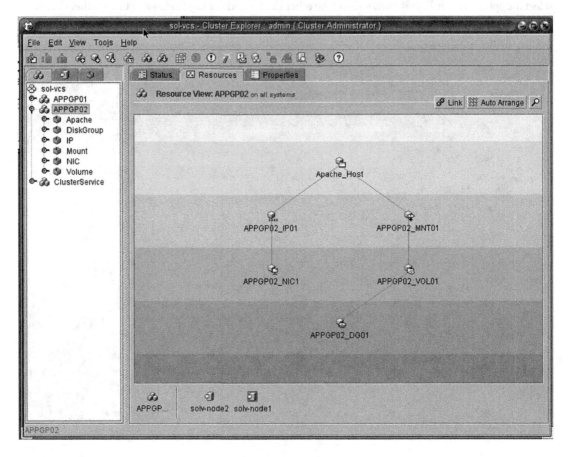

Next, to switchover a cluster resource group, right-click on the resource group (APPGP01 here) and select the option Switch To and further select the other cluster node or any (to failover to any other cluster node). Here in two-node cluster we have only solv-node2 host available to failover to and confirm as below:

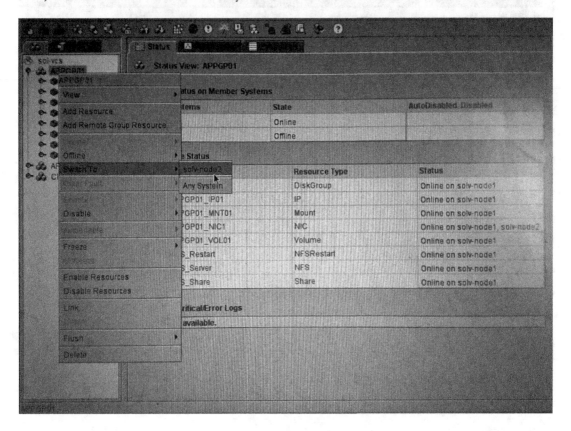

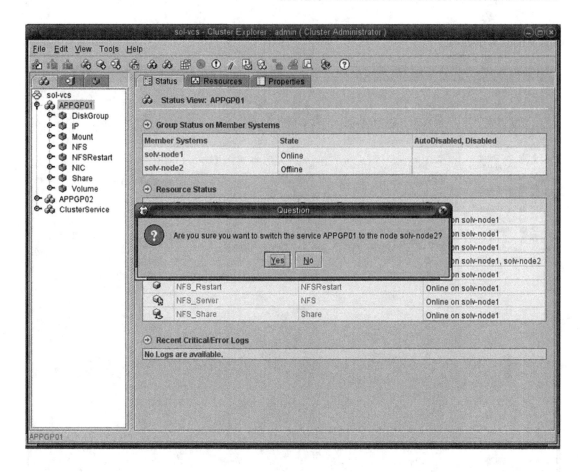

Post successful failover of services, the next screen will confirm the service group online on the other cluster node as below:

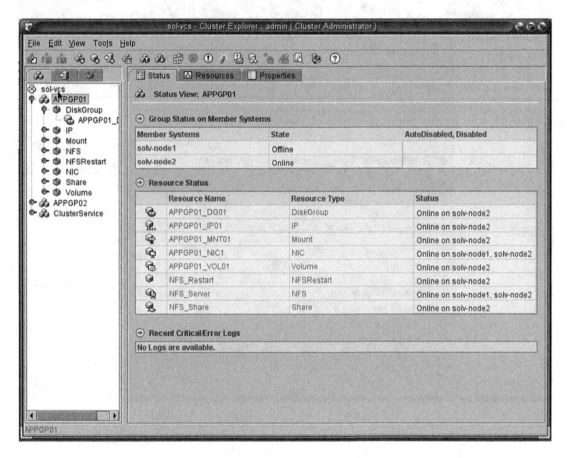

And then fail back to the same host by repeating the steps above and by selecting the node solv-node2:

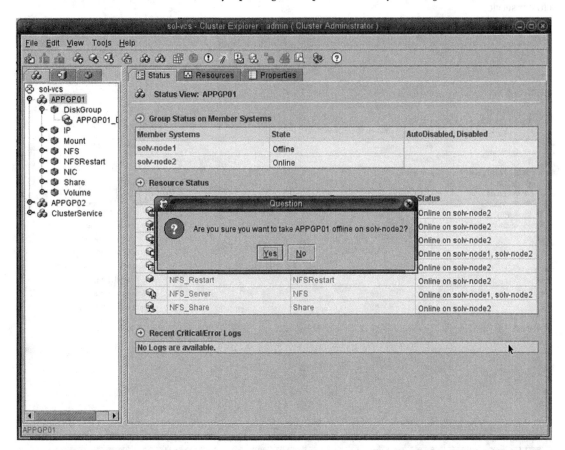

The status will first be at Pending Online and then will change to Online after successful failover of cluster services.

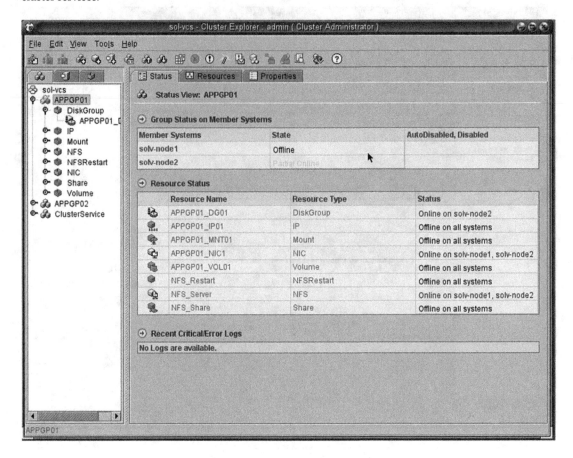

The next screen shows the successful failover of the cluster resource group.

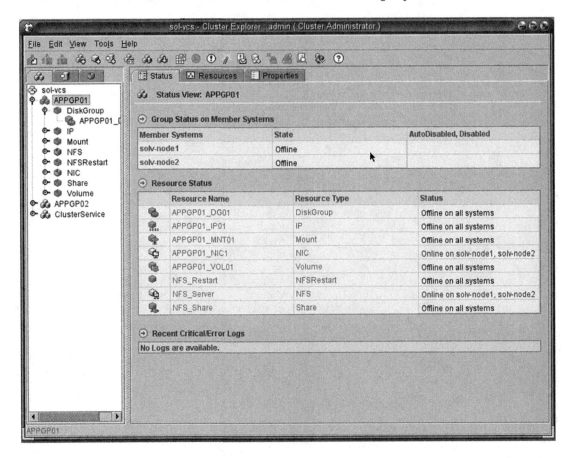

CHAPTER 9

■ ■ ■

Additional Examples – Cluster Configurations

In this chapter, some additional examples of Oracle Solaris and Veritas cluster configuration setups will be shown. These are practice examples and can be used on this configuration.

Oracle Solaris Geographic Cluster

Geographic cluster is spanned across two sites that are geographically distant. This type of cluster configuration, which is set up for disaster recovery, uses data replication between these clusters and treats one of the sites as redundant or standby and becomes an active or primary site during disasters. In this configuration, Oracle Solaris Geographic cluster requires an additional geographic cluster software layer called Oracle Solaris Geographic Edition. Below is an example of high-level Geographic Cluster design.

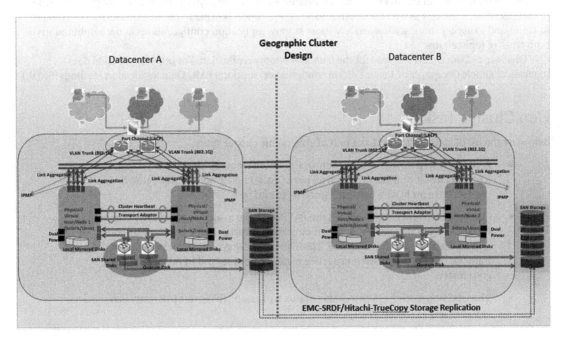

Figure 9-1. *An example of high-level Geographic Cluster design*

There are two scenarios of disaster recovery:

Planned Disaster Recovery (DR)

This occurs for planned maintenance activity such as enhancement of network capabilities or fixing network issues, storage capabilities changes, application or OS or cluster patching ,or any other cluster configuration changes. Once the maintenance activity is planned for the primary site, post business approval of the primary cluster is temporarily failed over to the DR site and failed back. Oracle Solaris Geographic Cluster Edition treats this as **switchover** activity. Disaster Recovery drills are another example of planned DR activity.

Unplanned Disaster Recovery (DR)

This occurs due to natural or uncontrolled disasters, such as earthquake, floods, tornados, fires, etc. In such scenario, one of the sites goes offline, so applications on the DR site (standby site) are brought online and temporarily treat the DR site as the primary site. Oracle Solaris Geographic Cluster Edition calls this a **takeover** process. In this situation, there are possibilities of data loss depending upon the type of disaster recovery configuration for storage replication.

Oracle Geographic cluster provides availability by having geographically separated secondary/standby sites; applications are installed and configured on the secondary site the same way as in the primary site; and, finally, storage replication mechanisms ensure the same copy of the data is available any time.

Geographic cluster performance is highly dependent on the distance between sites, which increases both network- and storage-level latency. The larger the distance, greater are the possibilities of data or network packet losses at the time of disasters.

Storage replication in Geographic cluster configuration uses two types of data replication methods: Synchronous and Asynchronous. Synchronous replication guarantees that every write on the primary site is first written on the second site to ensure data is synchronized, while asynchronous may not guarantee the data replication. Although as a tradeoff, synchronous replication is expected to have performance concerns as compared to asynchronous. Alternatively some storage replication configurations allow combinations of both types of replications.

Oracle uses Data Guard software for the database remote replication. For other application data replication, Oracle Geographic Cluster Edition configuration supports EMC Data Replication Methods (SRDF).

Geo Cluster Tasks

Below are the list of tasks performed as a part of geographic cluster setup.

- A very first step for Geo Cluster setup is to Install Geographic Cluster Edition as a part of cluster build software on all participant cluster nodes. Make sure both clusters have an FQDN name assigned (e.g., clus_site1, clus_site2).

- Once the software is installed, set the PATH variable to access geo cluster commands. Log in to any of the cluster nodes on one site and run **geoadm start** command and do the same on the other site. This will build the geo cluster configuration framework, create and start respective resource groups, and build resources for geo cluster.

- The next step is to check geo cluster status and establish cluster trust between the two sites and verify the cluster trust.

- Once the trust is created, create cluster partnership on one site and join the partnership by the other site. By now the geo cluster framework should be up and running.

- Create a protection group (PG) under the partnership setup in the previous step. For this purpose, first go offline and unmanage application cluster resource group/groups, which are to be brought under protection group on both sites. Once PGs are created, add application resource group/groups to the respective PG and update protection group configuration on the other site.

- Finally, start protection groups globally to activate the PG globally and check the PG and underlying application Resource group/groups and resources status.

To test and verify the geo cluster configuration, run **geopg switch** command to ensure respective resource group/groups under PG successfully failover from a primary site to a secondary site, in case of controlled disaster. And a final test on **geopg takeover** is to ensure that cluster runs on either site, in case of disaster (i.e., one site is not available).

Business Value of Geographic Cluster

Geographic cluster setup helps in ensuring maximum business uptime. In other words, Geographic cluster contributes to the business continuity.

Geographic cluster also helps in a faster return of business services during disasters. With regard to the automated replication and cluster dependencies set, immediately after the start of the DR trigger, all other recovery processes start with no manual intervention, thereby reducing the time of recovery.

Geographic cluster also helps in reduced loss of data during disasters. As the data is replicated and synchronized cross-site, chances are that business data losses are minimized.

Oracle Geographic Cluster Setup

Once the planning listed above is completed, let's create a geographic cluster framework using the following command line:

Enable Geographic Edition Infrastructure on both sites

> #geoadm start

Check geo cluster status

> #geoadm status
> Check cluster names for both nodes

Add trust between two sites

> Log on to one of the nodes on one site and add trust
> #geops add-trust -c clus_site1
> Log in to one of the node on other site
> #geops add-trust –c clus_site2

Verify cluster trust between two sites

> Log on to one of the node on one site
> #geops verify-trust –c <remote-cluster>
> Log on to one of the node on the other site
> #geops verify-trust –c <remote-cluster>

Create cluster partnership on one site

Log in to one of the nodes on one site
geops create –c clus_site1 nfs-ps

Join partnership by other site

Log in to one of the node on one site
geops join-partnership clus_site1 nfs-ps

Verify partnership

#geops list

Create protection group (PG) under the partnership defined above

Log in to one of the nodes
#geopg create –s nfs-ps –o primary nfs-pg

Offline and unmanage cluster resource group/groups, to be brought under protection group on both sites.

#clrs disable <resource>
#clrg offline <resource group> (clrg offline nfs-rg)
#clrg unmanage <resource group> (clrg unmanage nfs-rg)

Bring the respective resource group/groups under the protection group.

#geopg add-resource-group <resource group to be added under PG> <resourcegroup-pg>
#geopg add-resource-group nfs-rg nfs-pg

Retrieve protection groups configuration on other site.

Login to one of the node
#geopg get –s nfs-ps <resourcegroup-pg>
#geopg get –s nfs-ps nfs-pg

Start protection group globally to activate the PG under globally.

#geopg start –e global <resourcegroup-pg>
#geopg start –e global nfs-pg

Check the PG and Resource group/groups status.

#geopg list
#geoadm status
#clrg status (It should show cluster resource group up and running on the primary node)
And this completes the geo cluster configuration and brining cluster resource groups under
partner groups.

To test and verify run switchover and failover tests to ensure respective resource group/groups under PG, a successful failover from primary site to secondary site.

#geopg switchover –m <whichever cluster need to fail to > <resourcegroup-pg>
#geopg takeover <resourcegroup-pg>

Setting Up NFS Using Solaris ZFS File System (Oracle Solaris Cluster)

Add nfs shared disk (steps already covered):

#devfsadm –C (Command to re-create device tree)

#scgdevs (Command to rebuild did device)

#scdidadm -L : Look for the newly added disk for zpool for nfs

#vi /etc/hosts - Update nfs-lh IP to both hosts

Set up storage for NFS shared filesystem

#zpool create nfspool

#zfs set mountpoint=/nfs-dshare nfspool

Create Cluster resource

clresourcetype register SUNW.HAStoragePlus

clresourcetype register SUNW.nfs

Create nfs-rg resource group

clresourcegroup create -p PathPrefix=/nfs-dshare nfs-rg

Create NFS Logical hostname

#clreslogicalhostname create -g nfs-rg -L -h nfs-lh nfs-lh

Create HAStorage for ZFS Mountpoint

#clresource create -g nfs-rg -t SUNW.HAStoragePlus -p Zpools=nfspool nfs-hasp-res

Setting up NFS environment

#mkdir /nfs-dshare/SUNW.nfs

#vi dfstab.nfs-rs (Insert below line to the file)

share -F nfs -o rw,anon=0 -d "Nfs Home Dir" /nfs-dshare

#clresource create -g nfs-rg -t SUNW.nfs -p Resource_dependencies=nfs-hasp-res nfs-rs

Test NFS mount on one of the hosts

#mount nfs-lh:/nfs-dshare /mnt

Setting Up Zone Cluster

A zone cluster is a cluster of non-global cluster environments: in other words, a zone cluster is having multiple virtual clusters in a main cluster framework.

Clzonecluster utility is used for setting up zone cluster environments.

Creating zone cluster

For creating a zone cluster, have cluster framework setup as discussed in Chapter 4. Also have the information below available prior to creation:

Unique name for zone cluster

Zone path zones cluster will be using

Each physical node name

Zone public hostname

Configure zone cluster (named zoneclus) environments

bash-3.2# clzonecluster configure zoneclus

zoneclus: No such zone cluster configured

Use 'create' to begin configuring a new zone cluster

clzc:zoneclus> create

clzc:zoneclus> set zonepath=/zones/zoneclus

clzc:zoneclus> add node

clzc:zoneclus:node> set physical-host=demo-host1

clzc:zoneclus:node> set hostname=zone1

clzc:zoneclus:node> add net

clzc:zoneclus:node:net> set address=10.0.0.45

clzc:zoneclus:node:net> set physical=e1000g0

clzc:zoneclus:node:net> end

clzc:zoneclus:node> end

clzc:zoneclus:node> add net

clzc:zoneclus:node:net> set address=10.0.0.55

clzc:zoneclus:node:net> end

physical not specified

clzc:zoneclus:node:net> set physical=e1000g0

clzc:zoneclus:node:net> end

clzc:zoneclus> add sysid

clzc:zoneclus:sysid> set root_password=NDKuhJEb0eW.Y

clzc:zoneclus:sysid> end

clzc:zoneclus> commit

clzc:zoneclus> exit

Add second zonecluster host on the host demo-host2

bash-3.2# clzonecluster configure zoneclus

clzc:zoneclus> add node

clzc:zoneclus:node> set physical-host=vij-host2

clzc:zoneclus:node> set hostname=zone2

clzc:zoneclus:node> add net

clzc:zoneclus:node:net> set address=10.0.0.46

clzc:zoneclus:node:net> set physical=e1000g0

clzc:zoneclus:node:net> end

clzc:zoneclus:node> end

clzc:zoneclus> commit

clzc:zoneclus> exit

Extended config

clzc:zoneclus> add sysid

clzc: zoneclus:sysid> set root_password=<encrypted passwd from /etc/shadow>

clzc: zoneclus:sysid> set name_service="NIS {domain_name=scdev.example.com

name_server=timber(1.2.3.4)}"

clzc: zoneclus:sysid> set nfs4_domain=dynamic

clzc: zoneclus:sysid> set security_policy=NONE

clzc: zoneclus:sysid> set system_locale=C

clzc: zoneclus:sysid> set terminal=xterms

clzc: zoneclus:sysid> set timezone=US/Pacific

clzc: zoneclus:sysid> end

clzc:zoneclus>

Verify Zone Cluster hosts

bash-3.2# clzonecluster verify zoneclus

Waiting for zone verify commands to complete on all the nodes of the zone cluster "zoneclus"...

bash-3.2# clzonecluster status zoneclus

```
=== Zone Clusters ===
--- Zone Cluster Status ---
Name       Node Name    Zone Host Name    Status    Zone Status
----       ---------    --------------    ------    -----------
zoneclus   demo-host1   zone1             Offline   Configured
           demo-host2   zone2             Offline   Configured
```

Install the zone cluster

bash-3.2# clzonecluster install zoneclus

Waiting for zone install commands to complete on all the nodes of the zone cluster "zoneclus"...

bash-3.2#

Boot zone cluster

bash-3.2# clzonecluster boot zoneclus

Waiting for zone boot commands to complete on all the nodes of the zone cluster "zoneclus"...

bash-3.2#

Add UFS file system as a highly available file system

clzonecluster configure zoneclus

clzc:zoneclus> add fs

clzc:zoneclus:fs> set dir=/app01

clzc:zoneclus:fs> set special=/dev/md/app-ds/dsk/d20

clzc:zoneclus:fs> set raw=/dev/md/app-ds/rdsk/d20

clzc:zoneclus:fs> set type=ufs

clzc:zoneclus:fs> end

clzc:zoneclus> exit

#

Add the Oracle Solaris ZFS storage pool zpool1 as highly available

clzonecluster configure zoneclus

clzc:zoneclus> add dataset

clzc:zoneclus:dataset> set name=zpool1

clzc:zoneclus:dataset> end

clzc:zoneclus> exit

Setting Up Custom Application in Veritas Cluster and Oracle Solaris Cluster

The steps below are only focused to create resource groups and resources under the cluster environment and assuming all other necessary framework components (Interface, IP, Device, Device Group, Mirroring, Data Set, Filesystem) have been created.

For this purpose, let's create a dummy application as dummy.sh, which is a shell script and will run in infinite loop as a daemon as below:

```
#dummy.sh
#!/bin/bash
while true
do
        echo "This is a dummy test"
        sleep 100
done
```

We are assuming the application is installed inside the directory as /opt/app.

Next is to create start, stop. and probe scripts, which will be used as a part of the cluster.

```
#dummp_start.sh
#!/bin/bash
PIDFILE=/var/log/app-pid
sh /opt/app/dummy.sh &
echo $! | tee $PIDFILE
exit 0
```

And to create stop script, write:

```
#dummp_stop.sh
#!/bin/bash
apppid=`ps -eaf | grep dummy.sh | grep -v grep`
if [ -z $apppid ]
then
        exit 0
fi
kill -9 $apppid
rm /var/log/app-pid
exit 0
```

And probe script:

```
#dummy_probe.sh
#!/bin.bash
PS=`ps -ef | grep -v grep | grep -v vi | grep -v probe | grep dummy.sh`
if ["$PS" -gt "0" }] then
# echo "Found $PS processes"
exit 0
else
echo "Found no processes"
exit 1
fi
```

Give execution permission to all these scripts as below:

```
#chmod 755 /opt/app/dummy.sh /opt/app/dummy_start.sh /opt/app/dummy_stop.sh and /opt/app/
dummy_probe.sh
```

Copy them to all the participant cluster nodes.
Now create cluster resources.
For Veritas Cluster create cluster resource as below:

```
#haconf -makerw
#hagrp –add dummy-rg
#hagrp –modify dummy-rg –SystemList demo-host1 0 demo-host2 1
#hares –add dummy_app Application dummy-rg
#hares –modify dummy_app User root
#hares –modify dummy_app StartProgram "/opt/app/dummy_start.sh"
#hares –modify dummy_app StopProgram "/opt/app/dummy_stop.sh"
#hares –modify dummy_app CleanProgram "/opt/app/dummy_stop.sh"
#hares –modify dummy_app PidFiles "/var/log/app-pid"
#hares –modify dummy_app Enabled 1
#haconf –dump -makero
```

For Oracle Solaris Cluster:

```
#clrg create dummy-rg
#clresource create -g dummy_rg -t SUNW.gds
 -p Scalable=false -p Start_timeout=120 \
 -p Stop_timeout=120 -p Probe_timeout=120 \
 -p network_aware=FALSE \
 -p Start_command="/opt/app/dummy_start.sh" \
 -p Stop_command="/opt/app/dummy_stop.sh" \
 -p Probe_command="/opt/app/dummy_probe.sh" \
 -p Child_mon_level=0 -p Failover_enabled=TRUE \
 -p Stop_signal=9 dummy_rs
```

■ ■ ■

## CHAPTER 10

Command-Line Cheat Sheet

Oracle Solaris Cluster Commands

Commands mentioned here are just a few of the commands, and in some cases not all options are mentioned. Set MANPATH environment variable to /usr/cluster/man as below to get more options in addition to the commands mentioned here.

```
MANPATH=/usr/cluster/man
export MANPATH
```

Cluster Configuration Information and Status

Cluster configuration files are located at
    /etc/cluster/ccr directory and
    /etc/cluster/ccr/infrastructure directory contains all the cluster configuration information, starting from devices to resource group to quorum etc.

Show cluster information

#scstat –pv (older version)

#cluster show

#cluster status

Cluster nodes

#scstat –n (older version)

#clnode list

#clnode show

#clnode status

Quorum

#scstat –q (Older version)

#clq list

#clq status

#clq show

Devices

#scstat –D (Older version)

#cldevice list

#cldevice show

#cldevice status

Transport Adapter

#scstat –W (Older version)

#clintr show

#clintr status

Resource group and resources

#scstat –g

#clrg list

#clrg status

#clrg show

#scstat –pv

#clrs show

#clrs status

Resource Type

#scrgadm

#clrst show

#clrst list –v

Cluster Setup

#scsetup

#clsetup

Cluster configuration check

#sccheck

#cluster check

Cluster interconnects

#clintrshow

#clintrdisable

Adding and Removing Cluster Node

Adding cluster node

> #clnode add –c <clustername> -n <nodename> -e endpoint1,
> endpoint2 –e endpoint3 endpoint4

Remove cluster node

> #clnode remove <nodename>

List cluster nodes

> #clnode list

Status of cluster nodes

> #clnode status

Setting cluster node properties

> #clnode set –p

Adding and Removing Resource Groups and Resources

Resource Groups

clrg create <rg name>	-> Create resource group
clrg add-node -n <node> <rg name>	-> Add cluster nodes to resource group
clrg delete <rg name>	-> Delete resource group
clrg online <rg name>	-> Online resource group
clrg offline <rg name>	-> Offline resource group
clrg switch –n <rg name>	-> Failover resource group
clrg suspend/resume <rg name>	-> Suspend or resume resource group

Resources

clrs create <res name>	-> Create resource
clrs delete <res name>	-> Removing resource
clrs set -p <property> <res name>	-> Setting or changing resource parameters
clrs list-props <res name>	-> Listing resource properties
clrs enable <res name>	-> Enable resource
clrs disable <res name>	-> Disable resource
clrs clear <res name>	-> Clear the fault state of cluster resource

Adding and Removing Resource Types

clusterresourcetype register	-> Register cluster resource type
clusterresourcetype add-node	-> Register resource type to the specific node
clustersourcetype unregister	-> Remove/delete cluster resource type
clusterresourcetype list	-> List cluster resource types

Device Management

cldev populate	-> Reconfigure device database by rebuilding device tree with new instances
cldev monitor	-> Turning device monitoring on
cldev check	-> Check for the devices
cldev set -p	-> Set the properties for the device
cldev repair	-> Repair or update cluster paths
cldg create	-> Create device group
cldg delete	-> Delete device group
cldg add-device/remove-node	-> Add/remove device to device group
cldg add-node/remove-node	-> Add/remove cluster node to device group
cldg switch	-> Switch over device groups
cldg online/offline	-> Online or offline cluster device groups

Quorum Add and Remove

To add or remove a quorum device, first bring the cluster into maintenance mode as shown below:

cluster set -p installmode=enabled

clq add	-> Adding a quorum device
clq add -t quorumserver	-> Adding quorum server
clq add -t netapp_nas	-> Adding NAS device as quorum
clq remove	-> Remove a quorum device
clq enable/disable	-> Enable or disable quorum device to put them into maintenance

Post adding or removal bring the cluster back out of install mode using option as

```
cluster set -p installmode=disabled
```

Quorum Server

To set up a quorum server follow these steps:

Install quorum server software on the host chosen as quorum server.

On the cluster host/node, run the command

```
/usr/cluster/lib/sc/scqsd [-d quorumdirectory] [-i instancename] -p port
Quorum directory - Directory where quorum server can store quorum  data
Instance Name - A unique name for quorum server instance
Port - A port used for quorum server to listen requests from cluster nodes. (default 9000)
```

To start/stop quorum server – clq start/stop   (clq is short form command of clquorumserver)

Transport Interconnects

clintr add	-> Adding cluster interconnects
clintr remove	-> Removing cluster interconnects configuration
clintr enable/disable	-> Enable or disable cluster interconnects for maintenance
clintr status	-> Show the interconnect stat

Veritas Cluster Commands

Cluster Configuration Files

/etc/VRTSvcs/conf/config/main.cf

/etc/VRTSvcs/conf/config/types.cf

/etc/llthosts

/etc/habtab

/etc/lltab

Cluster Information

haclus –display	-> Detailed information about cluster
hasys – display	-> Display system attributes
hastatus –sum	-> Display cluster summary

Adding and Removing Nodes

hasys –add	-> Adding host to the cluster
hasys –delete	-> Removing node from the cluster
hasys –force	-> Force a system to start
hasys –state	-> Finding the cluster node status
hasys –list	-> List cluster nodes

Add and Remove Service Group
Managing Cluster Resource Groups

haconf –makerw – to make main.cf file read+write

hagrp –add	-> Add a service group in cluster
hagrp –modify	-> Modify a service group
hagrp –delete	-> Delete a service group
hagrp –list	-> List of service groups configured
hagrp –dep	-> List resource group dependencies
hagrp –state	-> Status of resource group
hagrp –online	-> Bring the cluster resource group online
hagrp –offline	-> Bring the cluster resource group offline
hagrp –switch	-> Switch cluster resource groups from one node to other

Managing Cluster Resources

hares –add	-> Adding cluster resource
hares –modify	-> Modify cluster resource properties
hares –delete	-> Delete cluster resource
hares –list	-> List cluster resources
hares –display	-> Display the details of cluster resource parameters
hares –state	-> Cluster resource status

haconf –dump –makero (to make main.cf file read-only)

Add and Remove Resource Type

hatype –add	-> Adding Resource Type
hatype –delete	-> Deleting cluster resource type
hatype –display	-> Display parameters on resource type
hatype –list	-> List resource types
hatype –value	-> Change resource type parameter values

LLT Commands

lltstat –n	-> Verify link status (up/down)
lltstat –nvv	-> Verbose status of the link
lltstat –c	-> Configuration status of the link
lltstat –p	-> Open ports for LLT
lltconfig –c	-> Configuration information
lltconfig –U	-> Stopping LLT
lltstat –l	-> List of LLT configured

GAB Commands

gabconfig –U	-> Stop GAB
gabconfig –c –n <no of nodes>	-> Start GAB

References

- **Oracle™ Solaris Cluster documentation** – http://www.oracle.com/technetwork/documentation/solaris-cluster-33-192999.html
http://www.oracle.com/technetwork/server-storage/solaris-cluster/documentation/index.html

- **VirtualBox Documentation** – https://www.VirtualBox.org/wiki/Documentation

- **Veritas ™ Cluster Server Administrator Guide** –https://sort.symantec.com/public/documents/sfha/6.0/linux/productguides/pdf/vcs_admin_60_lin.pdf

- **Clusters for High Availability (by Peter S. Weygant)** – https://www.symantec.com/en/in/cluster-server/),

- **Oracle Solaris Cluster (by Tim Read)** – http://www.Data Centerknowledge.com/archives/2014/04/20/data-center-fire-leads-outage-samsung-devices/)

- **VirtualBox Definition** – https://en.wikipedia.org/wiki/VirtualBox

- **Cluster Analysis Definition** – https://en.wikipedia.org/wiki/Cluster_analysis

- **Missed Alarms and 40 Million Stolen Credit Card Numbers: How Target Blew It** – (by Michael Riley, Ben Elgin, Dune Lawrence, and Carol Matlack on March 13, 2014) http://www.bloomberg.com/bw/articles/2014-03-13/target-missed-alarms-in-epic-hack-of-credit-card-data

- **'Ocean's 11' Data Center Robbery in London (by Rich Miller on December 8, 2007)** – http://www.Data Centerknowledge.com/archives/2007/12/08/oceans-11-data-center-robbery-in-london/

- **VCS : Veritas Cluster Step by Step Implementing 2 Node VCS Setup (by Ejaj Mansuri)** http://www.em-dba.com/emvcs01.html

- **Downtime, Outages and Failures – Understanding Their True Costs –** http://www.evolven.com/blog/downtime-outages-and-failures-understanding-their-true-costs.html

- **The cost of critical application failure** – http://www.stratus.com/assets/Cost-Of-Critical-App-Downtime1.pdf

- **Beginners Lesson – <u>Veritas Cluster Services for System Admin</u> –** http://unixadminschool.com/blog/2011/07/beginners-lesson-veritas-cluster-services-for-solaris/

- **<u>Sun Clusters – Adding New Disk and Extending Filesystem</u> –** http://unixadminschool.com/blog/2011/10/sun-clusters-adding-new-disk-and-extending-filesystem/

Index

Get the eBook for only $5!

Why limit yourself?

Now you can take the weightless companion with you wherever you go and access your content on your PC, phone, tablet, or reader.

Since you've purchased this print book, we're happy to offer you the eBook in all 3 formats for just $5.

Convenient and fully searchable, the PDF version enables you to easily find and copy code—or perform examples by quickly toggling between instructions and applications. The MOBI format is ideal for your Kindle, while the ePUB can be utilized on a variety of mobile devices.

To learn more, go to www.apress.com/companion or contact support@apress.com.

Printed in the United States
By Bookmasters